Walkers', Cyclists' and Horse Riders'

LightFoot Guide to the Via Domitia Arles to Vercelli

(Linking the St James Way and the Via Francigena)

Copyright 2010 Pilgrimage Publications All rights reserved.
ISBN: 9782917183144
Pilgrimage Publications www.pilgrimagepublications.com

Also by Babette Gallard and Paul Chinn
Riding the Milky Way - Long Riders' Press 2006
Riding the Roman Way - Pilgrimage Publications 2007
Reflections - A Pictorial Journey Along the via Francigena 2008
LightFoot Guide to the via Francigena - Canterbury to Besançon 2008/9/10/11
LightFoot Guide to the via Francigena - Besançon to Vercelli 2008/9/10/11
LightFoot Guide to the via Francigena - Vercelli to Rome 2008/9/10/11
LightFoot Guide to the Three Saints Way - Winchester to Mont St Michel 2008
LightFoot Guide to the Three Saints Way - Mont St Michel to St Jean d'Angely 2008
Companion Guides to the Via Francigena and Via Domitia 2010/2011

The authors have done their best to ensure the accuracy and currency of the information in the LightFoot Guide to the Via Francigena, however they can accept no responsibility for any loss, injury or inconvenience sustained by any traveller as a result of information contained in the guide. Changes will inevitably occur within the lifespan of this edition and the authors welcome notification of such changes and any other feedback that will enable them to enhance the quality of the guide.

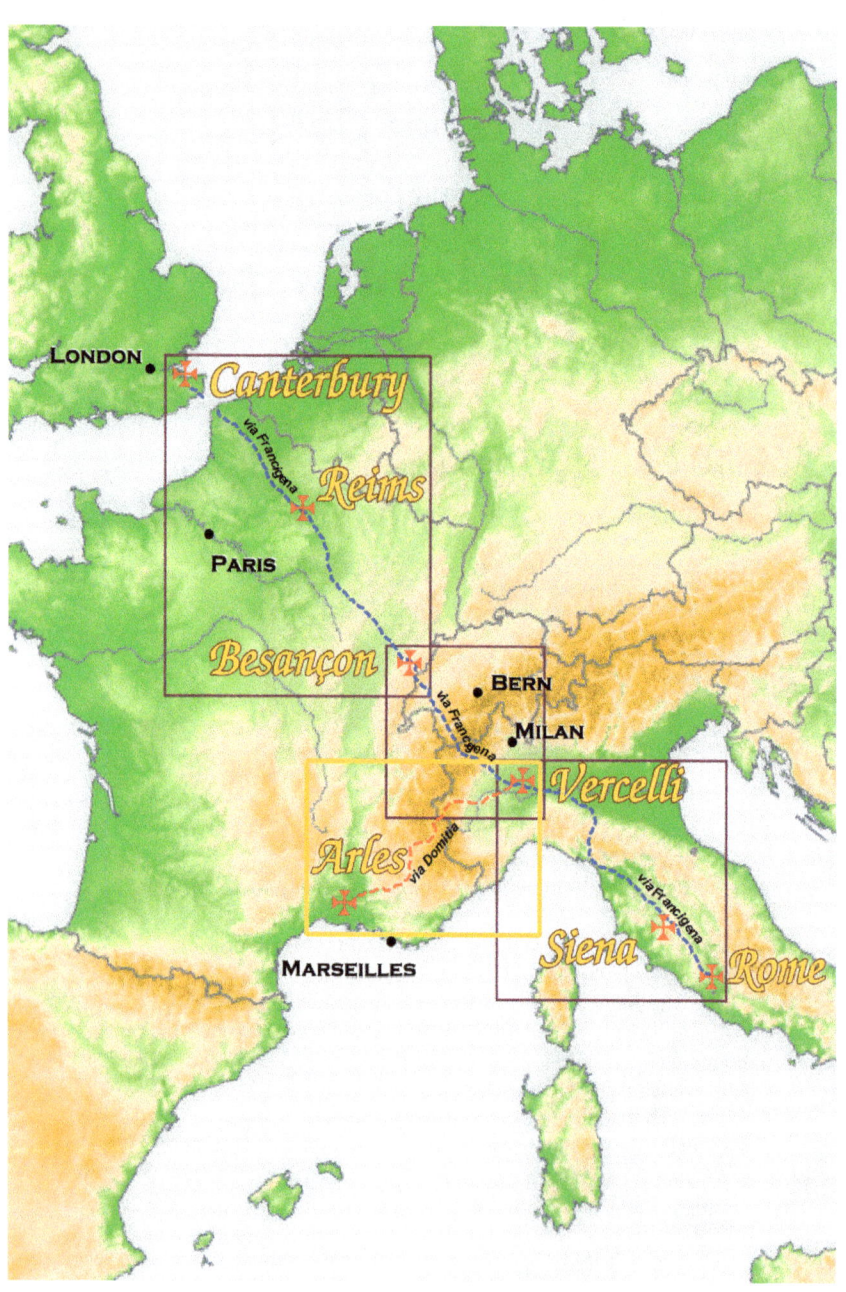

Contents

Page	Stage N°	Stage	Length (km)
5		About Your Authors	
6		About Your Guide	
7		Symbol Key	
8		The Basics in France	
9		The Basics in Italy	
10		Useful Links & Recommended Reading	
11		The Via Domitia	
12	01	Arles - Fontvieille	12.2
19		*Alternate Route #01.A1 12.6km*	
23	02	Fontvieille - Saint-Rémy-de-Provence	22.6
31	03	Saint-Rémy-de-Provence - Eygalières	13.0
36	04	Eygalières - Cavaillon	15.9
41	05	Cavaillon - Beaumettes	16.3
48	06	Beaumettes - Apt	18.8
54	07	Apt - Céreste	21.2
60	08	Céreste - Moulin-de-Lincel	13.2
66	09	Moulin-de-Lincel - Forcalquier	17.6
74	10	Forcalquier - Prieure-de-Ganagobie	22.2
82	11	Prieure-de-Ganagobie - Peipin	23.6
89		*Alternate Route #11.A1 7.7km*	
91	12	Peipin - Saint-Geniez	23.7
98		*Alternate Route #12.A1 15.6km*	
99	13	Saint-Geniez - la-Motte-du-Caire	16.3
103		*Alternate Route #13.A1 10.8km*	
104		*Alternate Route #13.A2 8.2km*	
106	14	la-Motte-du-Caire - Tallard	24.2
110		*Alternate Route #14.A1 5.5km*	
112	15	Tallard - Gap	17.9

Contents

Page	Stage N°	Stage	Length (km)
120	16	Gap - Notre-Dame-de-Laus	11.0
124	17	Notre-Dame-de-Laus - Chorges	15.4
130	18	Chorges - Abbaye-de-Boscodon	24.6
136	19	Abbaye-de-Boscodon - Embrun	12.5
144	20	Embrun - Châteauroux-les-Alpes	10.3
149	21	Châteauroux-les-Alpes - Saint-Crépin	19.4
153		*Alternate Route #21.A1 5.4km*	
159	22	Saint-Crépin - l'Argentière-la-Bessée	13.1
163	23	l'Argentière-la-Bessée - Briançon	23.1
169		*Alternate Route #23.A1 9.2km*	
171	24	Briançon - Cesana-Torinese	24.3
177		*Alternate Route #24.A1 2.7km*	
179	25	Cesana-Torinese - Oulx	13.8
184	26	Oulx - Susa	27.7
190	27	Susa - Sant'Antonio-di-Susa	21.2
196	28	Sant'Antonio-di-Susa - Rosta	17.2
201	29	Rosta - Turin	20.4
206	30	Turin - Gassino-Torinese	15.9
213	31	Gassino-Torinese - Chivasso	11.6
217	32	Chivasso - Lamporo	21.2
223	33	Lamporo - Sali-Vercellese	29.9
228	34	Sali-Vercellese - Vercelli	10.0
			621.3

Average Stage length = 18.3km
Total number of Waypoints = 1354
Average distance between Waypoints = 459m

About the Authors

We are two very ordinary people who quit the world of business and stumbled on the St James Way during our search for a more viable, rewarding alternative to our previous lifestyle. Since then we have completed four pilgrimages, one of which was particularly tough and finally prompted us to create Pilgrimage Publications and the LightFoot guide series. We have no religious beliefs, but share a 'wanderlust' and need to know about and contribute to the world we occupy.

Pilgrimage Publications is a not-for-profit organisation dedicated to the identification and mapping of pilgrim routes all over the world, regardless of religion or belief. Any revenue derived from the sale of guides or related activities is used to further enhance the service and support provided to pilgrims.
The ethos of Pilgrimage Publications is based on 4 very basic aims:
  To enable walkers, cyclists and riders to follow pilgrim routes all over the world
  To ensure LightFoot guides are as current and accurate as possible, using pilgrim feedback as a major source of information.
  To use eco-friendly materials and methods for the publication of LightFoot guides and Travel Books.
  To promote eco-friendly travel.

As with all the routes presented in our LightFoot Guide series, we have followed every centimetre of the via Domitia ourselves - this time, accompanied by our horse, Nellie, and our dog, Flea. You can read about how we did it on our blog: http://burkinaschool.blogspot.com/

We welcome suggestions for the improvement of our guides and rely on updates from pilgrims to ensure that our guides are as up to date and accurate as possible - mail@pilgrimagepublications.com

LightFoot Guides are designed to enable everyone to meet their personal goals and enjoy the best, whilst avoiding the worst, of following ancient pilgrimage routes. Written for Walkers, Cyclists and Horse Riders, every section of this LightFoot guide provides specific information for each group.

We would like to emphasise that we have made great efforts to use only public footpaths and to respect private property. Historically, pilgrims may not have been so severely restricted by ownership rights and the pressures of expanding populations, but unfortunately this is no longer the case. Today, even the most free-spirited traveller must adhere to commonly accepted routes. Failure to do so will only antagonise local residents, encourage the closure of routes and inhibit pilgrims following on behind.

This book traces the Via Domitia from Arles to Vercelli. You will find an introductory section followed by 34 chapters, each of which covers a segment of the route. **Each chapter contains a route summary, detailed instructions, a map and an altitude profile**.
Historical and cultural data is included in the Companion edition.

Accommodation

In general we try to select budget accommodation, unless nothing else is available in the area. Prices may or may not include breakfast and some establishments charge a tariff for dogs. We have listed opening/closing information where we have been able to get it. In general, dogs are not welcome in Youth or Religious Hostels. The general rule for accommodation in Religious Houses is that reservations must be made 24 hours ahead of arrival.

Price bands, B1, B2, B3 are based on one double room per night - accurate at the time of entry, but subject to change.

B1 0-40 €/£   **B2** 40-60 €/£   **B3** 60+ €/£

Look out for the **PR** - Pilgrim Recommended- in front of listings

Our special thanks go to Barbara Edger for her tireless and ever vigilant proof-reading.

Symbol Key

Main Route and Waypoint Number
---------------- 1 ----------------

Alternate Route and Waypoint Number
---------------- 2 ----------------

🛏	B&B, Hotel, Gite d'Etapes	U	Farrier
P	Pilgrim Accommodation Co-ordinator	🍴	Restaurant
🏠	Religious Hostel	✝	Place of Worship
🏠	Youth Hostel	🚆	Railway Station
⛺	Camping	🚌	Bus Station
🐎	Equestrian Centre	i	Tourist Information
🏠	Pilgrim Hostel	⚕	Doctor
🏠	Diocesan House	🐾	Veterinary
⭐	Historical Site	🏛	Museum

7

Currency: **Euro**. Standard banking Hours: Monday-Friday 09.30-12.00 and 14.00-16.00. Closed on Sundays and usually Monday, with half day opening on Saturday morning

Post Offices (La Poste): Standard opening hours Mon - Fri - 09.30-12.00 and 14.00-17.00. Half day opening on Saturday morning.

You can make domestic and international **phone calls** from any public telephone box and can receive calls where there is a new logo of a ringing bell.
Emergencies - 112 will give you access to the emergency services. This is free and can be dialled from any telephone (including mobile phones).

Basic **Business Hours** - 08.00-12.00 and 14.00-18.00. Almost everything in France - shops, museums, tourist offices etc. - closes for two hours at midday. Food shops often don't reopen until half way through the afternoon, but close at 19.30 or 20.00. The standard closing days are Sunday and Monday in small towns, but you will find that many large supermarkets are now staying open throughout the day.

All EU citizens are eligible for free **health care** if they have the correct documentation. The UK's NHS care includes free visits to the local **doctor**, and paying a standard charge for prescriptions and dental treatment.

In France, the best way of **eating** breakfast is in a bar or café, at a fraction of the cost charged by most hotels. Expect a croissant or some bread with coffee or hot chocolate. At lunchtime and sometimes in the evenings you'll find most cafés and restaurants offering a *plat du jour*, which is by far the cheapest alternative if you don't fancy cooking yourself.

In country areas, in addition to standard hotels, you will come across **chambre d'hôte**s and *ferme auberge*, bed and breakfast accommodation in someone's house or farm. These are rarely an especially cheap option, usually costing the equivalent of a two star hotel. Youth hostels (***auberges de jeunesse***) are great for travellers on a budget. They are often beautifully sited and they allow you to cut costs by preparing your own food in their kitchens or eating in cheap canteens. The majority will require that you are a member of the International Youth Hostel Federation.

Gites d'étape are basic but do not require membership and provide bunk beds with primitive kitchen and washing facilities at a reasonable price.

Campsites in France are nearly always clean and have plenty of hot water. On the coast there are superior categories of campsite where you will pay prices similar to those of a hotel for the facilities -bars, restaurants and usually elaborate swimming pools too. For horses, it is useful to know that campsite owners often allow horses to be tethered at the edge of the site.

Currency: **Euro**. Standard banking Hours: 08.30–13.30 and 14.30-16.00, Monday to Friday. Closed on Sundays.

Post Offices - Standard Opening Hours: 08.30-19.30 and 13.45-18.30, Monday to Friday. Branches in smaller towns and villages close for an hour, 13.00-14.00.

Numbers beginning with 800 are free.
170 - English-speaking operator.
176 - International Directory Enquires.
 12 - Telephone Directory Assistance Number
112 - *Carabinieri* (national-level police who also perform military police duties)
113 - Emergency Police Help Number (also ambulance and fire)
115 - Fire Department
116 - A.C.I. (Italian Automobile Club) road assistance.
118 - Medical Emergencies
Note: Italian telephone numbers can include 4, 5, 6, 7, or even 8 digits, so don't automatically assume you have the wrong number if it looks strange. Since December 1998, calls to land lines must include a leading '0' regardless of whether the call originates within or outside of Italy.

Basic Business Hours 08.00-13.00 and 16.00-19.00, Monday to Friday. Shops in smaller towns may close on Saturday afternoons and Monday mornings.

All EU citizens are eligible for free **health care** in Italy, if they have the correct documentation. Non EU Citizens need personal health insurance.

Traditionally **Italian food** consists of lunch (*pranzo*) and dinner (*cena*) starting with *antipasto* (literally before the meal), a course consisting of cold meats, seafood and vegetables. The next course, *primo,* involves soup, risotto or pasta, followed by *secondo* - the meat or fish course, usually served alone. Vegetables - *contorni* - are ordered and served separately.
Public Holidays - August, particularly during the weeks either side of *Ferragosto* (August 15) is a difficult time for travellers, because many towns are deserted, with shops, bars, hotels and restaurants shut.

Italian **hotels** fall into a number of categories, though the difference between each is gradually decreasing. **Locanda** - historically the most basic option, but now tending to charge more for 'traditional' facilities. **Pensione, albergo** or hotel - prices vary greatly between tourist hotspots and rural areas. Expect an additional charge for breakfast. **Hostels** usually charge 15€. Virtually all hostels (excepting Religious Hostels) are members of the International Youth Hostel Association and you'll need to be a member. **Agritourismo** - basically an upmarket B&B in a rural area and usually a working farm **Camping** in Italy is popular and the sites are generally well equipped.

General

British Tourist Authority, Thames Tower, Black's Road, London W6 9EL
Tel: 0044 (0) 20 8846 9000 www.uktouristinfo.com info@uktouristinfo.com

Youth Hostel Association, 0870 770 8868 (UK) 0044 1629 592700 (Outside UK)
customerservices@yha.org.uk   www.yha.org.uk

French Tourist Board, 300 High Holborn, London WC1V 7JH
Tel: 0044 (0)9068 244 123   info.uk@franceguide.com
http://uk.franceguide.com

French Youth Hostelling Association, FUAJ - National Centre Office, 27 rue Pajol, 75018 Paris Tel: 0033 (0)1 44 89 87 27

IGN Maps http://ign.fr

Further Reading

Europe's Monastery and Convent Guest Houses	Kevin J. Wright
Guide St. Christophe - Comprehensive Guide for lodging in monasteries and convents (French only)	Available from: GSC, 163 blvd Malesherbes 75859 PARIS CEDEX
The Art of Pilgrimage	Phil Cousineau
Have Saddle Will Travel	Don West
The Essential Walker's Journal	Leslie Sansone
Pilgrimage to Rome in the Middle Ages: Continuity and Change (Studies in the History of Medieval Religion)	Debra J. Birch
The Age of Pilgrimage: The Medieval Journey to God	Jonathan Sumption
The Pilgrim's France - A Travel Guide to the Saints	James & Colleen Heater
Along the Templar Trail	Brandon Wilson
Via Francigena - Impressions of a Pilgrimage	Publisher: Eurovia
The Christian's Guide to Rome	S.G.A Luff
Rome: a pilgrim's companion	David Baldwin (Catholic Truth Society, London)
In Search of a Way: two journeys of spiritual discovery	Gerard Hughes
Sigeric's Journey to Rome	Heather Burnley

"Omnes Viae Romam Perducunt"   **All roads lead to Rome ...**

Even with the wealth of historical data available to us today, we can only offer an approximate version of yesterday's reality and we claim to do nothing more in this book. The route described runs roughly parallel with a section of the via Domitia between Arles and Montgenévre (a large portion of the original route having been subsumed by the A51), continues along a variety of roads and tracks that together form a modern-day branch of the via Francigena and rejoins the official main route (to Rome) in Vercelli.

The via Domitia

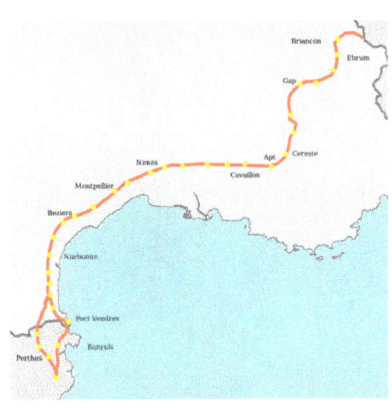

Nearly a century before Caesar, the Roman presence in the Midi region of France was consolidated with the construction of the first Roman road built outside Italy. The via Domitia was constructed in 118 BC by the proconsul, Gnaeus Domitius Ahenobarbus, whose name it bore. It linked Italy and Hispania through Gallia Narbonensis, across what is now southern France. Nevertheless, it was not entirely new, parts traced the mythic route travelled by Hercules and then, more probably, by Hannibal on his way to Italy. The via Domitia crossed the Alps via the Col de Montgenèvre (1850m), followed the valley of the Durance to cross the Rhône in Beaucaire, passed through Nîmes (Nemausus) and proceeded along the coastal plain. Today the via Domitia between Arles and Montgenévre is largely subsumed by a series of major roads, with only a few small sections preserved and still visible. Today its major legacy is in the buildings and bridges left behind - cathedrals in Embrun, Gap, Sisteron, Forcalquier, Apt, Cavaillon and Arles, monasteries or convents in Boscodon, Ganagobie, Salagon, Montmajour, Roman bridges such as Pont Julien, where the via Domitia crosses the Calavon river in Bonnieux.

Arles - Fontvieille 12.2 km

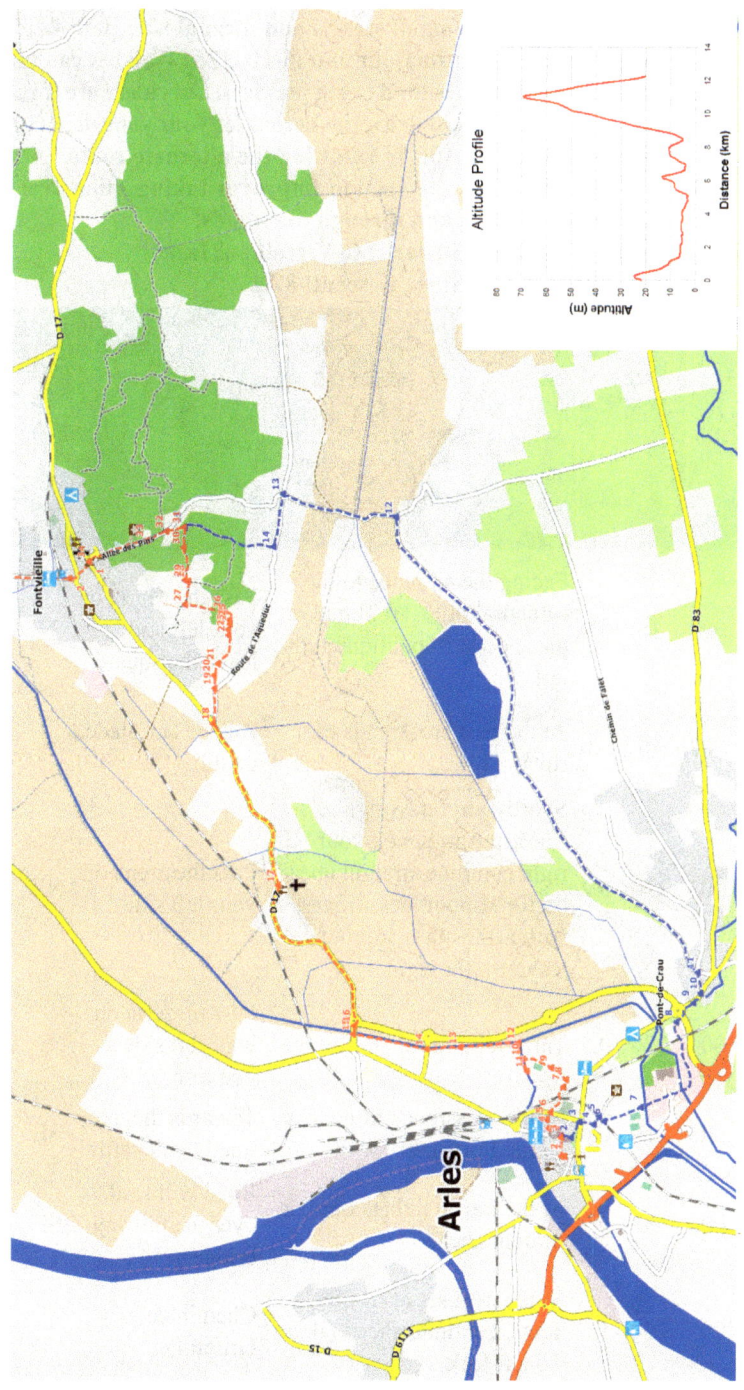

The exit from Arles follows small streets and a canal-side path before joining the busy road to Montmajour and Fontveille. Walkers can take some shelter from the traffic behind crash barriers, but riders are forced into the road. We advise choosing a quiet period for your your departure to avoid the worst of the traffic or following the alternate route. After the Abbey of Montmajour the section improves taking quiet tracks beside the Roman aqueduct and through the woods.

Distance from Arles: 0km   Distance to Vercelli: 621km
Stage Ascent: 85m   Stage Descent: 87m

	Waypoint	Distance Between Waypoints (m)	Total (km)	Directions	Verification Point	Compass	Altitude (m)
Arles - Fontvieille 12.2 km	01.001	0	0,0	Facing the entrance to the cathedral of St Trophime in place de la République turn left	Pass the Marie on your left and leave the square	N	22
	01.002	40	0,0	At the first crossroads turn right	Rue de la Calade, up hill	E	22
	01.003	210	0,2	Shortly after passing the Théâtre Antique on your right continue straight ahead on Rond-point des Arènes. **Note:-** the alternate route leaves to the right	Pass the arena on your left side	NE	24
	01.004	220	0,5	Turn right on rue du Refuge	Pass pizzeria on your left side as you turn	E	20
	01.005	110	0,6	At the crossroads turn right on rue Portagnel	Towards the tree lined boulevard	SE	17
	01.006	90	0,7	At the traffic lights continue straight ahead	Road will lead over the railway bridge	SE	14
	01.007	400	1,0	At the next set of traffic lights, continue ahead taking the left fork	Chemin de Grifeuille	E	11

Waypoint	Distance Between Waypoints (m)	Total (km)	Directions	Verification Point	Compass	Altitude (m)
01.008	80	1,1	Turn left on rue Nicolas Saboly	Pass the clinic on your right side	NE	10
01.009	230	1,3	At the crossroads, continue straight ahead on chemin de la Tour	Pass the sports ground on your left	N	7
01.010	400	1,7	At the T-junction turn left	Proceed with the canal on your right	W	6
01.011	140	1,8	Turn right to cross the canal on the pedestrian bridge and then right again. **Note:-** horse riders should continue beside the canal and take the road bridge and return on the far side of the canal	Keep canal on your right side	E	6
01.012	400	2,2	At the end of the track turn left at the junction of the canals	Keep canal on your right	N	6
01.013	700	2,8	Continue straight ahead beside the canal	Pass blue metal bridge on your right	N	5
01.014	400	3,2	Cross over the main road and continue on the track beside the canal	Pass green metal barrier	N	6
01.015	900	4,1	At the junction with the main road, turn right across the bridge	Towards the roundabout	E	5

Arles - Fontvieille 12.2 km

Waypoint	Distance Between Waypoints (m)	Total (km)	Directions	Verification Point	Compass	Altitude (m)
01.016	90	4,2	Cross the roundabout and take the second exit. **Note:-** the route ahead follows the GR653D, beside the busy and dangerous main road. Pedestrians can walk behind the crash barriers, but horse riders and cyclists must unfortunately follow the road	Signed D17/Fontveille /Abbaye le Montmajour	NE	5
01.017	2100	6,3	Continue straight ahead on the main road	Entrance to Abbaye le Montmajour on the right	NE	12
01.018	2000	8,3	Turn right on the D82	Direction Aqueduc Romain	E	6
01.019	400	8,7	Fork left on the track	Direction Centre Equestre	E	8
01.020	150	8,8	Pass through the Centre Equestre and climb the small hill on the stony track		E	10
01.021	140	8,0	Cross the road and continue straight ahead on the track	Ball Trap on the left	E	15
01.022	400	9,4	Take the right fork		E	27
01.023	60	9,4	Continue straight ahead	Pass aqueduct on the right	E	28

Arles - Fontvieille 12.2 km

Waypoint	Distance Between Waypoints (m)	Total (km)	Directions	Verification Point	Compass	Altitude (m)
01.024	60	9,5	Take the left fork	Following GR sign	E	30
01.025	50	9,5	Take the right fork	Following GR sign	NE	31
01.026	150	9,7	Take the left fork	Continuing to follow the GR	N	36
01.027	500	10,1	At the T-junction turn right	Small house on the left	E	48
01.028	270	10,4	At a T-junction in the track turn left	Keep olive trees to the left	N	53
01.029	40	10,4	Turn right direction Fontvieille Village	Chemin Raymond	E	53
01.030	400	10,8	Continue straight ahead on the broad track	Chemin Raymond	E	64
01.031	220	11,1	At the T-junction in the track turn left. The alternate route joins from the right	Towards the road	N	69
01.032	210	11,3	At the road junction, follow the road to the left	Pine woods on both sides of the road	NW	59
01.033	240	11,5	Continue straight ahead beside the road	Moulin de Daudet to the right	N	50
01.034	700	12,2	Arrive at Fontvieille in the square beside the cafés and Patisserie	Traffic lights at the crossroads with the D17		20

Arles - Fontvieille 12.2 km

17

Stage Ascent: 134m   Stage Descent: 86m

Waypoint	Distance Between Waypoints (m)	Total (km)	Directions	Verification Point	Compass	Altitude (m)
01A1.001	0	0,0	At the top of the hill, turn right	Keep the Théâtre Antique on your right	S	24
01A1.002	110	0,1	Bear left and take the lower road, Montée Vauban	Park immediately on your right	SE	23
01A1.003	210	0,3	At the traffic lights turn right on Avenue des Alyscamps	Pass Police station on your right	S	20
01A1.004	160	0,5	At the bottom of the hill turn left	Keep trees on your left	SE	11
01A1.005	120	0,6	Cross the disused railway track and bear right on the road	Pass the entrance to the Alyscamps Necropolis on your left	SW	9
01A1.006	80	0,7	Take the second turning to the left and then quickly bear right on Avenue du Maréchal Lyautey	Pass sports ground on your right	S	8
01A1.007	500	1,1	At the traffic lights, continue straight ahead remaining on the road as it passes through the commercial district of Fourchon	Cross canal bridge and continue straight ahead at the subsequent small roundabouts	SE	4

Arles - Fontvieille 12.2 km

Waypoint	Distance Between Waypoints (m)	Total (km)	Directions	Verification Point	Compass	Altitude (m)
01A1.008	1400	2,5	After passing under the railway bridge and following the road as it bends to the right, turn right onto the cycle track	Cycle track passes through a subway ahead	SE	3
01A1.009	280	2,8	Continue on the cycle track as it passes under the ancient stone causeway and turns right beside the main road	Enter the village of Pont de Crau	SE	6
01A1.010	160	2,9	At the traffic lights, turn left	Sign Salle Polyvalente	E	11
01A1.011	220	3,2	At the crossroads turn left	Direction Fontvieille	NE	9
01A1.012	6400	9,6	At the crossroads with the D33, turn left	Direction Fontvieille	N	13
01A1.013	1400	10,0	After passing the château de Barbegal, turn left at the next crossroads	Direction Abbaye de Montmajour, route de l'Aqueduc	W	19
01A1.014	600	11,5	Turn right onto the track towards the woods	Low stone wall above drainage ditch on the left at the junction	N	20
01A1.015	1100	12,6	Continue straight ahead on the track. **Note:-** the main route joins from the left	GR sign		71

Alternate 12.6 km

B&B, Hotel, Gite d'Etapes	Price/ Opening
Le Camarguais, 44 Rue Amédée Pichot 13200 Arles, Bouches du Rhône, France Tel:+33(0)4 90 96 01 23	B2
Hotel Voltaire, 1 Place Voltaire 13200 Arles, Bouches du Rhône, France Tel:+33(0)4 90 96 49 18 www.hotel-de-provence.net/?/Hotel-Arles/258-Hotel-Voltaire	B2
14 Rue Rouget de Lisle (Mme Graziella Lopez) 13200 Arles, Bouches du Rhône, France Tel:+33(0)4 90 96 70 87	B2
Les Iris (M. Marcel Manin), 33 Chemin du Fort d'Herval 13990 Fontvieille, Bouches du Rhône, France Tel:+33(0)4 90 54 83 75 Mobile:+33(0)6 30 35 02 17 irisfontvieille@aol.com	B2
Auberge des Balastres, 90 Avenue de Tarascon 13990 Fontvieille, Bouches du Rhône, France Tel:+33(0)4 90 54 68 72 www.auberge-balastres.com/	B2
Pilgrim Accommodation	
Babette Gallard & Paul Chinn, 8 Rue des Vinatiers, 13200 Arles,Bouches du Rhône,France Tel:+33(0)4 90 91 70 01 babette_gallard@hotmail.com **Note:** Credentials available	Donation Open all year
Bénédicte Rata, 32 Rue de la Madeleine 13200 Arles, Bouches du Rhône, France Tel:+33(0)4 90 96 18 16 Mobile:+33(0)6 17 98 18 85 bjp.rata@free.fr **Note:** Credentials available	B1 Open all year
Martine Piriou, 26 Chemin de Bigot 13200 Arles, Bouches du Rhône, France Tel:+33(0)4 90 93 07 49 Mobile:+33(0)6 63 00 28 27 pmartine13@gmail.com **Note:** Credentials available	B1 Open all year
Eric Grandin, 4 Rue François Arago 13200 Arles, Bouches du Rhône, France Tel:+33(0)9 50 80 25 13 Mobile:+33(0)6 11 86 55 31 lauberginerouge@hotmail.fr	B1 Open all year

Arles - Fontvieille 12.2 km

Pilgrim Accommodation co-ordinator	
Marie-Françoise, 4 Rue Savérien 13200 Arles, Bouches du Rhône, France Tel:+33(0)4 90 96 75 21 mf.rives@yahoo.fr **Note:** Credentials available	B1 Open all year
Annie Guillot, 104 Avenue de la Camargue 13200 Arles, Bouches du Rhône, France Tel:+33(0)4 90 43 37 06 Mobile:+33(0)6 19 97 42 19 jmaguillot@hotmail.fr	B1 Open all year
Renée Debard, 30 Avenue de Pskov 13200 Arles, Bouches du Rhône, France Tel:+33(0)4 90 96 29 09 Mobile:+33(0)6 83 26 13 16 renee.debard@wanadoo.fr **Note:** Credentials available	Donation
Sophie Berton, Les Ruchers de la Cala Melosa, Vallon de la Lèque 13990 Fontvieille, Bouches du Rhône, France Tel:+33(0)4 90 54 66 83 Mobile:+33(0)6 07 54 56 69 cala.melosa@free.fr **Note:** Accommodation for 2 people	B1 Closed 1/02 - 30/11
Yourte accommodation 13990 Fontvieille, Bouches du Rhône, France Mobile:+33(0)6 07 54 56 69	Donation

Religious Hostel	
Pierre de Bénédictin, Gageron 13200 Arles, Bouches du Rhône, France Tel:+33(0)4 90 97 00 55 hotelleriebouchaud@orange.fr **Note:** 7km outside Arles and 2 km from the beginning of the St James Way	Donation

Youth Hostel	
Auberge de Jeunesse, 20 Rue du Maréchal Foch 13200 Arles, Bouches du Rhône, France Tel:+33(0)4 90 96 18 25 arles@fuaj.org	B1 Open 10/02 - 15/12

Camping	
Arles Camping Club, Route nationale Pont de Crau 13200 Arles, Bouches du Rhône, France Tel:+33(0)9 62 09 95 83	B1
Camping Camp Municipal Des Pins, Rue Michelet 13990 Fontvieille, Bouches du Rhône, France Tel:+33(0)4 90 54 78 69	B1
Camping Le Gardian, 100 Rue des Anciens Combattants d'Afrique du Nord et d'Outre-Mer 13200 Arles, Bouches du Rhône, France Tel:+33(0)4 90 98 46 51	B1

Arles - Fontvieille 12.2 km

Pilgrim Hostel	Price
Communauté Emmaüs, Route Saintes Maries de la Mer 13200 Arles, Bouches du Rhône, France Tel:+33(0)4 90 49 79 76	Donation

Tourist Office

Office de Tourisme, Avenue Moulins 13990 Fontvieille, Bouches du Rhône, France   Tel:+33(0)4 90 54 67 49
www.fontvieille-provence.com/

Office de tourisme d'Arles, Boulevard des Lices 13200 ARLES, Bouches du Rhône, France   Tel:+33(0)4 90 18 41 20   www.arlestourisme.com/

Doctor

Mollard Barre Frédérique, 6 Impasse Jules Auvergne 13990 Fontvieille, Bouches du Rhône, France   Tel:+33(0)4 90 54 75 67

Sayn Urpar Véronique, 9 Rue Liberté 13200 Arles, Bouches du Rhône, France   Tel:+33(0)4 90 49 89 91

Veterinary

Clinique Vétérinaire des Remparts, 26 Boulevard Emile Combes 13200 Arles, Bouches du Rhône, France   Tel:+33(0)4 90 96 64 06

Arles - Fontvieille 12.2 km

View from Montmajour Abbey direction Fontvieille

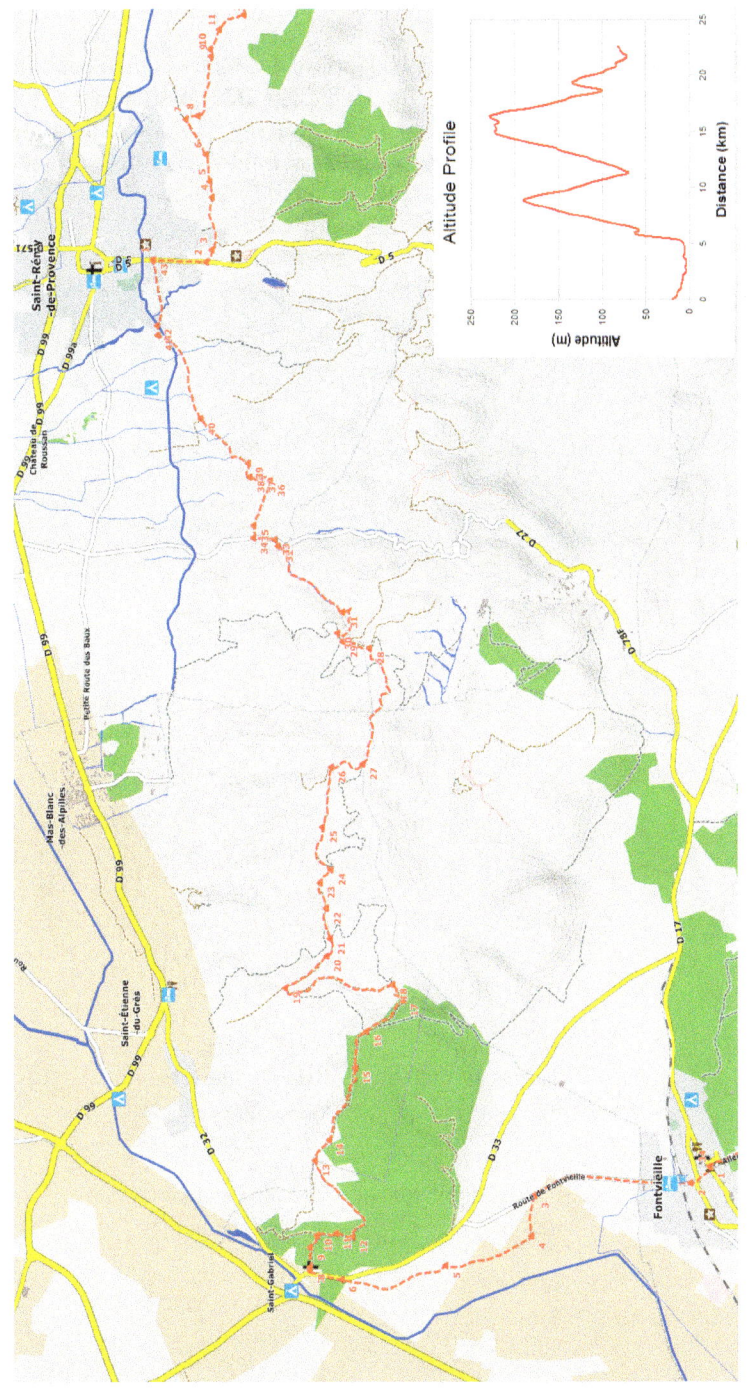

After 2kms on the sometimes busy D33, the route follows quieter country roads and tracks before briefly rejoining the D33 for the entry to St Gabriel. From here the route climbs into the Alpilles and follows beautiful woodland tracks to the outskirts of Saint-Rémy-de-Provence.
Distance from Arles: 12km   Distance to Vercelli: 609km
Stage Ascent: 409m   Stage Descent: 347m

Fontvieille - Saint-Rémy-de-Provence 22.6 km

Waypoint	Distance Between Waypoints (m)	Total (km)	Directions	Verification Point	Compass	Altitude (m)
02.001	0	0,0	At the traffic lights in Fontvieille continue straight ahead	Direction Saint Etienne du Grès, D33	NW	20
02.002	300	0,3	At the roundabout bear right	Direction Saint Etienne du Grès following the GR signs	N	15
02.003	1900	2,2	Turn left off the main road	Direction Mas de la Grande Visclède, following the GR sign	W	7
02.004	500	2,6	Turn right onto the track	Shortly before reaching the farm buildings on the left side of the road	N	4
02.005	1100	3,7	At the T-junction turn left	Pumping station on the left at the junction	N	7
02.006	1300	4,0	At the junction with the major road, bear left	Direction Chapelle St Gabriel	N	7

Waypoint	Distance Between Waypoints (m)	Total (km)	Directions	Verification Point	Compass	Altitude (m)
02.007	400	5,4	From the parking area beside the chapelle of St Gabriel, take the steps on the right. **Note:-** horse and bike riders can enter the chapelle grounds via the embankment to the left of the gates	Towards the chapelle entrance	E	15
02.008	30	5,4	Skirt around the chapelle and climb the hill on the path at the rear		E	17
02.009	250	5,6	Turn right	Keep the ruined tower on your left side	SE	46
02.010	170	5,8	At the T-junction, turn right	GR sign	S	60
02.011	230	6,0	Bear right on the track	GR sign	S	61
02.012	190	6,2	Turn left up the hill	GR sign	NE	58
02.013	1200	7,4	At the crossroads in the track, continue straight ahead	Sign "GR 6, St Etienne du Grès"	SE	117
02.014	280	7,6	Continue straight ahead across the tarmac patch	Sign "Citern 142"	E	138
02.015	900	8,5	Continue straight ahead	Sign GR6	E	180
02.016	500	9,0	Take the left fork, down the hill	GR and "Citern 276" signs	SE	187
02.017	600	9,6	Turn sharp left on the track	Cottage to the right	NE	154

Fontvieille – Saint-Rémy-de-Provence 22.6 km

Waypoint	Distance Between Waypoints (m)	Total (km)	Directions	Verification Point	Compass	Altitude (m)
02.018	270	9,9	Turn left on the track	Sign "GR 6, St Etienne du Grès"	N	136
02.019	1400	11,3	At the junction in the hamlet of mas de Pommet, turn right on the tarmac road	Direction les Baux en Provence	SE	70
02.020	600	11,9	Continue straight ahead on the track	Ignore right fork to Auzepy	E	85
02.021	220	12,1	Take the left fork	Sign GR6	E	94
02.022	400	12,5	Take the left fork	Sign GR6	E	111
02.023	300	12,8	Continue straight ahead	Pass la Cabane du Garde on your left	SE	121
02.024	190	12,0	Bear left on the track	GR 6	E	131
02.025	600	13,6	Continue straight ahead	Sign "les Quatre Termes"	E	154
02.026	700	14,2	At the crossroads in the track turn right	GR sign	S	195
02.027	500	14,7	At the crossroads in the tracks continue straight ahead and following the ridge	The valley towards les Baux de Provence on the right	E	217
02.028	1600	16,2	At the junction in the track, turn left	Take the broad track down the hill	N	228
02.029	300	16,5	At the junction continue straight ahead	Direction Saint Rémy	NE	222
02.030	110	16,7	Take the right fork downhill	Rock outcrop on the left	E	217
02.031	600	17,2	At the junction in the tracks, bear right	Down hill	NE	173

Fontvieille - Saint-Rémy-de-Provence 22.6 km

Waypoint	Distance Between Waypoints (m)	Total (km)	Directions	Verification Point	Compass	Altitude (m)
02.032	1100	18,4	Cross the stream and bear right on the tarmac road	Down hill	NE	114
02.033	80	18,4	At the T-junction with the D27 turn left	GR sign	N	108
02.034	250	18,7	Turn right onto the stony track into the woods. **Note:-** the route ahead involves steep descents over loose stone paths, riders should continue on the road for 1.5 km and turn right at the crossroads on the vieux chemin d'Arles for 2.5 km to reach the end of this section	200 metres after passing small stone building on the right	E	100
02.035	140	18,8	Continue straight ahead across the clearing and take the broad stone path	Following the GR signs	E	106
02.036	600	19,4	At the top of the rise turn left	Following the GR signs	N	134
02.037	130	19,5	Turn left	Follow GR signs	N	131
02.038	140	19,6	Continue straight ahead	Follow GR signs	E	128
02.039	180	19,8	At the T-junction turn left onto the road	White rock face ahead	NE	123

Fontvieille - Saint-Rémy-de-Provence 22.6 km

Waypoint	Distance Between Waypoints (m)	Total (km)	Directions	Verification Point	Compass	Altitude (m)
02.040	800	20,6	Continue straight ahead on the road	Chemin de Servières at des Cadenières	NE	90
02.041	1100	21,7	At the crossroads between the vieux chemin d'Arles and the chemin de Servières et des Cadenières, turn right on the narrow road between hedges	Chemin de la Croix d'Arles	E	71
02.042	110	21,8	Turn right to cross the canal bridge	GR sign	E	73
02.043	800	22,6	Arrive at Saint-Rémy-de-Provence, town centre to the left	Crossroads with Avenue van Gogh		82

B&B, Hotel, Gite d'Etapes	Price /Opening
Mas de Bigau (M. André Denante) 13210 Saint Rémy de Provence, Bouches du Rhône, France Tel:+33(0)4 90 92 24 15 andre.denante@orange.fr	B2
Mas Les Floralies (Mme Annie Gros), Avenue Durand Maillane 13210 Saint Rémy de Provence, Bouches du Rhône, France Tel:+33(0)4 90 92 10 38 Mobile:+33(0)6 88 42 26 48	B2
Hotel de la Caume, Route de Cavallon 13210 Saint Rémy de Provence, Bouches du Rhône, France Tel:+33(0)4 90 92 43 5 www.hoteldelacaume.com/	B2
Hôtel du Cheval Blanc, 6 Avenue Fauconnet 13210 Saint Rémy de Provence, Bouches du Rhône, France Tel:+33(0)4 90 92 09 28 www.hotelduchevalblanc.com/	B2
Hotel Mas Vidau, 5 Avenue N D du Château 13103 Saint Etienne du Grès, Bouches du Rhône, France Tel:+33(0)4 90 47 63 71 www.mas.vidau.monsite.wanadoo.fr/	B3

Fontvieille - Saint-Rémy-de-Provence 22.6 km

B&B, Hotel, Gite d'Etapes	Price/ Opening
Hotel Mas Vidau, 5 Avenue N D du Château 13103 Saint Etienne du Grès, Bouches du Rhône, France Tel:+33(0)4 90 47 63 71 www.mas.vidau.monsite.wanadoo.fr/	B3
Mas Les Floralies (Mme Annie Gros), Avenue Durand Maillane 13210 Saint Rémy de Provence, Bouches du Rhône, France Tel:+33(0)4 90 92 10 38 Mobile:+33(0)6 88 42 26 48	B2
Hôtel du Cheval Blanc, 6 Avenue Fauconnet 13210 Saint Rémy de Provence, Bouches du Rhône, France Tel:+33(0)4 90 92 09 28 www.hotelduchevalblanc.com/	B2
Hotel de la Caume, Route de Cavallon 13210 Saint Rémy de Provence, Bouches du Rhône, France Tel:+33(0)4 90 92 43 59 www.hoteldelacaume.com/	B2
Mas de Bigau (M. André Denante) 13210 Saint Rémy de Provence, Bouches du Rhône, France Tel:+33(0)4 90 92 24 15 andre.denante@orange.fr	B2
Camping	
Camping Municipal De Saint Etienne Du Gres, 2 avenue Du Dr Barberin 13103 Saint etienne du grès, Bouches du Rhône,France Tel: +33(0)4 90 49 00 03	B1 Open all year
Camping Municipal des Romarins, Route de St. Rémy/D 5 13520 Maussanne les Alpilles, Bouches du Rhône, France Tel:+33(0)4 90 54 33 60 www.maussane.com/	B1
Camping Tartarin, Route Vallabrègues 13150 Tarascon, Bouches du Rhône, France Tel:+33(0)4 90 91 01 46 www.campingtartarin.fr/	B1 Open all year
Saint-Gabriel, Carrefour St Gabriel 13150 Tarascon, Bouches du Rhône, France Tel:+33(0)4 90 91 19 83 **Note:** Horses accepted	B1
PR Camping à la Ferme, Vieux chemin d'Arles 13210 Saint Rémy de Provence, Bouches du Rhône, France Tel:+33(0)4 90 92 27 22 tgperrot@orange.fr **Note:** Accepts horses	B1 Open 15/03 - 15/10
Camping Monplaisir, Chemin Monplaisir 13210 Saint Rémy de Provence, Bouches du Rhône, France Tel:+33(0)4 90 92 22 70 www.camping-monplaisir.fr/	B1

Fontvieille – Saint-Rémy-de-Provence 22.6 km

Camping

Camping Pegomas, 3 Avenue Jean Moulin 13210 Saint Rémy
de Provence, Bouches du Rhône, France B1
Tel:+33(0)4 90 92 01 21   www.campingpegomas.com/

Camping le Mas de Nicolas, Avenue de Plaisance-du-Touch
13210 Saint Rémy de Provence, Bouches du Rhône, France B1
Tel:+33(0)4 90 92 27 05   www.masdenicolas.celeonet.fr/

Tourist Office

Mairie 13103 Saint Étienne du Grès, Bouches du Rhône, France
Tel:+33(0)4 90 49 16 46
Note: Information about local accommodation,

Office du Tourisme, Place Jean Jaurès 13210 Saint Rémy de Provence,
Bouches du Rhône, France   Tel:+33(0)4 90 92 05 22
www.mairie-saintremydeprovence.fr/

Mairie, Place Jules Pélissier 13210 Saint Rémy de Provence, Bouches du
Rhône, France   Tel:+33(0)4 90 38 61 31

Veterinary

Clinique Vétérinaire des Alpilles, Route Plan d'Orgon 13210 Saint Rémy
de Provence, Bouches du Rhône, France   Tel:+33(0)4 90 92 01 91

Farrier

Mistral guillaume, Route de Châteaurenard 13690 Graveson, Bouches du
Rhône, France   Mobile: +33 (0)6 07 13 68 74,

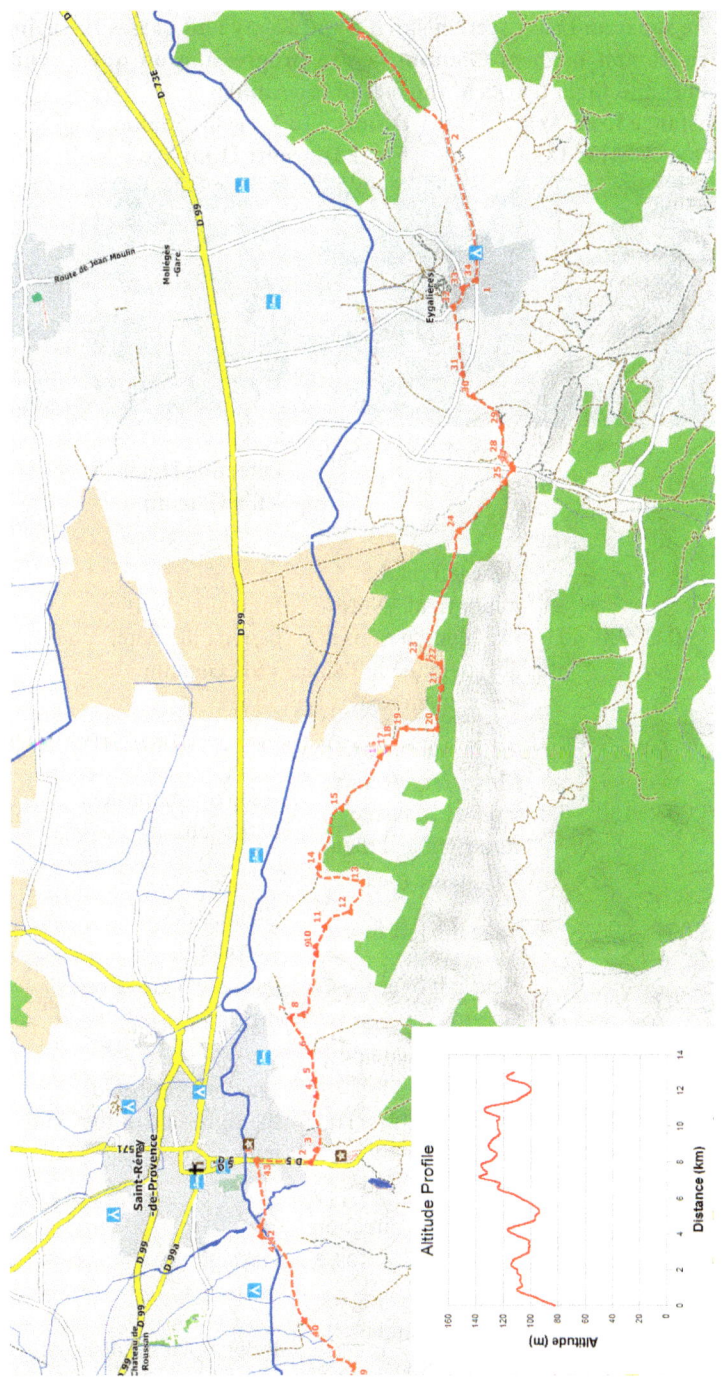

The short and easy section skirts Saint Rémy and passes the ruins of pre-Roman town of Glanum before progressing on quiet country roads and farm tracks at the foot of the Alpilles.

Distance from Arles: 35km   Distance to Vercelli: 586km
Stage Ascent: 143m   Stage Descent: 113m

Saint-Rémy-de-Provence to Eygalières 13 km

Waypoint	Distance Between Waypoints (m)	Total (km)	Directions	Verification Point	Compass	Altitude (m)
03.001	0	0,0	From the crossroads take the D5, Avenue van Gogh	Direction Hotel Villa Glanum	S	82
03.002	600	0,6	Bear left on the minor road. **Note:-** the Glanum ruins are ahead on the left-side of the main road	Immediately after passing the hotel Villa Glanum	SE	102
03.003	150	0,8	At the entrance to the Monastery of Saint Paul de Mausole, turn right and then left on the road	Keep the monastery to the left	E	107
03.004	600	1,4	Take the left fork	Chemin des Carrièrs	E	107
03.005	160	1,6	Bear left over the stream	Pass olive grove on the right	E	107
03.006	300	1,9	At the crossroads continue straight ahead: **Note:-** GR6 crosses the track, GR653D ahead	Line of trees beside the right side of the track	NE	110
03.007	500	2,3	Turn right, direction Boucle de la Grosse Galine	GR sign	S	114
03.008	170	2,5	Turn left on the broad track	Pylons overhead	E	113

Waypoint	Distance Between Waypoints (m)	Total (km)	Directions	Verification Point	Compass	Altitude (m)
03.009	700	3,2	Take the left fork	GR sign	E	101
03.010	80	3,3	At the tarmac road turn right	Slightly uphill with houses to the right	SE	101
03.011	250	3,5	Take the left fork on the track	Opposite road to mas de Calabrun	SE	101
03.012	400	3,9	At junction turn left	Keep the Alpilles to the right	E	109
03.013	400	4,3	At the T-junction turn left		N	116
03.014	600	4,9	Continue straight ahead on the track	Direction Eygalières	E	96
03.015	800	5,6	Take the left fork	GR and yellow footpath signs	SE	99
03.016	700	6,3	At the metal gate, bear right on the track	Between trees	SE	114
03.017	140	6,5	Take the right fork	Pass small building on your right	SE	123
03.018	100	6,6	Take the right fork	Towards the Alpilles and the vineyards	SE	124
03.019	230	6,8	After skirting the farm buildings, continue straight ahead	Towards the Alpilles avoiding right fork through vineyards	S	122
03.020	400	7,2	Bear left on the broad track	Towards Château de Romanin	E	137
03.021	500	7,6	Take the left fork	Château de Romanin to the right	E	135

Saint-Rémy-de-Provence to Eygalières 13 km

Waypoint	Distance Between Waypoints (m)	Total (km)	Directions	Verification Point	Compass	Altitude (m)
03.022	280	7,9	Continue straight ahead on the long straight track	Towards Eygalières	N	136
03.023	230	8,1	At the T-junction turn right	Metal gate	E	128
03.024	1500	9,6	Continue straight ahead on the track	House to your left	SE	122
03.025	800	10,3	Bear left over the stone bridge	Towards parking area	SE	124
03.026	180	10,5	Cross the main road, D24, and continue on the stony track		NE	123
03.027	40	10,6	Take the left fork		NE	124
03.028	140	10,7	Take the right fork	GR sign	E	130
03.029	300	11,0	Take the left fork	GR sign	NE	133
03.030	500	11,5	Bear left and then right on the track		NE	108
03.031	300	11,8	At the junction with the main road, D24b, cross over and continue on the small tarmac road	Crucifix to the right	E	102
03.032	800	12,6	At the crossroads turn right into Eygalières	Rue des Ecoles	SE	115
03.033	260	12,8	At the next crossroads turn right with caution	No entry sign, rue de la République	SE	117
03.034	170	13,0	Arrive at Eygalières centre	Brasserie on the left		122

Saint-Rémy-de-Provence to Eygalières 13 km

B&B, Hotel, Gite d'Etapes	Price/ Opening
L'Oustaoude Vérane (Michelle et Pierre Viaud), Chemin des Véranes 13210 Saint Rémy de Provence, Bouches du Rhône, France Tel:+33(0)4 90 95 14 48 loustaou.verane@wanadoo.fr	B2
La Sarriette (Monique et René Marcellin), Route du Mas des Mauniers 13810 Eygalières, Bouches du Rhône, France Tel:+33(0)4 90 95 94 50 Mobile:+33(0)6 74 68 23 44 renemarcellin@wanadoo.fr **Note:** also equestrian centre	B1
Chemin du Contras (Danielle et Maurice Pernix) 13810 Eygalières, Bouches du Rhône, France Tel:+33(0)4 90 95 04 89 Mobile:+33(0)6 19 01 28 77 pernix.maurice@orange.fr	B2

Camping	
Camping Les Oliviers, Avenue Jean Jaurès 13810 Eygalières, Bouches du Rhône, France Tel:+33(0)4 90 95 91 86 reservation@camping-les-oliviers.com	B1 Open 1/04 - 15/10

Tourist Office	
Office Tourisme Syndic Initiative Orgo, Place Liberte 13660 Orgon, Bouches du Rhône, France Tel:+33(0)4 90 73 04 56	

Saint-Rémy-de-Provence to Eygalières 13 km

Eygalières

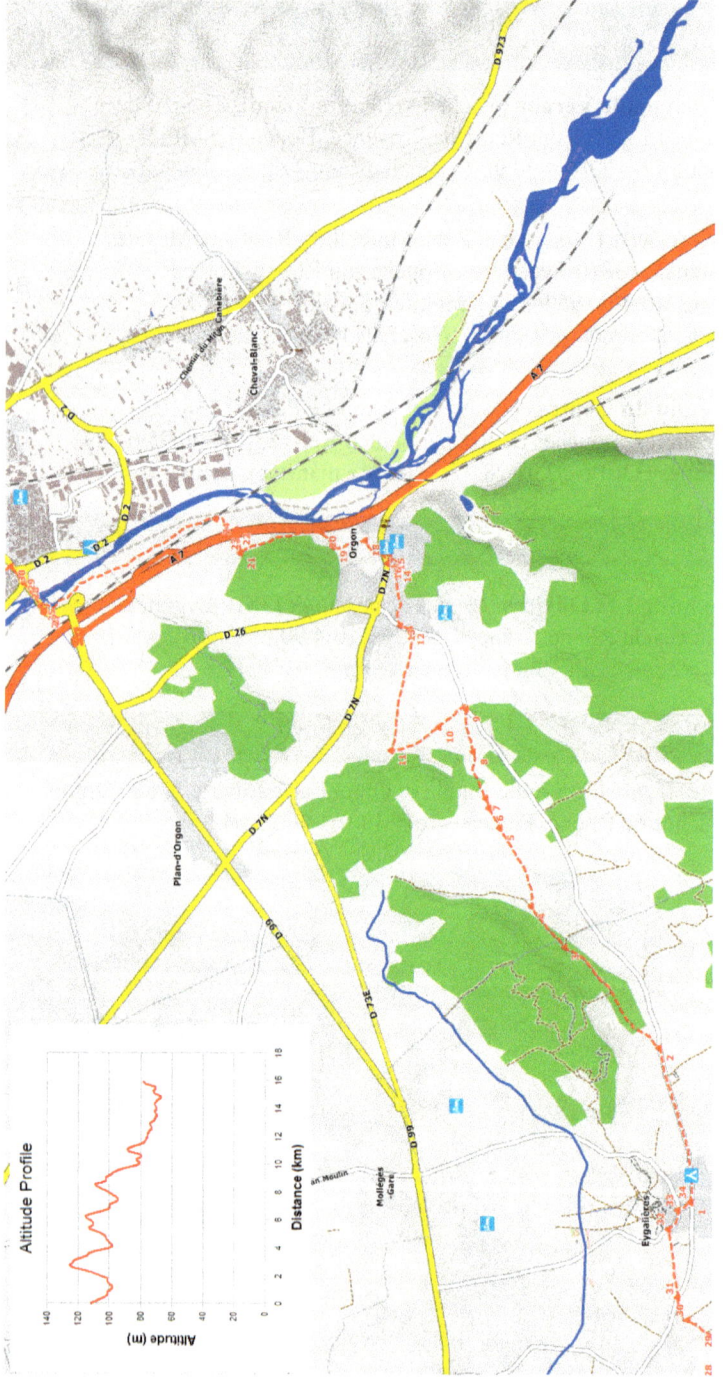

Eygalières - Cavaillon 15.9 km

The exit from Eygalières initially proceeds besides the D24b before returning to farm and forest tracks and then quiet minor roads leading to Orgon. After passing through Orgon, the route continues on farm tracks parallel to the river Durance, before crossing the river, the autoroute and TGV line on a very busy road bridge.

Distance from Arles: 48km **Distance to Vercelli: 573km**
Stage Ascent: 91m   **Stage Descent: 125m**

Waypoint	Distance Between Waypoints (m)	Total (km)	Directions	Verification Point	Compass	Altitude (m)
04.001	0	0,0	From the crossroads in the centre of Eygalières, turn left on avenue Jean Jaurés	Direction Orgon	E	112
04.002	1700	1,7	Bear left onto a track	Sign "Domaine de Coste Bonne", GR sign	NE	101
04.003	1600	3,3	Take the left fork	GR sign	NE	118
04.004	600	3,9	Bear right following the GR sign	Rocks ahead	NE	104
04.005	1000	4,8	At the crossroads continue straight ahead	Sign "Domaine de Valdition"	NE	102
04.006	240	5,1	At the crossroads with the tarmac road continue straight ahead on the stony track	Yellow gas pipeline markers beside the track	E	106
04.007	110	5,2	Take the left fork	Continuing beside the yellow markers and following the GR signs	E	108
04.008	600	5,7	At the crossroads, continue straight ahead on the track	Olive grove to the left	E	110
04.009	500	6,2	At the T-junction with the D24b, turn left and then immediately left again onto a small road	Cross small bridge, leaving the yellow markers	NW	115

Eygalières – Cavaillon 15.9 km

Waypoint	Distance Between Waypoints (m)	Total (km)	Directions	Verification Point	Compass	Altitude (m)
04.010	400	6,6	Continue straight ahead on the small road	Cross small bridge, leaving the yellow markers	NW	105
04.011	600	7,2	At the T-junction turn right	GR sign	E	97
04.012	1300	8,6	At the crossroads with the main road, D24b, cross over and turn left beside the main road	Factory entrance ahead at the junction	N	109
04.013	120	8,7	Turn right on the road	Direction Notre Dame de Beauregard, GR sign	E	105
04.014	700	9,3	At the crossroads turn left	Montée du Paradis	NE	98
04.015	150	9,5	At the crossroads, turn sharp left	Rue du Faubourg Sainte Anne	W	96
04.016	100	9,6	At the T-junction, turn sharp right on avenue de la Victoire	Direction Marseille	NE	94
04.017	120	9,7	Turn left into the small road, chemin de la Mine, and then immediately turn right on chemin des Perriéres	Cross canal	NE	91
04.018	280	9,0	Bear left on chemin des Pelliettes	Keep small waterway on the left	N	82
04.019	400	10,4	Take the right fork	Keeping waterway on your left	NE	82

Eygaliéres - Cavaillon 15.9 km

Waypoint	Distance Between Waypoints (m)	Total (km)	Directions	Verification Point	Compass	Altitude (m)
04.020	200	10,6	At T-junction turn left on the tarmac road	Keep autoroute on the right	N	79
04.021	1000	11,5	Shortly after passing the farm of la Baume, turn right	Towards bridge over the autoroute	E	78
04.022	260	11,8	After bridge turn left		N	76
04.023	150	11,9	Turn sharp right and skirt the field	Keep the field to your left	NE	75
04.024	270	12,2	Bear right, proceed between river and railway	Pass under the railway	NW	75
04.025	2300	14,5	Pass under the road bridge and bear left	Industrial building	SW	70
04.026	90	14,5	Turn left at the T-junction with the road		SE	69
04.027	30	14,6	At the T-junction with the main road, turn left and keep to the left side of the road, direction Cavaillon	Take the bridge over the river	NE	69
04.028	400	14,0	Bear left onto the cycle track	GR sign	NE	69
04.029	100	15,0	Take the zebra crossing over the road and continue straight ahead	Remain on cycle track	NE	71
04.030	150	15,2	Turn left on Allée Guende	Direction Stade Pagnetti, GR sign	NW	72
04.031	300	15,5	At the T-junction turn right and then immediately left	Follow GR signs, avenue du Général Leclerc	N	70
04.032	160	15,7	T-junction turn right	GR sign	NE	75
04.033	240	15,9	Arrive in Cavaillon centre	Place François Tourel		78

Eygalières – Cavaillon 15.9 km

B&B, Hotel, Gite d'Etapes	Price/ Opening
Hôtel Le Relais Des Fumades, RN 7 13660 Orgon, Bouches du Rhône, France Tel:+33(0)4 90 73 00 81	B2
Au Petit Pavé, RN 7 13660 Orgon, Bouches du Rhône, France Tel:+33(0)4 90 59 00 22 www.aubergeauxpetitspaves.com/	B2
L'Atelier du Peintre (Mme Charlotte Novitz), 2 Rue Paul Berthe 13660 Orgon, Bouches du Rhône, France Tel:+33(0)4 90 73 01 85 Mobile:+33(0)9 53 44 25 00 charlottenovitz@gmail.com	B2
La Maison de Chichui, 8 Impasse des Remparts 13660 Orgon,Bouches du Rhône, France Tel:+33(0)4 90 53 95 70 Mobile:+33(0)4 90 53 95 70 jacquelinefourquaux@orange.fr **Note:** Pilgrim price reduction	B2
Etap Hotel Cavaillon, 175 Avenue du Pont 84300 Cavaillon, Vaucluse, France Tel:+33(0)8 92 68 07 91 www.accorhotels.com/accorhotels/lien_externe.svlt?goto=fiche_hotel&code_hotel=2718	B2
Le Splendid, 35 Avenue Germain Chauvin 84300 Cavaillon, Vaucluse, France Tel:+33(0)4 90 71 68 69	B2
Logis Hotel Toppin, 70 cours gambetta 84300 Cavaillon, Vaucluse, France Tel:+33(0)4 90 71 30 42 www.hotel-toppin.com/	B2
Religious Hostel	
Paroisse Cathédrale Ste Bernadette (P. Vincent de Martino), Avenue Albin Durand 84300 Cavaillon, Vaucluse, France Tel:+33(0)4 90 78 03 44 **Note:** Only in an emergency	Donation
Camping	
Camping de la Durance, 495 Avenue Boscodomini 84300 Cavaillon, Vaucluse, France Tel:+33(0)4 90 71 11 78 www.camping-durance.com/ **Note:** price reduction for pilgrims with credential	B1 Open 1/04 - 30/09
Tourist Office	
Mairie, Rue Eglise 84460 Cheval Blanc, Vaucluse, France Tel:+33(0)4 90 71 01 17	
Doctor	
Calafat Gérard, 6 Hameau Lucien Martin 13750 Plan d'Orgon, Bouches du Rhône, France Tel:+33(0)4 90 73 15 26	

Eygalières - Cavaillon 15.9 km

After leaving Cavaillon, this flat and easy section follows generally quiet country roads before a brief period on the busy D900. From there the route follows a disused railway track to the villages of Coustellet and Beumettes. Accommodation is very limited on this section and so planning ahead is highly recommended.

Distance from Arles: 64km Distance to Vercelli: 558km
Stage Ascent: 64m   Stage Descent: 16m

Cavaillon - Beaumettes 16.3 km

Waypoint	Distance Between Waypoints (m)	Total (km)	Directions	Verification Point	Compass	Altitude (m)
05.001	0	0,0	Continue straight ahead across the square	Towards the cathedral spire	NE	77
05.002	120	0,1	Turn right on the road, place du Clos	Trees on right, cafés on left, GR sign	E	77
05.003	60	0,2	Turn left into the covered passage way	Sign "Circuit du Vieux Cavaillon"	N	76
05.004	120	0,3	Directly beside the Cathedral bear left	Keep Cathedral on your right side	N	77
05.005	70	0,4	After passing the Cathedral turn right	Rue de Diderot	E	78
05.006	60	0,4	At the end of the road, turn left	Grande Rue	N	78
05.007	280	0,7	Pass through the archway and turn right into Cours Gambetta	Church on the right	SE	77
05.008	120	0,8	Turn left, direction les Condamines	GR sign	NE	76
05.009	120	0,9	At the roundabout, continue straight ahead	Road progresses parallel and closer to the railway track	NE	75

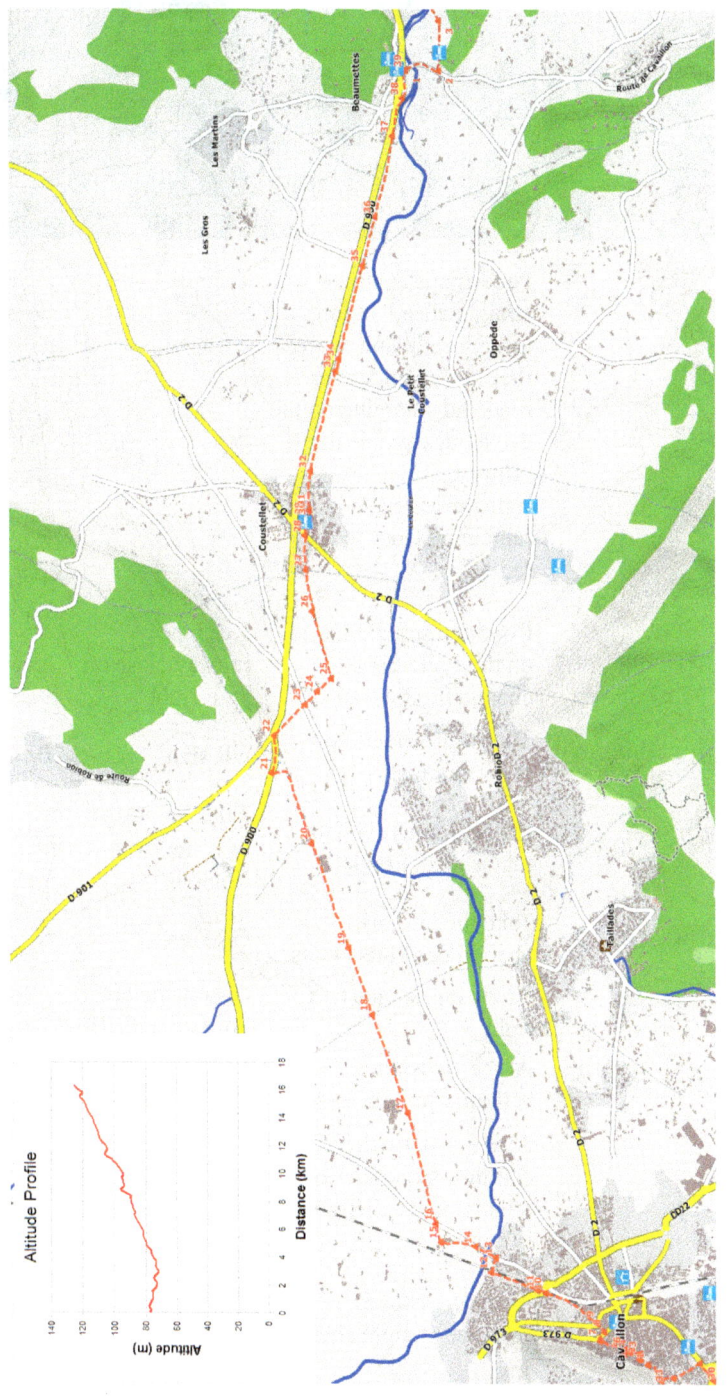

Waypoint	Distance Between Waypoints (m)	Total (km)	Directions	Verification Point	Compass	Altitude (m)
05.010	700	1,6	Pedestrians continue straight ahead, before turning right and taking the subway under the road and emerging on the cycle track beside the railway. Riders bear right, direction Avignon, remaining close to the railway		N	75
05.011	90	1,7	Continue straight ahead on the cycle track, chemin du Ratacan	Keep the railway close on your right	N	74
05.012	600	2,2	Turn right under the railway bridge	GR sign	E	73
05.013	170	2,4	At the T-junction with a major road, turn left	Take the bridge over the river, le Coulon	NE	74
05.014	250	2,6	Take the left fork, chemin des Puits Neufs	GR sign	N	74
05.015	400	3,0	At the crossroads turn right	Chemin de la Tour	E	72
05.016	200	3,2	At the crossroads continue straight ahead	GR sign	E	73
05.017	1200	4,4	At the crossroads, continue straight ahead remaining on chemin de la Tour	GR sign	E	76
05.018	1100	5,5	At the crossroads, continue straight ahead	GR sign, stream to the right of the road	E	81

Cavaillon - Beaumettes 16.3 km

Waypoint	Distance Between Waypoints (m)	Total (km)	Directions	Verification Point	Compass	Altitude (m)
05.019	800	6,3	At the crossroads with the D31, continue straight ahead	Yellow GR sign, chemin de la Tour Sabran	E	83
05.020	1200	7,4	At the crossroads, continue straight ahead	Camping des Cerisiers to the right	NE	88
05.021	1000	8,4	At the T-junction with the main road, D900, turn right	Direction la Tour de Sabran	E	90
05.022	400	8,8	Shortly before the next T-junction, turn right on the small road	GR sign, chemin du Four à Chaux	SE	96
05.023	500	9,3	At the crossroads, continue straight ahead on chemin du Four à Chaux	GR sign, towards large barn	SE	94
05.024	200	9,5	At crossroads, continue straight ahead, avoid the GR signs (GR6) to the right and left	Chemin des Pendus to the left	SE	94
05.025	210	9,7	Turn left on the stony track	GR sign, just before crossroads	E	95
05.026	700	10,4	Turn right and immediately left	Pass between the supports of a derelict railway bridge	E	97
05.027	500	10,9	Continue straight ahead into the town of Coustellet on chemin des Guillaumets	Tarmac road	E	100

Cavaillon - Beaumettes 16.3 km

Waypoint	Distance Between Waypoints (m)	Total (km)	Directions	Verification Point	Compass	Altitude (m)
05.028	400	11,2	At the junction with Allée de Commerce, continue straight ahead	Narrow road, with car park to your left, shops and restaurant on right	E	105
05.029	180	11,4	Shortly after passing the former railway station, turn right	GR sign	S	106
05.030	50	11,5	T-junction turn left	Cave Cooperative at junction, route des Caves	E	106
05.031	80	11,5	At the junction, continue straight ahead	Direction Zone d'Activités la Tourail	E	105
05.032	400	11,0	Continue straight ahead on the track	Déchetterie to the right	E	105
05.033	1100	13,0	At the junction with the tarmac road, bear left on the road	Continue parallel to the main road	E	110
05.034	130	13,2	Leave the road and continue straight ahead on the track	Pass disused railway bridge on the left	E	111
05.035	1000	14,2	Cross the tarmac road and continue straight ahead	Towards tower, les Hermitants to the right	E	115
05.036	500	14,7	At a crossroads in the track, straight ahead	GR sign, parallel to the main road	E	117
05.037	900	15,6	Continue straight ahead on the tarmac road	Village of Beaumettes to the left	E	122
05.038	500	15,0	At the T-junction with the main road, turn right	Direction Ménerbes	E	122
05.039	300	16,3	Arrive at Beaumettes	Subway on the left leads to the village centre		125

Cavaillon - Beaumettes 16.3 km

B&B, Hotel, Gite d'Etapes	Price/ Opening
Mairie 84660 Maubec, Vaucluse, France Tel:+33(0)4 90 76 50 34	B1
Les Biguières (M. Max Vialis), Route d'Oppède 84660 Maubec,Vaucluse, France Tel:+33(0)4 90 76 90 62	B2
Le Relais du Luberon (Mme Marianne Nieuwenhuis), Quai des Entreprises 84660 Maubec, Vaucluse, France Tel:+33(0)4 32 52 91 54 Mobile:+33(0)6 70 37 51 22 contact@relaisduluberon.fr **Note:** Pilgrim price reduction	B1
Moise Francoise Nee Krajcer, Chemin Alafoux 84560 Ménerbes,Vaucluse, France Tel:+33(0)9 71 56 10 47	B1
La Providence (M. Ickherrbouchene) 84220 Beaumettes,Vaucluse, France Tel:+33(0)4 90 72 20 61	B2
Au Ralenti du Lierre 84220 Gordes,Vaucluse, France Tel:+33(0)4 90 72 39 22 www.auralentidulierre.com/	B3
Lochon Francois, La Bégude 84220 Goult,Vaucluse, France Tel:+33(0)9 65 37 68 09	B3
Farrier	

Gaspar Carlos,Mirabel 30260 Brouzet lès Quissac, Gard, France
Tel:+33(0)4 66 77 40 23,

Cavaillon - Beaumettes 16.3 km

Pont Saint-Julien

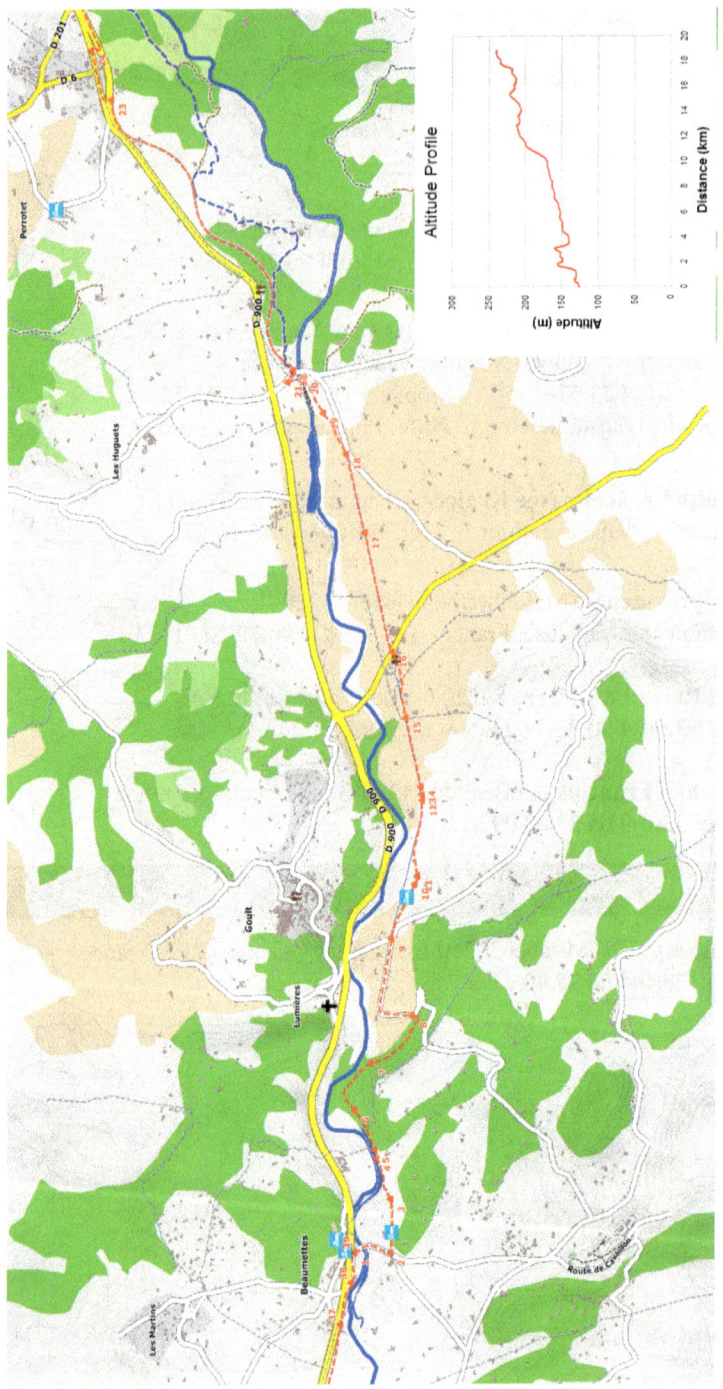

From Beaumettes the route briefly climbs to follow a pretty track above the river, le Coulon, and then returns to the old railway track. At the Roman bridge of Pont Julien the route forks with the choice of following the tarmac covered cycle route along the old railway line or taking to forest paths. The routes merge on the cycle track for the final approach to Apt. For long distance walkers we recommend the shorter and easier cycle route.

Distance from Arles: 80km Distance to Vercelli: 541km
Stage Ascent: 170m Stage Descent: 57m

Waypoint	Distance Between Waypoints (m)	Total (km)	Directions	Verification Point	Compass	Altitude (m)
06.001	0	0,0	Beside the subway continue straight ahead on the minor road		S	125
06.002	400	0,4	Beside la Bastide de Soubeyras, turn left off the tarmac road	GR sign	E	130
06.003	500	0,9	Take the left fork onto the track	GR sign, vines and then olive groves to the left	E	129
06.004	400	1,3	After crossing a stream, continue straight ahead at the junction	Parallel to the river	E	133
06.005	80	1,4	At a fork in the tracks, keep left	Remaining parallel to the river	NE	136
06.006	500	1,9	Continue straight ahead	Main road visible to the left	E	154
06.007	600	2,5	Continue straight ahead on track	Track bears away from the river	SE	152
06.008	800	3,2	At the junction with the tarmac road, continue straight ahead on the road	Large house immediately to the left at the junction	E	154
06.009	1100	4,3	At the crossroads, continue straight ahead on the track	Pylon on the right, ditch to the left	SE	144

Beaumettes to Apt 18.8 km

49

Waypoint	Distance Between Waypoints (m)	Total (km)	Directions	Verification Point	Compass	Altitude (m)
06.010	600	4,8	At the junction in the tracks, continue straight ahead	Shortly after passing la Grande Bégude	E	149
06.011	80	4,9	Continue straight ahead	Towards "la Porte des Etoiles"	E	148
06.012	800	5,7	Continue straight ahead on the tarmac	Direction Bonnieux	E	152
06.013	50	5,7	Continue straight ahead on the unmade road	GR sign	E	152
06.014	80	5,8	Take the left fork onto the grass track	Former railway track close on the left	E	151
06.015	700	6,5	At the crossroads, continue straight ahead	Towards farm buildings "le Coucourdon"	E	154
06.016	700	7,1	After passing the Gare de Bonnieux, cross the road, D36 and continue straight ahead on the old railway track. **Note:-** improvements are taking place to the track and it is possible that the surface and detailed directions may change, between this point and Pont St Julien	GR sign, direction Bonnieux	E	160
06.017	1200	8,3	At the crossroads continue straight ahead on the stony track		E	162
06.018	800	9,1	Bear slightly left on the grass track	Tarmac road and disused railway to your right	NE	167

Beaumettes to Apt 18.8 km

Waypoint	Distance Between Waypoints (m)	Total (km)	Directions	Verification Point	Compass	Altitude (m)
06.019	500	9,6	At the junction with a minor road, keep right	Towards the bridge	NE	170
06.020	400	9,0	At the T-junction turn left and cross the Roman bridge	Pont St Julien	N	169
06.021	160	10,1	Turn sharp right	Take the pedestrian and cyclist underpass	SE	171
06.022	180	10,3	Immediately after the underpass remain on the cycle track - Veloroute du Calavon. **Note:-** the GR653D turns left away from the cycle track and initially parallel to the main road.	Tarmac track	NE	173
06.023	3500	13,8	Bear left and then immediately right	Pass under the road bridge	NE	206
06.024	600	14,4	Turn right to leave the road	Pass under road again and turn left	E	207
06.025	1400	15,7	At the junction with the road, turn left and then right to continue on the cycle track. **Note:-** the GR653D rejoins the veloroute from the right	Roundabout on your left as you cross the road	E	215
06.026	2300	18,0	Shortly before the old railway station, horse riders should leave the track turning left onto the parallel road	Station ahead to the right	SE	233

Beaumettes to Apt 18.8 km

Beaumettes to Apt 18.8 km

Waypoint	Distance Between Waypoints (m)	Total (km)	Directions	Verification Point	Compass	Altitude (m)
06.027	190	18,2	At the end of the cycle track turn left to cross the road and continue on the veloroute. **Note:-** horse riders rejoin the veloroute here	Chalk embankment to the left of the track	E	236
06.028	400	18,6	Cross the road and continue on the veloroute	Bridge ahead	E	239
06.029	260	18,8	Arrive at Apt. To visit the centre of the town turn left downhill and follow the red and white GR signs. **Note:-** the GR653D takes a circuitous route via the village of Saignon before returning to the cycle track	The path to the town centre passes under the cycle track		238. 364 591

B&B, Hotel, Gite d'Etapes	Price/ Opening
Relais du Lubéron, Avenue Tilleuls 84480 Bonnieux, Vaucluse, France Tel:+33(0)4 90 75 80 84	B2
Le Moulin du Lavon (Isabelle et Gilles Geynet), Perrotet 84400 Gargas, Vaucluse, France Tel:+33(0)4 90 74 34 54 gilles.geynet@wanadoo.fr	B1
Bastide dela Peyrolière (M. Franck Mura), La Peyroulière 84400 Apt, Vaucluse, France Tel:+33(0)4 90 74 40 50 la.peyroliere@wanadoo.fr	B2
Maison de la Boucheyronne, Plan d'Eau de la Riaille 84400 Apt, Vaucluse, France Tel:+33(0)4 90 04 77 66 boucheyronne@apt.fr	B1

B&B, Hotel, Gite d'Etapes	Price/ Opening
Hotel Du Mont Ventoux, 785 Avenue Victor Hugo 84400 Apt, Vaucluse, France Tel:+33(0)4 90 04 74 60 www.hotelventoux-apt.com/	B2
Hôtel Le Palais, 24 bis place Gabriel Péri 84400 Apt, Vaucluse, France Tel:+33(0)4 90 04 89 32	B2
Josette Briffa, 72 Boulevard du Maréchal Joffre 84400 Apt, Vaucluse, France Tel:+33(0)4 90 74 31 78	B2
Hôtel L'Aptois 84400 Apt, Vaucluse, France Tel:+33(0)4 90 74 02 02 www.aptois.fr/	B2
Chambres chez l'habitant (Mme Françoise Garnier), Rue Courtine 84400 Saignon, Vaucluse, France Tel:+33(0)4 90 74 41 53	B1

Religious Hostel	
Cathédrale, 104 Rue René Cassin 84400 Apt, Vaucluse, France Tel:+33(0)4 90 04 85 44 **Note:** Accommodation for one person only, with credential,	Donation

Camping	
Camping Les Cèdres, 63 Impasse de la Fantaisie 84400 Apt, Vaucluse, France Tel:+33(0)4 90 74 14 61 www.camping-les-cedres.fr/	B1
Camping la Clé des Champs, Quartier des puits, Chemin des Abbayers 84400 Apt, Vaucluse, France Tel:+33(0)4 90 74 41 41 www.camping-luberon.com/	B1
Camping le Luberon, Avenue de Saignon 84400 Apt, Vaucluse, France Tel:+33(0)4 90 04 85 40 www.camping-le-luberon.com/	B1

Tourist Office
Tourist Office, 20 Avenue Philippe de Girard 84400 Apt, Vaucluse, France

Doctor
Lipari Fabien, 53 Boulevard Elzéar Pin 84400 Apt, Vaucluse, France Tel:+33(0)4 90 04 77 44

Veterinary
Docteurs Bassine Yves et Pfister Gilles SCP, Lançon 84400 Apt, Vaucluse, France   Tel:+33(0)4 90 74 29 98

Farrier
Barghout Eric, Collet Redon 84160 Puyvert, Vaucluse, France Tel:+33(0)4 90 08 40 57

Beaumettes to Apt 18.8 km

Apt to Céreste 21.2 km

From Apt we chose to continue on the cycle track. The GR653D crosses Apt and takes the road to the hill-top village of Saignon before returning by a rough track to the main route. At the end of the cycle track we continue by quiet roads and tracks over farm land at the foot of the Grand Luberon.

Distance from Arles: 99km **Distance to Vercelli: 522km**
Stage Ascent: 349m **Stage Descent: 196m**

Waypoint	Distance Between Waypoints (m)	Total (km)	Directions	Verification Point	Compass	Altitude (m)
07.001	0	0,0	Continue straight ahead on the cycle track	Direction Céreste	E	238
07.002	1100	1,1	Continue straight ahead on the cycle track to leave the town of Apt	Beside the main road - Rue de la Madeleine, D900	E	231
07.003	4300	5,4	Continue straight ahead on the veloroute. **Note:-** the GR653D rejoins from the right	GR sign	SE	263
07.004	800	6,1	Bear left over the river bridge and then right on the cycle track	Remain parallel to the D900	SE	262
07.005	1000	7,1	Cross the road and continue straight ahead on the cycle track	St Martin de Castillon to the left	SE	274
07.006	600	7,7	Cross the main road and continue on the cycle track on the other side	GR sign	SE	282
07.007	2300	10,0	At the T-junction with the road turn right	D48, direction Castellet	SW	298
07.008	400	10,4	Turn left onto a gravel track	Uphill	SE	299
07.009	400	10,8	Continue straight through the farm	Les Gaudins	S	334

Apt to Céreste 21.2 km

Waypoint	Distance Between Waypoints (m)	Total (km)	Directions	Verification Point	Compass	Altitude (m)
07.010	180	10,0	At the crossroads with a minor road turn left	GR sign	E	340
07.011	600	11,6	Turn right onto the dirt track	Just before the road starts to descend	S	337
07.012	130	11,7	Take the left fork	GR sign	E	341
07.013	1600	13,3	At the junction with the road, continue straight ahead on the tarmac	Direction Cereste	E	405
07.014	500	13,8	At the top of the hill continue straight ahead	Pass the farm Glorivette on your left side	E	402
07.015	400	14,1	At the junction, continue straight ahead	Road joins at acute angle from the right	N	386
07.016	800	14,0	Take right fork on the road	Direction Céreste, GR sign	E	347
07.017	1400	16,3	Shortly after crossing a bridge over a small stream, turn sharp left	Direction Céreste	E	334
07.018	700	17,1	At the apex of a bend to the right in the road, turn left onto a track	GR sign	NE	333
07.019	1400	18,4	At the crossroads with a minor road, continue straight ahead on the track		E	342
07.020	300	18,7	At a T-junction in the tracks, turn left	Direction Cereste	E	351
07.021	500	19,3	At the junction in the tracks, turn left and continue up the hill	GR Sign	NE	388

Apt to Céreste 21.2 km

Waypoint	Distance Between Waypoints (m)	Total (km)	Directions	Verification Point	Compass	Altitude (m)
07.022	500	19,7	The track joins a tarmac road, continue straight ahead	Pass the sign for the entry to Céreste	E	437
07.023	1200	20,9	At a crossroads in Céreste, turn left	Boulevard Jean Jaurés, GR sign	N	401
07.024	110	20,0	At the roundabout turn right on the D4100	Direction Forcalquier	SE	398
07.025	210	21,2	Arrive at Céreste, Place de la République	Gîte Municipal on your right		392

Apt to Céreste 21.2 km

B&B, Hotel, Gite d'Etapes	Price/ Opening
Gite & Camping (Raymonde Bouscarle), Les Gaudins 84400 Castellet, Vaucluse, France Tel:+33(0)4 90 75 28 62 **Note:** Closed Easter and All Saints' Day	B1
Village Tourisme, Avenue des Plantiers 04280 Céreste, Alpes de Haute Provence, France Tel:+33(0)4 92 79 00 61 vtfcereste@vtf-vacances.com	B1
Les Souliers Magiques, Boulevard Jean Jaurès 04280 Céreste, Alpes de Haute Provence, France Tel:+33(0)4 92 79 06 52 Mobile:+33(0)6 84 09 15 88 genevieve.julien3@wanadoo.fr	B1
Gite Communale, Rue Bicentenaire 04280 Céreste, Alpes de Haute Provence, France Tel:+33(0)4 92 79 00 46 **Note:** Pilgrim price reduction	B1
Le Cours (Christina Van Geloven & Mathieu Custers) 04280 Céreste, Alpes de Haute Provence, France Tel:+33(0)4 92 73 28 06 app.cereste@gmail.com	B1
La Florentine (M. Olivier Malfait), Campagne Florent 04280 Céreste, Alpes de Haute Provence, France Tel:+33(0)4 92 79 05 64 Mobile:+33(0)6 70 73 70 67 olivier.malfait@gmail.com	B2
Sellam Georges, La Pourraque 04110 Reillanne, Alpes de Haute Provence, France Tel:+33(0)4 92 76 43 53	B3

Camping

Le Bois de Sibourg (Mme Agnès Vial-Ménard), Sibourg 04280 Céreste, Alpes de Haute Provence, France
Tel:+33(0)4 92 79 02 22   Mobile:+33(0)6 30 88 63 29
camping.sibourg@orange.fr
Note: pilgrim price reduction, credential required

B1
Open 15/04 - 30/09

Equestrian

Ferme Equestre (M. Olivier Malfait), Campagne Florent 04280 Céreste, Alpes de Haute Provence, France
Tel:+33(0)4 92 79 05 64   Mobile:+33(0)6 70 73 70 67
olivier.malfait@gmail.com
Note: Chambre d'hote that also takes horses

B2
Open all year

Tourist Office

Office de Tourisme Syndicat d'Initiative, Place République 04280 Céreste, Alpes de Haute Provence, France
Tel:+33(0)4 92 79 09 84   www.cereste.fr/

Doctor

Guillaume-Richand Françoise, Place St Michel 04280 Céreste, Alpes de Haute Provence, France
Tel:+33(0)4 92 79 05 52

Farrier

Helque Virgile Didier Gilbert, 31 Avenue Mar de Lattre de Tassigny 26700 Pierrelatte, Drôme, France   Tel:+33(0)4 75 49 72 81

The route quickly leaves the main road in Céreste and takes to farm tracks before climing by broad forest tracks to the town of Rellianne. After Rellianne the route continues on broad tracks before breifly following the busy N100

Distance from Arles: 120km **Distance to Vercelli: 501km**
Stage Ascent: 296m **Stage Descent: 241m**

Waypoint	Distance Between Waypoints (m)	Total (km)	Directions	Verification Point	Compass	Altitude (m)
08.001	0	0,0	Continue straight ahead on the main road	Direction Forcalquier	E	392
08.002	70	0,1	Turn left into rue de la Poste and immediately right on avenue de la Romane	Proceed with grassed area on the left	NE	387
08.003	280	0,3	At the end of the road, turn left on avenue Dr Guy Borty	GR sign	NE	374
08.004	270	0,6	Shortly after crossing the Roman bridge, take the right fork	GR sign	E	366
08.005	800	1,4	Take the left fork, up the hill	GR sign	N	373
08.006	500	1,9	Take the left fork on a grassy track	GR sign	N	396
08.007	600	2,4	At the junction with a minor road, bear right	Direction Reillanne	NE	426
08.008	700	3,1	Take the right fork onto a sandy track	Direction Carluc	E	463
08.009	280	3,4	After passing the large house, le Grand Carluc, on your right, continue straight ahead until the road begins to descend, then bear left on the track. **Note:-** riders can remain on the road to the next waypoint	Direction Carluc on the veloroute Forcalquier, then beside Prieuré de Carluc	E	457

Céreste to Moulin de Lincel 13.2 km

Waypoint	Distance Between Waypoints (m)	Total (km)	Directions	Verification Point	Compass	Altitude (m)
08.010	120	3,5	Rejoin the road and bear left, then take the track to the left	Follow the right hand side of the valley, with views of the Troglodyte settlement on your left	N	454
08.011	400	3,9	Take the right fork. **Note:-** the left fork is GR4	Follow direction Reillanne	NE	469
08.012	1200	5,1	Take the right fork	GR sign	NE	519
08.013	300	5,4	At the junction, bear left down hill	GR sign	N	527
08.014	170	5,6	At the crossroads in the tracks, turn sharp right up the hill	GR sign	S	531
08.015	400	5,0	At the fork in the tracks continue straight ahead	Up the hill	S	560
08.016	70	6,1	At the next fork in the tracks also continue straight ahead	Up the hill	E	565
08.017	210	6,3	At a complex junction take the centre track	"Reserve de Chasse" sign straight ahead	N	579
08.018	30	6,3	Bear right up the hill	Following the GR sign	NE	581
08.019	400	6,7	At a T-junction with a tarmac road, bear right down the hill	GR sign	E	610
08.020	1800	8,5	At the crossroads, continue straight ahead	Boulevard Jean Jaurés	E	559
08.021	400	8,8	At the T-junction, turn right	Boulevard Saint Joseph	S	557

Céreste to Moulin de Lincel 13.2 km

Waypoint	Distance Between Waypoints (m)	Total (km)	Directions	Verification Point	Compass	Altitude (m)
08.022	130	8,0	At the crossroads in the centre of the town of Reillanne with the church directly ahead, turn left on the D14	Pass the parking area below on your right	NE	555
08.023	280	9,2	After crossing bridge, take higher left fork	D14	SE	548
08.024	110	9,4	Take the right fork onto the smaller road	GR sign	SE	546
08.025	140	9,5	Continue straight ahead	Direction Saint Michel l'Observatoire	SE	542
08.026	270	9,8	The track rejoins the D14, bear right and then turn left	Chemin de Bissargues, GR sign	E	540
08.027	1300	10,0	Straight ahead		E	558
08.028	700	11,6	At the junction, straight ahead	Pass "le Coulet" on your right	E	560
08.029	600	12,2	At a junction in the tracks, take the second turning from the left, down hill	Grass track	E	528
08.030	400	12,5	Take the right fork	GR sign	SE	490
08.031	400	12,9	At T-junction turn right then at junction with main road turn left. **Note:** At the time of writing the GR keeps to the left of the road, but has been blocked close to the river with fencing		NE	451
08.032	240	13,2	Arrive at Moulin-de-Lincel	Gîte to the right		447

Céreste to Moulin de Lincel 13.2 km

B&B, Hotel, Gite d'Etapes	Price/
Chateau Pinet (Mme Anne de Salve), Le Petit Pinet 04110 Reillanne, Alpes de Haute Provence, France Tel:+33(0)4 92 76 69 60 Mobile:+33(0)9 64 28 27 76 château.pinet@free.fr	B1
Les Volets Verts (Madame Norol), Chemin des Bedauches 04110 Reillanne, Alpes de Haute Provence, France Tel:+33(0)4 92 76 46 99 Mobile:+33(0)6 75 41 40 16 **Note:** Pilgrim price reduction	B2
Le Farnet (Cathy et Pascal Depoisson), Route De Banon 04110 Reillanne, Alpes de Haute Provence, France Tel:+33(0)4 92 76 65 02 le-farnet@wanadoo.fr	B2
Carpe Diem (Mme Arlette Truffert), Place de la Libération 04110 Reillanne, Alpes de Haute Provence, France Tel:+33(0)4 92 76 47 62 Mobile:+33(0)6 88 18 30 78 etelra@free.fr	B1
Chambre des Poètes (M. Stéphan Lévy), Barruol 04110 Reillanne, Alpes de Haute Provence, France Tel:+33(0)4 88 02 43 26 Mobile:+33(0)6 76 06 36 12 levy.stephan@aliceadsl.fr	B2
PR Moulin de Lincel (Mme Anne-Lise Bador), Le Moulin du Largue 04870 Saint Michel l'Observatoire, Alpes de Haute Provence, France Tel:+33(0)4 92 76 46 34 Mobile:+33(0)6 16 09 81 78 moulindelincel@aliceadsl.fr www.moulindelincel.net/ **Note:** Accepts horses	B1
Le Pin Lyre (Mme Isabelle Murach), Rue Grande 04870 Saint Michel l'Observatoire, Alpes de Haute Provence, France Tel:+33(0)4 92 76 60 81 epinlyre@yahoo.fr **Note:** Pilgrim price reduction	B1
Hôtel de l'Observatoire, Place de la Fontaine 04870 Saint Michel l'Observatoire, Alpes de Haute Provence, France Tel:+33(0)4 92 76 63 62	B2
Les Chambres du Serre (Mme Chantal Heckenroth), Place du Serre 04870 Saint Michel l'Observatoire, Alpes de Haute Provence, France Tel:+33(0)4 92 76 65 20 chantal.heckenroth@aliceadsl.fr	B1

Céreste to Moulin de Lincel 13.2 km

B&B, Hotel, Gite d'Etapes	Price/
Le Plateau du Moulin à Vent (M. Vincent Alliaud), Route Banon 04870 Saint Michel l'Observatoire, Alpes de Haute Provence, France Tel:+33(0)6 86 81 42 40 alliaud.vincent0181@orange.fr **Note:** Camping also possible	B1
Le Barri (Mme Nicole Massel), Rue du Barri 04870 Saint Michel l'Observatoire, Alpes de Haute Provence, France Tel:+33(0)4 92 76 68 45 nicole.massel@free.fr **Note:** Pilgrim price reduction	B1

Tourist Office

Cours Thierry d'Argenlieu 04110 Reillanne, Alpes de Haute Provence, France   Tel:+33(0)4 92 76 45 37

Tourist Office, Place de la Fontaine 04870 Saint Michel l'Observatoire, Alpes de Haute Provence, France   Tel:+33(0)4 92 75 64 43

Farrier

Fabrice Deprey, Domaine de magny 13420 Gémenos, Bouches du Rhône, France   Tel:+33(0)6 83 13 72 85   www.fabricedeprey.fr/

Céreste to Moulin de Lincel 13.2 km

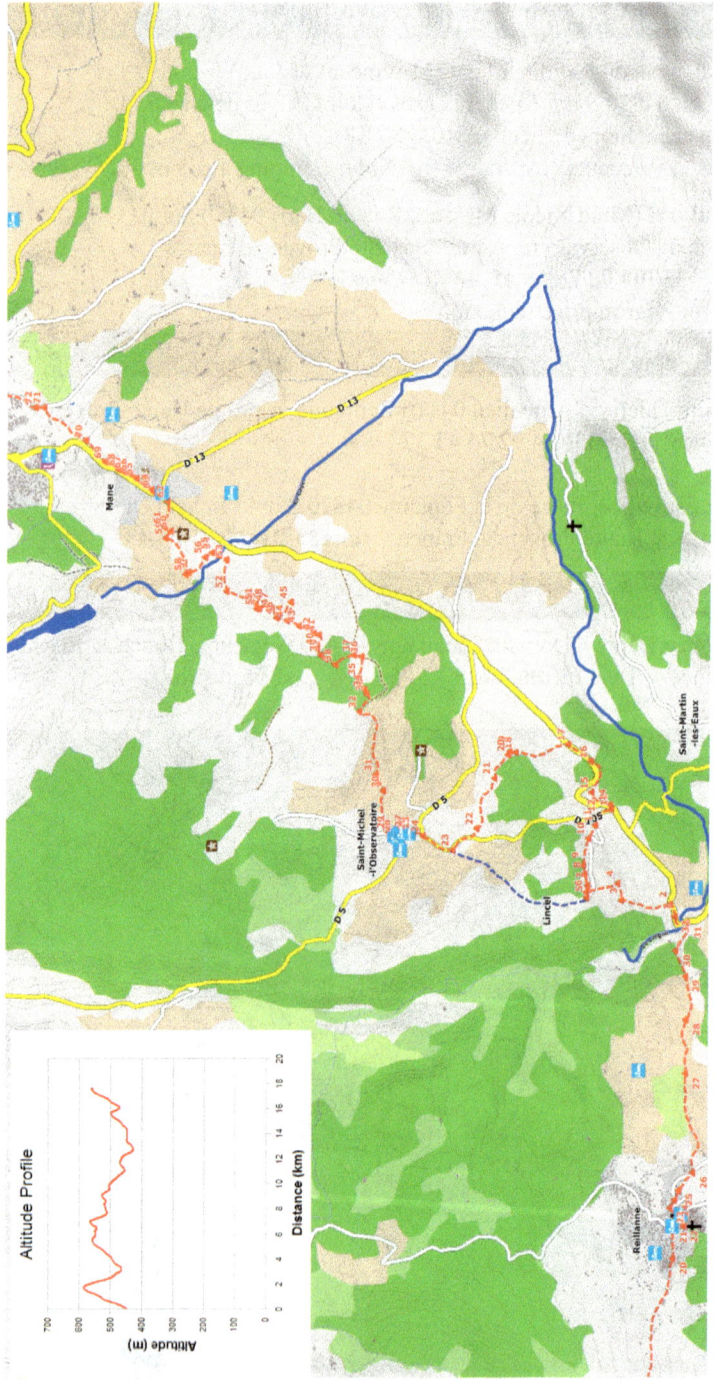

From the Moulin-de-Lincel the route climbs by farm tracks to the village of Lincel. Here there is the choice of a shorter route by a generally quiet country road to Saint-Michel-l'Obseravtoie or the pathway and tracks which pass the Gué de Reculon – part of the ancient via Domitia. Horse riders are advised to follow the shorter route. From Saint-Michel, the route continues on further farm and forest tracks to the town of Mane with short sections on a very busy section of the N100. The final approach to Forcalquier follows a narrow but busy winding road which should be followed with great care.

Distance from Arles: 133km   Distance to Vercelli: 488km
Stage Ascent: 464m   Stage Descent: 353m

Waypoint	Distance Between Waypoints (m)	Total (km)	Directions	Verification Point	Compass	Altitude (m)
09.001	0	0,0	Continue straight ahead beside the main road	N100 towards Forcalquier	E	447
09.002	220	0,2	Turn left on the track	Direction Saint Michel l'Observatoire, GR sign	N	457
09.003	600	0,9	At the T-junction in the tracks, turn right		E	524
09.004	220	1,1	At the T-junction with the road, turn left to continue up the hill	Towards the village of Lincel	NW	536

Moulin de Lincel to Forcalquier 17.6 km

Waypoint	Distance Between Waypoints (m)	Total (km)	Directions	Verification Point	Compass	Altitude (m)
09.005	500	1,5	Turn right in front of the church. **Note:-** the route can be reduced by 3km by continuing straight ahead on the generally quiet road, the GR will rejoin the road from the right before entering Saint Michel l'Observatoire. Horse-riders should follow the alternate route to avoid a very narrow bridge - le Gué de Reculon	GR sign	E	577
09.006	90	1,6	Take the right fork	Pass under the archway	E	582
09.007	90	1,7	At The T-junction, turn left up the hill	GR sign	E	585
09.008	130	1,8	Continue straight ahead	Road to the left is chemin des Genets	E	581
09.009	110	1,0	Take the right fork onto narrow grass track	Sign Saint Michel l'Observatoire	E	574
09.010	300	2,3	Continue straight ahead on the narrow track	Avoid the tarmac road to the right	SE	534

Moulin de Lincel to Forcalquier 17.6 km

Waypoint	Distance Between Waypoints (m)	Total (km)	Directions	Verification Point	Compass	Altitude (m)
09.011	170	2,4	Cross over the tarmac road and continue straight ahead on the track	Farm building immediately on your right	E	507
09.012	140	2,6	At the T-junction with a minor road turn right	Towards the main road	SE	494
09.013	160	2,7	Cross over the major road N100/D4100 and bear left on the track	Sign le Gué de Reculon	E	485
09.014	80	2,8	Take the left fork		NE	481
09.015	300	3,1	Cross the narrow stone bridge	Le Gue de Reculon	E	463
09.016	500	3,6	The track returns to the main road, bear right along the road	GR sign	NE	480
09.017	400	3,9	Turn left onto a track	Direction Saint Michel l'Observatoire	N	492
09.018	700	4,6	Bear right into the hamlet of les Craux	GR sign	N	518
09.019	90	4,7	Turn left on the grass track	Direction Saint Michel l'Observatoire	NW	522
09.020	60	4,7	After passing the last house in the hamlet turn right on the track	Pass through gap in the stone wall	NW	524

Moulin de Lincel to Forcalquier 17.6 km

Waypoint	Distance Between Waypoints (m)	Total (km)	Directions	Verification Point	Compass	Altitude (m)
09.021	400	5,1	At the junction in the tracks beside the house, keep right	Pass the house on your left side	W	546
09.022	700	5,8	Take the left fork and then immediately bear right on the road	Pass beside chapelle St Paul	NW	550
09.023	400	6,2	Bear right on the road. **Note:**- the alternate route from Lincel joins from the left	Towards the village of Saint Michel l'Observatoire	NE	549
09.024	400	6,6	Continue straight ahead on the small road	Towards the village centre	N	549
09.025	130	6,7	Continue straight ahead into the centre of the village	Direction "Information"	N	558
09.026	60	6,8	In the centre of Saint Michel l'Observatoire, turn right and cross the village square	Direction la Poste	NE	561
09.027	80	6,9	In front of la Poste turn left	Direction l'Observatoire de Haute Provence, rue du Barri	N	564
09.028	150	7,0	At the junction on the edge of the village take the right fork on the small road down hill	GR sign,	NE	563

Moulin de Lincel to Forcalquier 17.6 km

Waypoint	Distance Between Waypoints (m)	Total (km)	Directions	Verification Point	Compass	Altitude (m)
09.029	80	7,1	Take the right fork	Direction Forcalquier, GR sign	E	558
09.030	500	7,6	At the crossroads turn left	Towards pumping station, GR sign	NE	511
09.031	230	7,8	At the T-junction with a tarmac road, bear right		E	513
09.032	900	8,8	Turn left onto a smaller track into the trees	"Reserve de Chasse" and GR signs	SE	519
09.033	250	9,0	At the T-junction in the tracks turn right	GR sign	NE	527
09.034	50	9,1	Take the left fork on the grassy track	GR sign	NE	527
09.035	160	9,2	At the junction, bear right down the hill	GR sign	E	521
09.036	260	9,5	At a T-junction in the tracks turn left	GR sign	N	505
09.037	110	9,6	Turn left towards the derelict chapel	Sign "Resistance Porchères"	NW	502
09.038	280	9,9	Turn right on the grassy track	GR sign	NE	504
09.039	220	10,1	At the junction in the tracks continue straight ahead	GR sign	NE	497
09.040	100	10,2	Keep right	Towards the large rock outcrop	E	493
09.041	190	10,4	At the T-junction, turn left	GR sign	N	483
09.080	40	17,6	Arrive at Forcalquier centre	Place du Bourguet		558

Moulin de Lincel to Forcalquier 17.6 km

B&B, Hotel, Gite d'Etapes	Price/ Opening
Font Reynière (Mme Anne-Marie Esmiol), Les Escagnettes 04300 Mane, Alpes de Haute Provence, France Tel:+33(0)4 92 75 04 85 Mobile:+33(0)6 72 12 57 21 anne-marie-esmiol@orange.fr **Note:**Pilgrim price reduction	B1
Le Jardin des Glycines, Rue de la Bourgade 04300 Mane, Alpes de Haute Provence, France Tel:+33(0)4 92 75 13 98 www.lejardindesglycines.free.fr/	B2
Domakia (Mme André Galmiche), Lotissement Le Petit Briant 04300 Forcalquier, Alpes de Haute Provence, France Tel:+33(0)4 92 74 37 78 galmiche.andré@wanadoo.fr	B2
Le Couvent Des Minimes Hotel Et Spa, Chemin des Jeux de Maï 04300 Mane en Provence, Alpes de Haute Provence, France Tel:+33(0)4 92 74 77 77 www.couventdesminimes-hotelspa.com/	B2
Grand Hôtel, 10 Boulevard Latourette 04300 Forcalquier, Alpes de Haute Provence, France Tel:+33(0)4 92 75 00 35 www.grandhotel-forcalquier.com/	B2
La Parise (Claudette et Maurice Chabaud) 04300 Forcalquier, Alpes de Haute Provence, France Tel:+33(0)4 92 75 01 50	B1
Les Chevauchées du Soleil (M. Pierre-Jean Roche), Route de Sigonce 04300 Forcalquier, Alpes de Haute Provence, France Tel:+33(0)4 92 75 13 74 chevauchees-du-soleil@wanadoo.fr	B1
Le Bas Chalus 04300 Forcalquier, Alpes de Haute Provence, France Tel:+33(0)4 92 75 05 67 baschalus@orange.fr **Note:** Pilgrim price reduction, camping also possible, horses accepted	B2
Le Mas du Galoubet, Claude et Christiane Cuérel-Busi 04300 Pierrerue, Alpes de Haute Provence, France Tel:+33(0)4 92 75 31 70 www.mas-du-galoubet.com	B2
Camping	
Camping Indigo Forcalquier, Route de Sigonce 04300 Forcalquier, Alpes de Haute Provence, France Tel:+33(0)4 92 75 27 94 www.camping-indigo.com/	B1

Moulin de Lincel to Forcalquier 17.6 km

Equestrian

Les Chevauchées du Soleil (M. Pierre-Jean Roche), Route de
Sigonce 04300 Forcalquier, Alpes de Haute Provence, France   B2
Tel:+33(0)4 92 75 13 74   chevauchees-du-soleil@wanadoo.fr

Tourist Office

Tourist Office, 13 Place du Bourguet 04300 Forcalquier, Alpes de Haute
Provence, France   Tel:+33(0)4 92 75 10 02   oti@forcalquier.com

Doctor

Cabinet Médical Humbert et Sèchehaye, Avenue Verdun 04300
Forcalquier, Alpes de Haute Provence, France   Tel:+33(0)4 92 75 00 66

Veterinary

Couffon Emmanuelle, 2 Chemin Cèdres 04300 Forcalquier, Alpes de
Haute Provence, France   Tel:+33(0)4 92 75 00 39

Farrier

Diette Jean-Jérôme, Quartier Beaudine 04300 Forcalquier, Alpes de Haute
Provence, France Tel:+33(0)4 92 73 11 19 Mobile: +33(0)6 80 92 05 12

Moulin de Lincel to Forcalquier 17.6 km

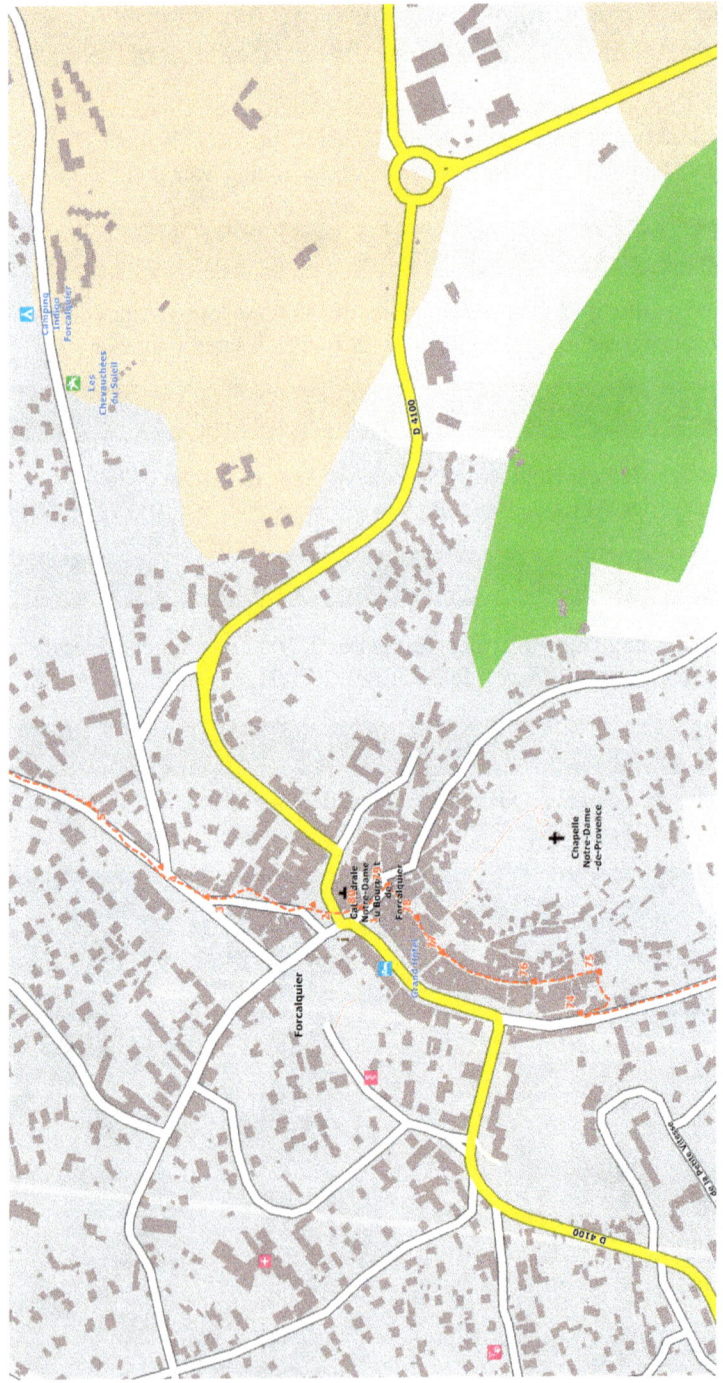

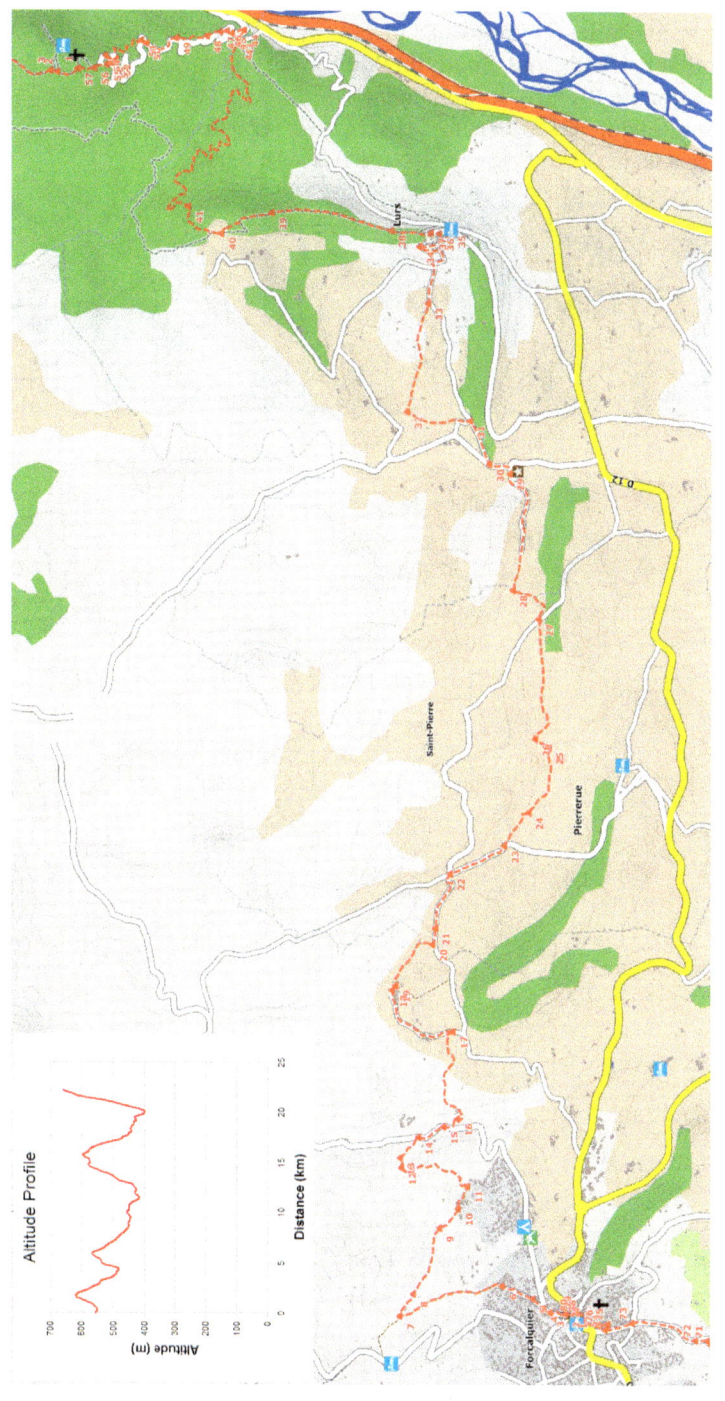

The route quickly climbs out of Forcalquier before meandering on woodland tracks and finally making a very steep climb on narrow tracks to the Prieure-de-Ganagobie

Distance from Arles: 151km   **Distance to Vercelli: 470km**
Stage Ascent: 639m   **Stage Descent: 538m**

Forcalquier to Prieure de Ganagobie 22.2 km

Waypoint	Distance Between Waypoints (m)	Total (km)	Directions	Verification Point	Compass	Altitude (m)
10.001	0	0,0	Bear right and cross the main road and enter place du Bourguet	Notre Dame du Bourguet on the right	N	558
10.002	80	0,1	Bear right and leave place du Bourguet on rue Louis Andrieux	Pass cinema on your left	N	555
10.003	130	0,2	At the crossroads, bear right	Pass school on the left	NE	551
10.004	70	0,3	Take the left fork	Avenue Fontauris, direction Cimetière	NE	549
10.005	120	0,4	Take the left fork	Chemin des Moureisses	N	549
10.006	290	0,7	At the top of a rise, continue straight ahead on the gravel track	The track will pass a cemetery on the right	N	560
10.007	900	1,6	At the top the hill, turn sharp right	Direction Lurs	SE	618
10.008	230	1,8	Take the left fork		E	616
10.009	600	2,4	At the end of the lane turn right	GR sign	SE	574
10.010	220	2,7	Bear left between the house and the farm buildings	Les Chambarels	SE	562
10.011	220	2,9	Turn sharp left onto the grass track	GR sign	N	545

Waypoint	Distance Between Waypoints (m)	Total (km)	Directions	Verification Point	Compass	Altitude (m)
10.012	700	3,6	At a junction in the tracks turn right	Stream on the left	E	500
10.013	100	3,7	After crossing the stream and climbing the rise, turn right	Buildings to the right of the track, "Beauregard"	SE	497
10.014	230	3,9	At the junction with the tarmac road, D16, turn right	Cross bridge	S	488
10.015	240	4,2	Turn left off the road onto a gravel track, slightly downhill towards the stream	GR sign	SE	485
10.016	160	4,3	Having crossed the stream, turn right on the track	"Le Moulin" to the left	E	479
10.017	900	5,2	At the T-junction with the tarmac road, turn left	Towards the hamlet of les Ecuyers	NE	538
10.018	800	5,0	In the hamlet of les Tourettes, turn right	Shortly after passing through an archway	SE	564
10.019	60	6,1	Turn left on the gravel track	GR sign	SE	561
10.020	500	6,6	At a T-junction with a road turn left		E	524
10.021	160	6,8	Continue straight ahead		E	518
10.022	500	7,3	At the junction with the D212 turn right across the bridge with the stone parapet	Equestrian Centre "mas de Bel Air" to the left	SE	492

Forcalquier to Prieure de Ganagobie 22.2 km

Waypoint	Distance Between Waypoints (m)	Total (km)	Directions	Verification Point	Compass	Altitude (m)
10.023	500	7,8	Take the left fork onto the smaller road	Direction "le Moulin"	SE	474
10.024	400	8,2	At the junction in the tracks, continue straight ahead	Direction Lurs	E	461
10.025	600	8,7	At the junction bear left	Direction Lurs	NE	449
10.026	140	8,9	Bear right on the track	Direction Lurs	E	451
10.027	1100	9,9	At the crossroads with a minor road, continue straight ahead	GR sign	NE	455
10.028	400	10,4	After crossing the stream turn right		E	449
10.029	1100	11,4	Cross the bridge and turn left on the road	Reservoir to the right, GR sign	NE	416
10.030	220	11,6	Take the right fork	Direction Lurs, GR sign	NE	419
10.031	400	12,0	Turn left	GR sign	N	430
10.032	600	12,6	Turn right on the track	Iron gates ahead at the junction	E	433
10.033	900	13,5	At the junction continue straight ahead on the road	The GR turns right and weaves towards the village	E	495
10.034	700	14,2	Turn sharp right up the hill	Towards the centre of the village of Lurs	SE	545
10.035	300	14,5	Turn left through the archway under the bell tower	Direction "Promenade des Evêques"	N	569
10.036	110	14,6	Bear right on the narrow street	Traverse de la Chapelle	N	576

Forcalquier to Prieure de Ganagobie 22.2 km

Waypoint	Distance Between Waypoints (m)	Total (km)	Directions	Verification Point	Compass	Altitude (m)
10.037	70	14,7	Turn left onto the gravel path "Promenade de Evêques"	Wall on your right side	N	577
10.038	400	15,1	Continue straight ahead	"Chapelle de Notre Dame de Vie" on the right	N	574
10.039	1100	16,1	Take the left fork, down the hill	GR sign	N	577
10.040	600	16,7	After emerging from the woodland, turn right on a track	Direction Bois de Lurs	NE	551
10.041	400	17,1	At a junction in the tracks, turn left on the wider track	Direction Monastère de Ganagobie, GR sign	E	450
10.042	2800	19,9	The track joins a minor road turn left	Cross stone bridge	E	397
10.043	50	19,0	Turn left on the track. **Note:**- riders should remain on the road until reaching the Monastery	Direction Monastère de Ganagobie	SE	396
10.044	100	20,1	At the junction with the road turn left		N	398
10.045	110	20,2	Turn right onto a small steep track		NE	406
10.046	80	20,3	Cross the road and continue on the small track		N	414
10.047	60	20,3	Cross the road and continue on the track on the other side	GR sign	N	421

Forcalquier to Prieure de Ganagobie 22.2 km

Waypoint	Distance Between Waypoints (m)	Total (km)	Directions	Verification Point	Compass	Altitude (m)
10.048	130	20,5	Bear right on the road and then turn right onto the track	GR sign	N	437
10.049	270	20,7	At the junction with the road and turn right and remain on the road		N	473
10.050	400	21,1	Turn left onto the track	GR sign, opposite les Ecoles	NE	516
10.051	70	21,1	Cross the road and continue on the path	GR sign	NW	526
10.052	500	21,6	Cross the road and continue on the path		NW	606
10.053	40	21,6	Rejoin the road and turn left on the road up the hill		NE	612
10.054	150	21,8	Turn left onto the track	Direction Monastère de Ganagobie	W	625
10.055	120	21,9	Turn right across the parking area	Follow the signposts for the Monastery	N	633
10.056	140	22,0	Take the left fork on the smaller path	GR sign	N	648
10.057	150	22,2	Arrive at Prieure-de-Ganagobie	Monastery complex to the right		659

Forcalquier to Prieure de Ganagobie 22.2 km

B&B, Hotel, Gite d'Etapes	Price/ Opening
Hotel le Seminaire, Lurs 04700 Lurs en Provence, Alpes de Haute Provence, France Tel:+33(0)4 92 79 94 19 www.hotel-leseminaire.com/	B3
PR Monastère de Ganagobie, Abbaye de Notre Dame 04310 Ganagobie, Alpes de Haute Provence, France Tel:+33(0)4 92 75 18 86 www.ndganagobie.com/ **Note:** Accepts horses, often full, advise advance reservation	B2
Gîte Communal 04310 Peyruis, Alpes de Haute Provence, France Tel:+33(0)4 92 33 21 00	B1
Camping	
Camping Les Cigales, Chemin de la Digue du Bevon 04310 Peyruis, Alpes de Haute Provence, France Tel:+33(0)4 92 68 16 04 www.camping-lescigales.fr/	B1

Forcalquier to Prieure de Ganagobie 22.2 km

Prieure de Ganagobie to Peipin 23.6 km

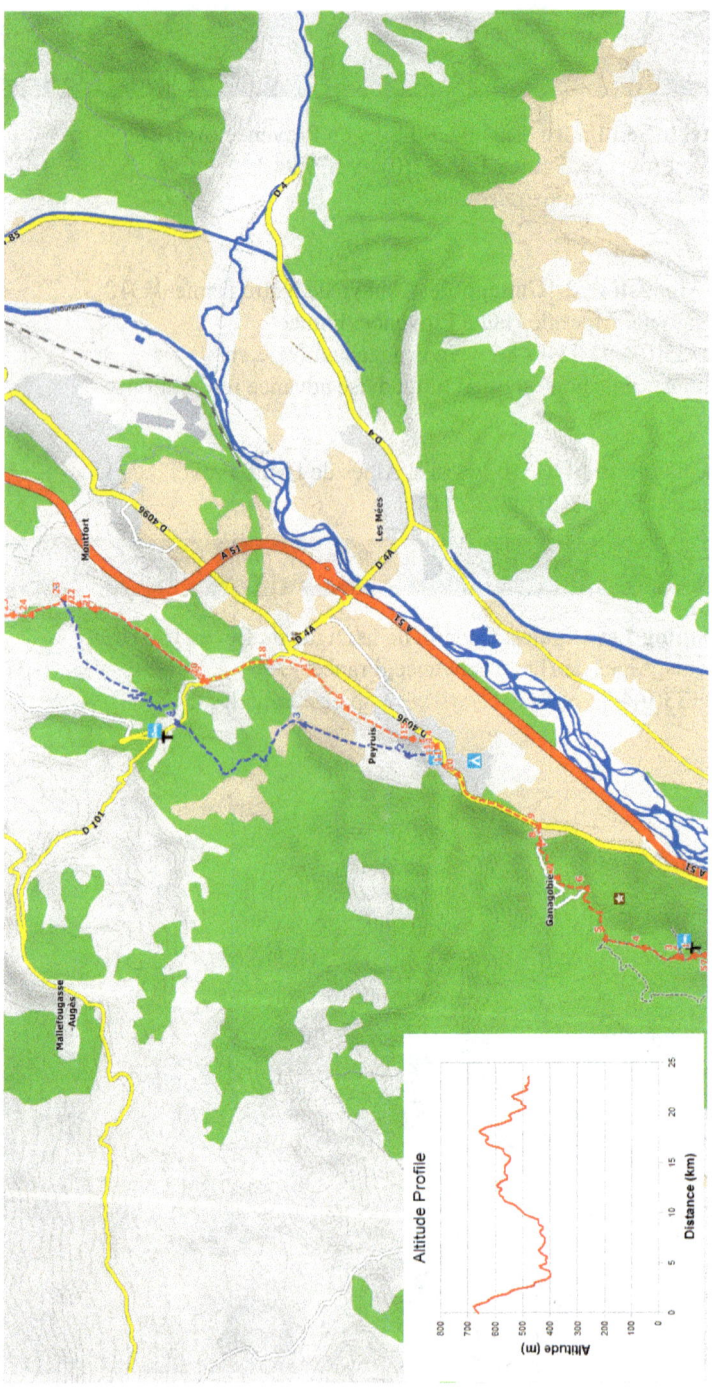

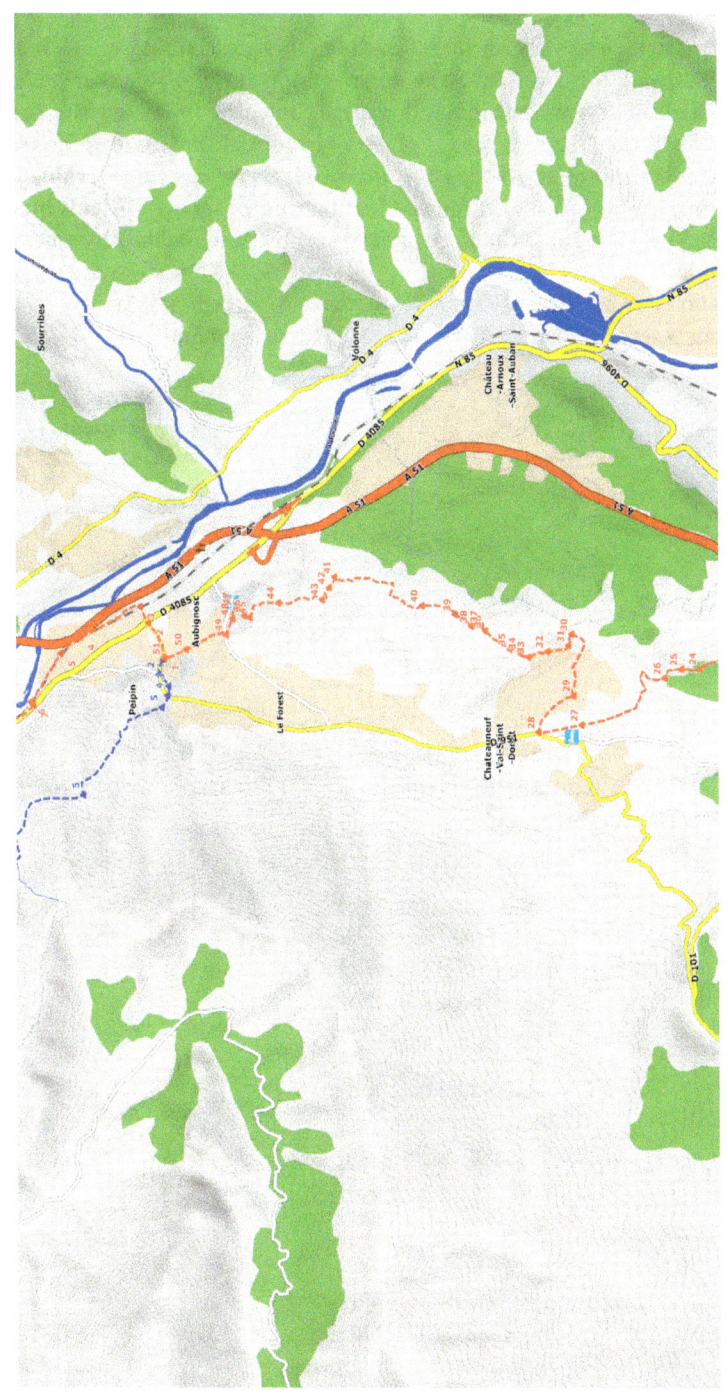

The track continues on forest paths before descending to follow the main road for 2km into the town of Peyruis. From Peryruis to Châteauneuf-Val-St-Donat there is a choice of following the forest tracks of the GR653D or our preferred route of the broad stone track of the via Domitia. At the time of writing there was considerable tree felling in the forest making navigation and progress difficult on the GR653D. The route then progress over often steep and stony tracks to Peipin.

Distance from Arles: 173km **Distance to Vercelli: 448km**
Stage Ascent: 502m **Stage Descent: 685m**

	Waypoint	Distance Between Waypoints (m)	Total (km)	Directions	Verification Point	Compass	Altitude (m)
Prieure de Ganagobie to Peipin 23.6 km	11.001	0	0,0	Pass between large stones and turn left	Direction l'Eglise	N	659
	11.002	200	0,2	Turn left on the grass track	Direction Ganagobie Village	N	669
	11.003	70	0,3	Bear left on the track	GR sign	N	671
	11.004	500	0,7	Continue straight ahead down the hill	Direction Ganagobie	N	670
	11.005	600	1,3	At the junction at the end of the track beside a wire barrier, turn right down the hill on the broad track	GR sign	E	623
	11.006	900	2,2	At the road junction in the village of Ganagobie turn left on the road and then left again onto the track into the woods	Beside Espace d'Activité, GR sign	N	539
	11.007	500	2,7	Take the right fork on the track, parallel to the road		NE	460

Waypoint	Distance Between Waypoints (m)	Total (km)	Directions	Verification Point	Compass	Altitude (m)
11.008	600	3,3	At the T-junction with the road turn right. **Note:-** The GR continues on the far side of the road making a steep climb into the hills before rejoining our route in Peyruis	Road proceeds with the river on the left	E	416
11.009	400	3,7	At the T-junction with the D4096, turn left and proceed with caution on the grass verge	Direction Peyruis	NE	398
11.010	1300	4,9	Continue straight ahead into the town of Peyruis. **Note:-** GR joins from the left	Tree lined parking area to the right	NE	414
11.011	210	5,2	Shortly after passing the fountain on the left, take the left fork	Narrow road rue du Grand Cabaret, GR sign	NE	415
11.012	150	5,3	At the junction, turn right through the archway and then bear left. **Note:-** our route will follow the Ancienne Voie Domitienne the Alternate route follows the GR653D straight ahead	Narrow road rue du Grand Cabaret, GR sign	NE	416
11.013	90	5,4	Bear right		E	414
11.014	100	5,5	At the T-junction turn left	Avenue de la Roche	N	411

Prieuré de Ganagobie to Peipin 23.6 km

Waypoint	Distance Between Waypoints (m)	Total (km)	Directions	Verification Point	Compass	Altitude (m)
11.015	300	5,8	Continue straight ahead	Cliffs on your left	NE	427
11.016	1000	6,8	At the crossroads, continue straight ahead	Remain on avenue de la Roche	NE	423
11.017	700	7,4	Continue straight ahead on the narrow road	Avenue de la Roche bears right	N	419
11.018	600	8,0	At the T-junction with the tarmac road, turn left on the road	D100, river below to the right	N	436
11.019	900	8,9	Bear right on the small road	Towards the farm "le Clos"	NE	443
11.020	140	9,1	After crossing the river, take the left fork onto the track - Ancienne Voie Domitienne	Track leads uphill	NE	442
11.021	2000	11,1	Take the left fork		N	555
11.022	230	11,3	Keep left on the broad track		N	569
11.023	200	11,5	Continue straight ahead on the broad track	GR653D joins from the left	NW	569
11.024	500	12,0	Continue straight ahead	Cross Roman bridge	N	585
11.025	260	12,3	Take the left fork	Upper track	NW	580
11.026	290	12,6	Continue straight ahead	Cross Roman bridge	NW	588
11.027	1600	14,2	At the crossroads continue straight ahead	Towards Châteauneuf centre	N	565
11.028	600	14,7	At the crossroads in the centre of Châteauneuf Val St Donat, turn right	Pass fountain on your left at the junction, GR sign	SE	563

Prieuré de Ganagobie to Peipin 23.6 km

Waypoint	Distance Between Waypoints (m)	Total (km)	Directions	Verification Point	Compass	Altitude (m)
11.029	700	15,4	At the T-junction turn left	Up the hill and away from the village	E	544
11.030	900	16,4	At a junction of tracks, turn left	Direction le Vieux Village, GR sign	W	573
11.031	190	16,6	Beside the building, take the small track to the left	GR sign	N	597
11.032	300	16,9	Take the left fork towards the old village. **Note:**- horse and bike riders should take the lower broad track to the next waypoint	GR sign on a cairn	N	628
11.033	270	17,1	Bear right on the small track	Direction Aubignosc, GRsign	NE	635
11.034	160	17,3	At the complex junction in the tracks turn right, then left and right again	GR sign, with a view of the old village to the right on the skyline	N	631
11.035	190	17,5	At the T-junction, turn right, down hill	GR sign	NE	625
11.036	400	17,9	Take the right fork on the smaller track	GR sign	NE	652
11.037	100	18,0	Bear left on the smaller track	Between stream bed and mounds of shale, GR sign	N	657
11.038	140	18,2	Bear right on the small track	GR sign	NE	656
11.039	270	18,4	Bear right down the hill		N	638
11.040	500	18,9	At a junction in the tracks, continue straight ahead	Direction Aubignosc, GR sign	N	573

Prieure de Ganagobie to Peipin 23.6 km

Waypoint	Distance Between Waypoints (m)	Total (km)	Directions	Verification Point	Compass	Altitude (m)
11.041	1600	20,5	Cross the river and bear left on the shale track	Pylon ahead, GR sign	NW	488
11.042	150	20,6	At the T-junction with a larger track, turn right	GR sign	NW	492
11.043	260	20,9	Continue straight ahead	Direction Aubignosc, GR sign	N	504
11.044	600	21,5	At the crossroads in the tracks, continue straight ahead	Direction Aubignosc	NW	538
11.045	500	22,0	Bear right on the wider track	Towards the village centre	N	503
11.046	80	22,1	Bear right on the tarmac road	Continue towards the centre of Aubignosc	NE	495
11.047	180	22,3	In place de la Fontaine, turn left	Montée du Bassin, GR sign	W	484
11.048	140	22,4	At the top of a steep rise, turn right onto a track to leave the village	GR sign	NW	488
11.049	230	22,6	At the T-junction with a tarmac road, turn right and then immediately left on the road	Parallel to overhead power line, GR sign	N	486
11.050	600	23,3	Continue straight ahead	Equestian centre and Gîte d'Etape can be seen across the fields to the right	N	478
11.051	300	23,6	Arrive at Peipin at the T-junction with route de Château Arnoux	Commercial centre to the right		476

Prieure de Ganagobie to Peipin 23,6 km

Stage Ascent: 288m   Stage Descent: 131m

Waypoint	Distance Between Waypoints (m)	Total (km)	Directions	Verification Point	Compass	Altitude (m)
11A1.001	0	0,0	Continue straight ahead up the hill	GR sign	N	423
11A1.002	400	0,4	Take the right fork		N	460
11A1.003	1500	1,9	On the crown of the bend to the right bear left	GR sign	N	492
11A1.004	2500	4,3	Cross the main road and continue straight ahead	River to the left	NE	466
11A1.005	3400	7,7	At the T-junction in the track turn left. **Note:-** main route joins from the right			580

Alternatre Route 7.7 km

B&B, Hotel, Gite d'Etapes	Price/
Les GrandesMollières (Cathy et Michel Raquet), Chemin de Mallefougasse à Saint-Julien-d'Asse 04600 Montfort, Alpes de Haute Provence, France Tel:+33(0)4 62 68 11 41 **Note:** Pilgrim price reduction	B2
Jas de Peguier (Hélène de Vilmorin) 04200 Châteauneuf Val Saint Donat, Alpes de Haute Provence, France Tel:+33(0)4 92 62 53 33 Mobile:+33(0)6 09 69 20 19 jasdp@orange.fr	B2
Hotel La Magnanerie, Les Filières 04200 Aubignosc, Alpes de Haute Provence France Tel:+33(0)4 92 62 60 11 ct@la-magnanerie.net www.la-magnanerie.net	B3
L'Oustalet (Marianne Barrois), Les Claux du Thor 04200 Sisteron, Alpes de Haute Provence, France Tel:+33(0)4 92 61 43 42 Mobile:+33(0)6 81 25 18 81 marianne.barrois@orange.fr	B2
Berte (Mme Bert), 168 Avenue Jean Moulin 04200 Sisteron, Alpes de Haute Provence, France Tel:+33(0)4 92 32 48 04 Mobile:+33(0)6 71 38 18 30 oubert04@gmail.com	B2
Le Tivoli, Place René Cassin 04200 Sisteron, Alpes de Haute Provence, France Tel:+33(0)4 92 61 15 16 www.hotel-tivoli.fr	B2
La Citadelle, 175 Avenue Paul Arène 04200 Sisteron, Alpes de Haute Provence, France Tel:+33(0)4 92 31 45 45 www.sisteron.com/	B2

Camping	
Camping Municipal, Chemin des Coudoulets 04200 Sisteron, Alpes de Haute Provence, France Tel:+33(0)4 92 61 19 69	B1 Open April - Sept

Tourist Office
Office de Tourisme, Place République 04200 Sisteron, Alpes de Haute Provence, France   Tel:+33(0)4 92 61 12 03   www.sisteron.com/

Doctor
Mondielli Jean-Marc, 10 Avenue Arcades 04200 Sisteron, Alpes de Haute Provence, France   Tel:+33(0)4 92 62 61 62

Veterinary
Debever Peter, 79 Rue Combes 04200 Sisteron, Alpes de Haute Provence, France   Tel:+33(0)4 92 61 24 89

Prieure de Ganagobie to Peipin 23.6 km

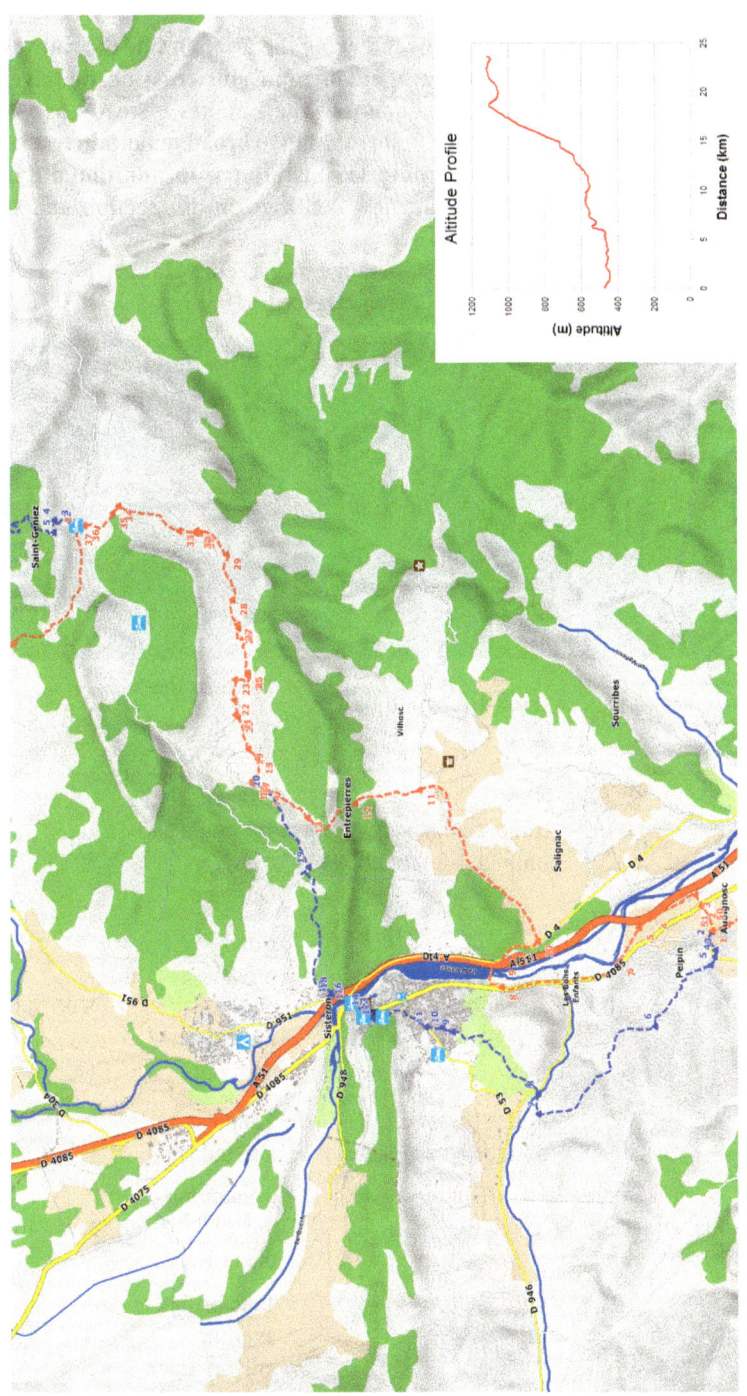

From Peipin we suggest initially following the track beside the railway before taking a small section of main road and crossing the river Durance. From there a quiet country road makes a steady ascent through dramatic countryside before taking to broad mountain tracks. The GR653 takes a longer route via Sisteron with additional and unnecessary climbs. There are few facilities on this section and so careful planning is necessary.

Distance from Arles: 197km **Distance to Vercelli: 425km**
Stage Ascent: 833m **Stage Descent: 193m**

	Waypoint	Distance Between Way-points (m)	Total (km)	Directions	Verification Point	Compass	Altitude (m)
Peipin to Saint-Geniez 23.7 km	12.001	0	0,0	At the T-junction turn right	Towards the Centre Equestre	NE	476
	12.002	500	0,5	At the roundabout, continue straight ahead	Towards the autoroute and the river Durance	NE	458
	12.003	250	0,8	Cross the level crossing and continue on the road as it bears left	Road progresses between railway and autoroute	NW	448
	12.004	900	1,7	At the crossroads, continue straight ahead	Tunnels to the left and right	NW	446
	12.005	400	2,0	Keep left	Remaining on the track beside the railway	NW	460
	12.006	700	2,8	Turn left	Take bridge over the railway track	SW	456

Waypoint	Distance Between Waypoints (m)	Total (km)	Directions	Verification Point	Compass	Altitude (m)
12.007	60	2,8	At the T-junction with the major road turn right and proceed with caution beside the road	D4085, direction Sisteron	N	456
12.008	2400	5,2	At the roundabout take the first exit and cross the bridge over the river	D4, blue signs for the autoroute	E	468
12.009	800	5,9	At the roundabout after the bridge take the second exit	Direction Entrepierres, D4	SE	482
12.010	900	6,8	At the top of the hill, turn left	Direction Entrepierres, D217	NE	524
12.011	4000	10,8	At the crossroads beside the Marie, continue straight ahead on the road	Direction Vieux Entrepierres	N	560
12.012	1300	12,2	After passing through Entrepierres, bear left onto a grass track. **Note:-** horse and bike riders should remain on the road	Yellow sign on wooden post	N	598
12.013	1300	13,4	Return to the road and bear left	River parallel on the right	NE	641
12.014	1000	14,4	In the hamlet of les Meuniers, bear right on the road. **Note:-** the GR653D and GR6 rejoin from the left	Direction St Geniez, GR sign	NE	715

Peipin to Saint-Geniez 23.7 km

Waypoint	Distance Between Waypoints (m)	Total (km)	Directions	Verification Point	Compass	Altitude (m)
12.015	270	14,7	Bear right onto a gravelled track. **Note:-** riders should continue on the road into the hamlet of Mezien and then straight ahead in the direction of the farm la Grande Bastide and the intersection the the GR653D	GR sign	E	716
12.016	120	14,8	Bear right after crossing the bridge and then left onto the narrow stone track	GR sign	SE	716
12.017	80	14,9	Continue straight ahead	Along stream bed	E	719
12.018	400	15,3	Turn right and then quickly left on a narrow track	GR sign	NE	767
12.019	290	15,6	At the intersection, cross the broad track and bear left on the narrow track. **Note:-** riders rejoin from the broad track on the left	Pass between a barn your right and fence on the left	E	806
12.020	700	16,2	At the T-junction between the path and a gravel track turn left	Farm to your right, GR sign	NE	884

Peipin to Saint-Geniez 23.7 km

Waypoint	Distance Between Way-points (m)	Total (km)	Directions	Verification Point	Compass	Altitude (m)
12.021	70	16,3	At the intersection with a tarmac road, turn right and then quickly left on the narrow track through the trees	GR sign	E	892
12.022	280	16,5	At the T-junction with the tarmac road, turn left on the road	Pass water station on the right	E	927
12.023	400	16,9	Turn right on the broad track	Cross the bridge over the stream	S	967
12.024	400	17,3	On a bend to the left, bear right on the narrow track	GR sign	E	994
12.025	40	17,3	At the T-junction, turn right on the broad track		E	998
12.026	1100	18,5	On the bend to the left, pedestrians bear right on the narrow track. **Note:**-riders should continue on the broad track to the next waypoint		E	1098
12.027	60	18,5	Rejoin the broad track and turn right		E	1103
12.028	500	19,0	Take the right fork down the hill, towards the hamlet of les Naux	GR sign	E	1084
12.029	1000	20,0	After passing through the hamlet of Sorine, bear right on the road		NE	1054

Peipin to Saint-Geniez 23.7 km

Waypoint	Distance Between Waypoints (m)	Total (km)	Directions	Verification Point	Compass	Altitude (m)
12.030	700	20,8	On the crown of the bend to the right, bear left on the stony track	GR sign	NE	1072
12.031	80	20,9	After passing the poly-tunnels bear left on the track	GR sign	W	1074
12.032	50	20,9	Turn right on the narrow path	Pass between 2 rocks, GR sign	N	1076
12.033	400	21,3	Cross the fence and continue straight ahead on the faint path	GR sign painted on a rock	N	1096
12.034	1300	22,6	With the village of St Geniez visible ahead, turn left on the small track	Direction Gîte d'Etape, GR sign	NW	1113
12.035	180	22,8	At the fork in the tracks, take the lower track towards the village	GR sign	NW	1111
12.036	700	23,5	At the crossroads in the tracks continue straight ahead on the tarmac road, towards the village	Pass Centre Equestre on the left, GR sign	NW	1100
12.037	180	23,7	Arrive at Saint-Geniez	Village centre to the right		1116

Peipin to Saint-Geniez 23.7 km

Stage Ascent: 853m   Stage Descent: 608m

Waypoint	Distance Between Waypoints (m)	Total (km)	Directions	Verification Point	Compass	Altitude (m)
12A1.001	0	0,0	To follow the GR653D via Sisteron, turn left at the T-junction	Route de Château-Arnoux	W	476
12A1.002	180	0,2	Turn left on route des Granges	Towards the centre of Peipin	SW	486
12A1.003	200	0,4	Take the right fork	Route des Granges	W	498
12A1.004	110	0,5	Cross the main road and continue straight ahead	GR sign	NW	496
12A1.005	170	0,7	Take the right fork	Chemin de Valbelle	NW	501
12A1.006	1800	2,4	After the long climb, at the T-junction with the broad track, turn right	GR sign	NW	791
12A1.007	3200	5,6	At the T-junction with the road, turn right		E	479
12A1.008	400	6,0	Cross the river bridge and the main road and continue on the track on the far side	GR sign	NE	469
12A1.009	2300	8,3	At the first crossroads in le Thor, continue straight ahead	Avenue Saint-Domnin	NE	549

Alternative Route 15.6km

Waypoint	Distance Between Waypoints (m)	Total (km)	Directions	Verification Point	Compass	Altitude (m)
12A1.010	210	8,5	At the junction, bear left	Av. Saint-Domnin	N	550
12A1.011	290	8,8	At roundabout, straight ahead	Avenue de Jabron	N	553
12A1.012	1100	9,9	In the centre of Sisteron, turn right across the square	Towards the roundabout	NE	494
12A1.013	130	10,1	At the roundabout turn left	Avenue Paul Arène	NE	490
12A1.014	190	10,2	Turn left and then right	Rue de Saunerie, parallel to river	NE	488
12A1.015	400	10,6	Turn right to cross the river bridge		NE	465
12A1.016	80	10,7	At the end of the bridge turn left	Towards la Baume	N	466
12A1.017	300	10,0	Turn right	Place saint Marcel	SE	483
12A1.018	70	11,1	At the T-junction turn left	Chemin d'Entrepieres	E	491
12A1.019	3000	13,0	Take the right fork		NE	821
12A1.020	1700	15,6	At the T-junction in les Meuniers, turn left. **Note:**- the main-route joins from the right	GR sign		722

Alternative Route 15.6km

B&B, Hotel, Gite d'Etapes	Price/
Chardavon (Marianne et Gino Devos) 04200 Saint Geniez, Alpes de Haute Provence, France Tel:+33(0)4 92 61 29 04 ginodevos@wanadoo.fr **Note:** Pilgrim price reduction	B2
PR Les Cavaliers de St Geniez (Marlène et Olivier Chabrand) 04200 Saint Geniez, Alpes de Haute Provence, France Tel:+33(0)4 92 61 00 87 o.chabrand@infonie.fr **Note:** Pilgrim price reduction	B1

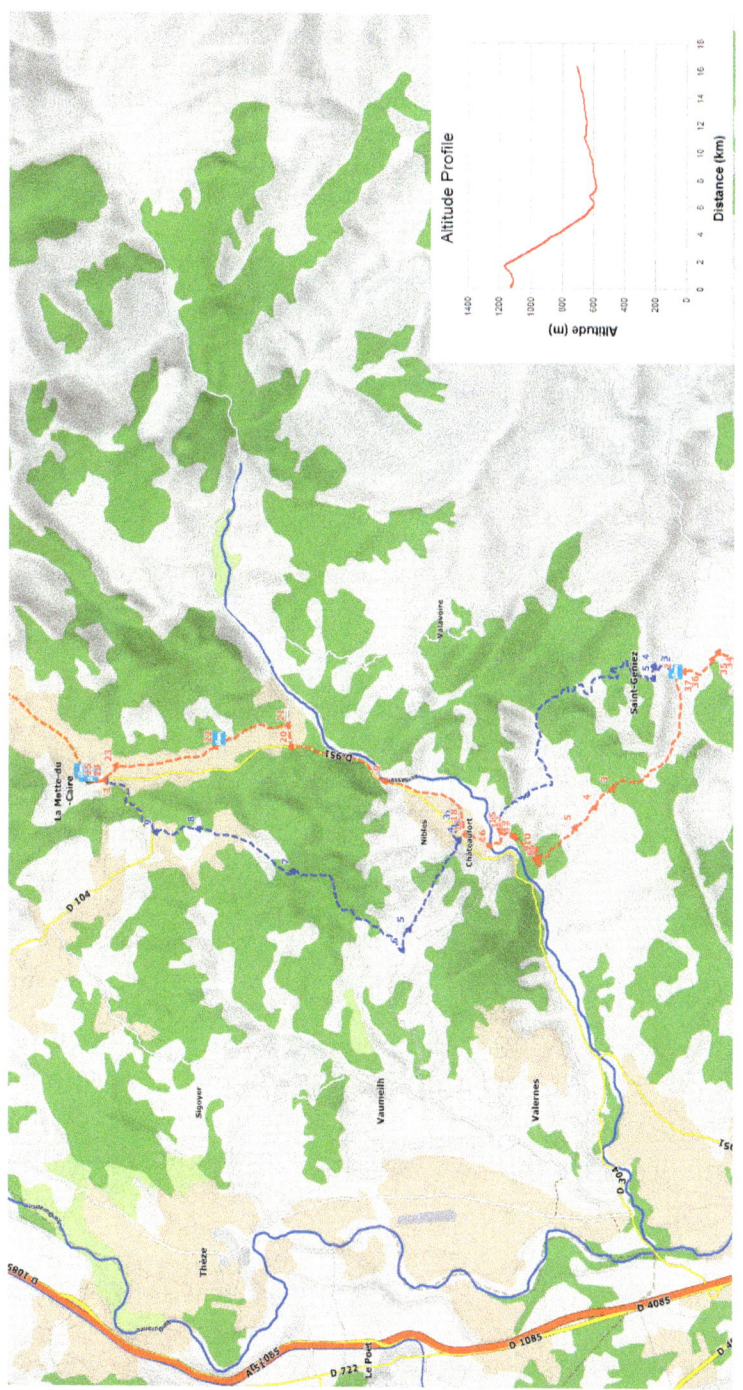

From Saint-Geniez the route returns to mountain tracks, which are often narrow, steep and exposed . The alternate route takes a broader and more gentle track to Châteaufort. From Châteaufort to la-Motte-du-Caire we prefer to remain in the river valley.
The GR takes a longer route through the mountains.
Distance from Arles: 220km   Distance to Vercelli: 401km
Stage Ascent: 237m   Stage Descent: 648m

Saint-Geniez to la-Motte-du-Caire 16.3 km

Waypoint	Distance Between Waypoints (m)	Total (km)	Directions	Verification Point	Compass	Altitude (m)
13.001	0	0,0	At the T-junction with the main road, turn right and immediately left. **Note:**- the route ahead, although indicated as a horse route by the signposts, contains many difficult and dangerous stretches for horse and bike riders who should consider taking the Alternate Route	Pass house close on your right	N	1117
13.002	20	0,0	At the T-junction, turn left on the track	Conical mountain to your right, GR sign	NW	1120
13.003	3300	3,3	Take the left fork. Caution:- junction may be easily missed	GR sign	NW	925
13.004	500	3,8	At the T-junction with a broad track, turn right on the track	GR sign, conical mountain, Mont de Hongrie, to the left	NW	869
13.005	600	4,4	Turn right on a wide track	Mont de Hongrie ahead, GR sign on a rock to the left	NW	784
13.006	1000	5,3	Take the left fork	GR sign	W	659

Waypoint	Distance Between Waypoints (m)	Total (km)	Directions	Verification Point	Compass	Altitude (m)
13.007	110	5,4	At the fork in the tracks, bear right		NE	648
13.008	20	5,5	Fork right	Along the ridge top, GR sign	NE	646
13.009	100	5,6	At the junction, continue straight ahead	GR sign	E	639
13.010	170	5,7	At a junction in the track, bear left	Downhill	NE	629
13.011	500	6,3	Take the pedestrian bridge over the river and turn right up the hill	GR sign	NE	592
13.012	40	6,3	Bear left on the small track	GR sign	NE	593
13.013	300	6,6	Bear left to pass between the houses and enter Châteaufort	GR sign	N	615
13.014	60	6,7	Continue straight ahead on the road through the village	GR and chemin de St Jacques signs	NE	619
13.015	80	6,8	At the T-junction, turn left on the road, downhill. **Note:-** Alternate route joins from the right	GR sign	NW	621
13.016	700	7,4	Cross the river bridge and immediately turn right on the track	GR sign, keep stream to your right	NE	581
13.017	500	7,9	Turn right	Cross the stream	E	586

Saint-Geniez to la-Motte-du-Caire 16.3 km

Waypoint	Distance Between Waypoints (m)	Total (km)	Directions	Verification Point	Compass	Altitude (m)
13.018	190	8,1	At the crossroads in the track, turn right and then follow the yellow marked path beside the irrigation channel. **Note:-** for the GR, proceed on the Alternate route to the next crossroads at the top of the hill.	Church visible on the hill ahead	NE	589
13.019	1900	10,0	At the junction, continue straight ahead with caution beside the main road, D951	River to the right	N	621
13.020	2000	11,0	Turn right over the bridge, D1	Direction Clamensane	E	643
13.021	400	12,4	Turn left between the farm buildings and proceed along the broad yellow marked track parallel to the main road and the river	Direction Bas Plan	N	643
13.022	1500	13,8	Continue straight ahead on the broad track	Pass Centre Equestre/Gîte d'Etape on the right	N	662
13.023	2000	15,8	Turn left across the bridge	Pass fruit packing plant on the right	NW	693
13.024	400	16,2	At the T-junction with the main road turn right. **Note:-** GR653D joins from the left	Follow the main road, towards the centre of la Motte du Caire	N	701
13.025	170	16,3	Arrive at la-Motte-du-Caire	Bar and pizzaria ahead		707

Saint-Geniez to la-Motte-du-Caire 16.3 km

Stage Ascent: 125m   Stage Descent: 617m

Waypoint	Distance Between Waypoints (m)	Total (km)	Directions	Verification Point	Compass	Altitude (m)
13A1.001	0	0,0	Turn right and follow the main road through the centre of the village	Pass gîte on the right	E	1119
13A1.002	110	0,1	Bear left to follow the road and then broad track	On the crown of the next bend to the right	NE	1125
13A1.003	60	0,2	Continue straight ahead	Pass cemetery on your left side	N	1131
13A1.004	700	0,8	On the apex of the second hairpin to the right, continue straight ahead on the track		W	1217
13A1.005	220	1,1	Take the right fork		NW	1210
13A1.006	7100	8,2	In the village of Châteaufort continue straight ahead. **Note:-** the main route joins from the left	GR sign		627

Alternate Route 8.2 km

Stage Ascent: 414m   Stage Descent: 303m

Waypoint	Distance Between Waypoints (m)	Total (km)	Directions	Verification Point	Compass	Altitude (m)
13A2.001	0	0,0	Continue straight ahead	Towards the centre of Nibles	NE	591
13A2.002	80	0,1	At the crossroads, turn left	Church on the right at the junction	NW	595
13A2.003	140	0,2	At the T-junction with the road turn left	D951	W	598
13A2.004	300	0,5	After crossing the river, bear right on the track	GR sign	NW	598
13A2.005	2200	2,7	At the junction with the tarmac road, turn right and then immediately left		W	763
13A2.006	400	3,2	At the T-junction turn right	Hamlet of Borelly	NE	767
13A2.007	3000	6,1	At the top of the hill turn left on the track	GR sign	NE	943
13A2.008	2100	8,2	At the junction with the minor road, continue straight ahead	Farm buildings on your left	N	813
13A2.009	1000	9,1	At the junction bear right towards the larger road and then bear right again and remain on the road	GR sign	NE	802
13A2.010	1700	10,8	At the junction with the main road turn left. **Note:-** the main route joins from the minor road opposite	Enter La Motte-du-Caire		701

Alternate Route 10.8 km

B&B, Hotel, Gite d'Etapes	Price/ Opening
PR Ferme la Bâtie Neuve (Eva et Holger Giersch) 04250 La Motte du Caire, Alpes de Haute Provence, France Tel:+33(0)4 92 68 36 51 labatie@wanadoo.fr **Note:** Pilgrim price reduction, also equestrian centre	B1
La Maison des Hôtes (Ingrid et Marc Linarès), Rue République 04250 La Motte du Caire, Alpes de Haute Provence, France Tel:+33(0)4 92 68 42 72 marc.linares@wanadoo.fr	B1
Conrad Dieter, Saint Georges 04250 LaMotte du Caire, Alpes de Haute Provence, France Tel:+33(0)4 92 68 35 55	B2

Camping	
Camping Municipal, Route Ste Catherine 04250 La Motte du Caire, Alpes de Haute Provence, France Tel:+33(0)4 92 68 33 30 Mobile:+33(0)6 43 73 80 94	B1

Saint-Geniez to la-Motte-du-Caire 16.3 km

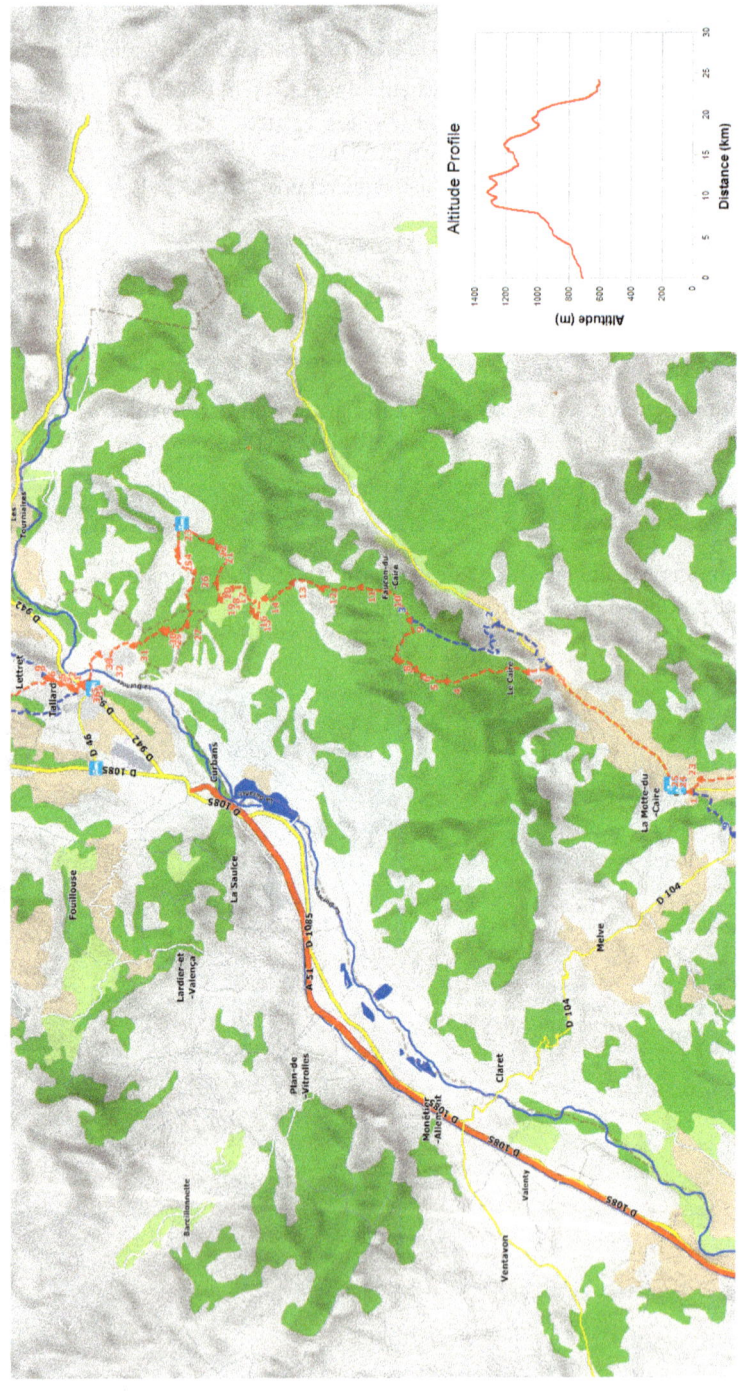

la-Motte-du-Caire to Tallard 24.2 km

The exit from la-Motte-du-Caire follows the route départementale to la Caire where there is the choice to continue on the road and take the GR653D and the steep climb to over 1400m or follow the initially gentle climb on the broad mountain track, before a brief, but steep ascent to rejoin the GR on the narrow forest tracks of the grand Vallon. Bikers will find both routes challenging and may wish to take the road route via Gigors, Bréziers and Rochebrune to Tallard. The descent to Tallard follows broad stone tracks and very quiet roads. There are again few facilities en route.

Distance from Arles: 237km   **Distance to Vercelli: 385km**
Stage Ascent: 882m   **Stage Descent: 979m**

Waypoint	Distance Between Waypoints (m)	Total (km)	Directions	Verification Point	Compass	Altitude (m)
14.001	0	0,0	Take the right fork, rue de la République	Pass bar and Pizzaria on your left	NE	707
14.002	4100	4,1	After crossing the bridge in le Caire, turn left on the road between the houses. **Note:-** the GR653D continues on the main road	Yellow footpath sign, "Campagne la Roche"	N	790
14.003	600	4,6	At the fork in the tracks keep right		N	340
14.004	2000	6,6	At a fork in the tracks, keep right and then turn right towards the river	Direction les Roches	N	924
14.005	600	7,1	At a fork in the track, turn right and cross the stream	Yellow signs painted on the trees	NE	949
14.006	280	7,4	Take the left fork	Bearing slightly away from the river	NE	969

la-Motte-du-Caire to Tallard 24.2 km

Waypoint	Distance Between Waypoints (m)	Total (km)	Directions	Verification Point	Compass	Altitude (m)
14.007	500	7,9	Take the right fork, away from the stream and up the hill	Direction les Roches	NE	989
14.008	90	7,0	Take the right fork, up the hill	Direction les Roches	E	996
14.009	1200	9,2	Bear right and then left	Rejoining the GR653D	NE	1287
14.010	800	9,0	Continue straight ahead	GR sign, direction Venterol	N	1260
14.011	600	10,6	At the junction with the gravel track, turn left	GR sign	N	1321
14.012	1000	11,6	At the junction, bear right beside the exposed rocks	GR sign	N	1257
14.013	800	12,4	On the crown of a bend to the right, turn left down a small track	GR sign	NW	1309
14.014	900	13,3	At the T-junction at the bottom of the hill, turn left on the broad track	Direction Venterol	NW	1170
14.015	500	13,7	At the T-junction at the bottom of the hill turn right	Direction Venterol, GR sign	NE	1129
14.016	140	13,9	At the next T-junction, turn right on the tarmac road	GR sign "les Garcins" ahead at the junction	NE	1118
14.017	1100	14,9	Take the left fork	Pass "les Marmets" on your right	NW	1478
14.018	180	15,1	Fork right on the road	Direction Venterol	NW	1149

la-Motte-du-Caire to Tallard 24.2 km

Waypoint	Distance Between Waypoints (m)	Total (km)	Directions	Verification Point	Compass	Altitude (m)
14.019	160	15,3	Continue straight ahead on the small road, after passing the farm	Sharp bend to the right ahead	E	1152
14.020	500	15,8	At the top of the rise, bear right	Direction Venterol	E	1181
14.021	900	16,7	Take the left fork down the hill	GR sign	NE	1197
14.022	210	16,9	Bear left down the hill	GR sign	NE	1182
14.023	900	17,8	In the centre of Venterol, turn left	Pass Gîte de France on the left, GR sign	W	1059
14.024	600	18,4	At the crossroads, continue straight ahead	Direction Tallard	W	1005
14.025	130	18,5	Take the left fork up the hill	Pass creche and tennis court	SW	997
14.026	600	19,1	Cross the stream and bear right	Up the hill on the broad track	W	1016
14.027	1400	20,4	Turn right	Direction Tallard, GR sign	N	988
14.028	600	20,0	Bear right down the hill	GR sign	SE	920
14.029	120	21,1	At the fork in the tracks, turn sharp left down the hill	GR sign	N	908
14.030	120	21,2	Take the right fork and then bear left	GR sign	NW	890
14.031	900	22,1	At the junction turn right and then left	GR sign	NW	675

la-Motte-du-Caire to Tallard 24.2 km

Waypoint	Distance Between Waypoints (m)	Total (km)	Directions	Verification Point	Compass	Altitude (m)
14.032	800	22,9	At the T-junction with the road, turn right	Château de Tallard ahead	NE	616
14.033	280	23,2	Turn left on the D46	Direction Tallard	W	618
14.034	700	23,9	Bear right on the road	Left fork leads to the historical centre of Tallard	NW	601
14.035	140	24,1	Turn left and across the place Charles de Gaulle towards the main road		SW	605
14.036	120	24,2	Arrive at Tallard centre	Marie to your right in the square		609

Alternate Route 5.5km   Stage Ascent: 634m   Stage Descent: 131m

Waypoint	Distance Between Waypoints (m)	Total (km)	Directions	Verification Point	Compass	Altitude (m)
14A1.001	0	0,0	Continue straight ahead on the main road	Towards Faucon du Caire	NE	789
14A1.002	1700	1,7	Turn left onto the track and climb the steep hill	GR sign	N	832
14A1.003	3800	5,5	At the T-junction in the tracks, turn right. **Note:-** the main route approaches from the left	GR sign		1293

la-Motte-du-Caire to Tallard 24.2 km

B&B, Hotel, Gite d'Etapes	Price/ Opening
La Grange, Petit Collet 05130 Tallard, Hautes Alpes, France Tel:+33(0)6 86 66 77 12	B1
Andalousie (Marie et José-Louis Narvaez), 9 La Placette 05130 Tallard, Hautes Alpes, France Tel:+33(0)4 92 56 00 25,Mobile:+33(0)6 71 89 34 67 marie.narvaez@libertysurf.fr **Note:** Pilgrim price reduction	B2
Le Château (Christophe Ubaud) 05130 Venterol, Hautes Alpes, France Tel:+33(0)4 92 54 01 85 Mobile:+33(0)6 64 22 27 85 contact@aucoeurdelamontagne.com	B2

Camping

Camping Le Chêne, Le Chêne 05130 Tallard, Hautes Alpes, France Tel:+33(0)4 92 54 13 31	B1

Tourist Office

Office de Tourisme du Pays de Tallard Barcillonnette, Place Château 05130 Tallard, Hautes Alpes, France   Tel:+33(0)4 92 54 04 29,

Doctor

Cabinet Médical Docteurs Favre Grégoire Grimaud, 31 Avenue Jacques Bonfort 05130 Tallard, Hautes Alpes, France   Tel:+33(0)4 92 54 10 01

Veterinary

Cabinet Vétérinaire, Les Lauzes Basses 05130 Tallard, Hautes Alpes, France   Tel:+33(0)4 92 54 06 77,

Farrier

Deprez Roger, Le Clot de Saigne 05400 Manteyer, Hautes Alpes, France Tel:+33(0)4 92 56 25 03,

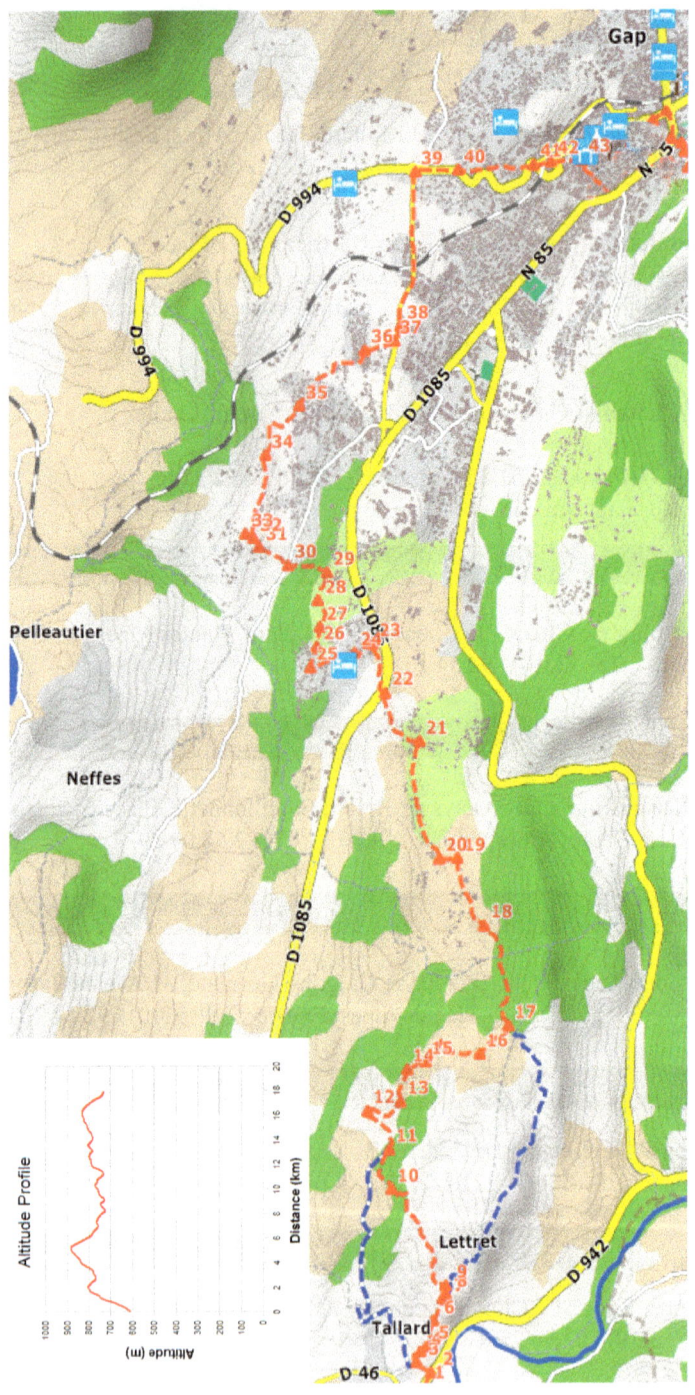

From Tallard the route initially follows quiet roads, before climbing on narrowing mountain tracks. The GR653D takes a narrow and potentially dangerous path over loose shale. We prefer to take the quiet roads via Châteauvieux, before rejoining the GR to make the approach to Gap. The final 4km to Gap follows busy roads.

Distance from Arles: 261km   **Distance to Vercelli: 361km**
Stage Ascent: 519m   **Stage Descent: 397m**

Waypoint	Distance Between Waypoints (m)	Total (km)	Directions	Verification Point	Compass	Altitude (m)
15.001	0	0,0	Proceed with care on the main road	D942 towards the Marie	NE	609
15.002	140	0,1	After passing the Marie on your right, turn left onto the stony road	Direction, Châteauvieux/Lettret, GR sign	NW	616
15.003	180	0,3	On the crown of the bend to the left, turn right on the track. **Note:-** the climb ahead may be difficult for mountain bikers an easier route is to remain on the road and take the next turning to the right and follow the road to rejoin our route in Châteauvieux		N	629
15.004	150	0,5	At the top of the hill, briefly join a tarmac road and then bear right on the narrow track up the hill	GR sign	NE	644
15.005	70	0,5	Continue on the broad track up the hill	GR sign	N	654
15.006	270	0,8	The track approaches a road, bear right to remain on the narrow track		NE	691

Tallard to Gap 17.9 km

Waypoint	Distance Between Waypoints (m)	Total (km)	Directions	Verification Point	Compass	Altitude (m)
15.007	210	1,0	The track joins a minor road, continue straight ahead	GR sign	NE	729
15.008	50	1,1	Bear left onto a small track. **Note:-** the GR653D leaves to the right, direction Lettret. However, the path is very narrow across unstable shale hillsides, we prefer to take the route via Châteauvieux and then rejoin the GR beside les Marinons	Signpost direction Châteauvieux	N	737
15.009	80	1,2	Take the left fork, up hill, on the smaller track	Right fork "Propriété Privé"	NW	745
15.010	1300	2,5	Join the tarmac road	Towards the hamlet of Valenty	N	779
15.011	400	2,9	At the T-junction with a minor road, turn right. **Note:-** the alternate cycle route joins from	Direction Châteauvieux	NW	770
15.012	500	3,4	After passing through the centre of the village of Châteauvieux turn right	Yellow footpath sign to Gap and Lettret	E	782
15.013	400	3,8	Turn sharp left onto a small track	Yellow footpath signs	N	816
15.014	400	4,1	Take the right fork towards the houses	Yellow sign	NE	840
15.015	190	4,3	Return to the road and turn left	Passing through the hamlet of "Bel-Air"	E	846

Tallard to Gap 17.9 km

Waypoint	Distance Between Waypoints (m)	Total (km)	Directions	Verification Point	Compass	Altitude (m)
15.016	700	5,0	Just before the top of the rise, bear left on the track	Farm just ahead on the right	NE	880
15.017	400	5,4	At the crossroads in the tracks, turn left. **Note:-** GR653D joins from the right	GR sign, direction Gap	N	877
15.018	1000	6,4	At a T-junction with a broad track, turn right	Direction Gap	NW	782
15.019	700	7,1	Bear left remaining on the road	GR sign	W	758
15.020	150	7,2	At the T-junction with a larger road turn right	Direction Gap	N	762
15.021	1100	8,3	Immediately after passing a bus garage, turn left	GR sign	NW	724
15.022	600	8,9	Take the green bridge over the main road	GR sign	N	741
15.023	500	9,4	In the village of la Tour Ronde, bear left up the hill on the road	GR sign	SW	745
15.024	230	9,6	At the crossroads continue straight ahead	Chemin des Chênes	W	751
15.025	400	10,0	Turn right on the road	GR sign, les Balcons	N	760
15.026	190	10,2	On the apex of a bend to the left, bear right on the path	GR sign	N	770
15.027	180	10,4	Turn right and immediately left	GR sign	N	768

Tallard to Gap 17.9 km

Waypoint	Distance Between Waypoints (m)	Total (km)	Directions	Verification Point	Compass	Altitude (m)
15.028	270	10,7	Turn right over a small stream	GR sign on tree to the right	N	760
15.029	270	10,0	At the T-junction with a minor road, turn left down the hill	GR sign	W	748
15.030	400	11,3	At the T-junction, turn left and immediately right	GR sign, proceed with stream on the right	NW	733
15.031	400	11,7	On the apex of a bend to the left, bear right on the path into the trees	GR sign	NW	761
15.032	90	11,8	At the T-junction with the road turn left on route de St Jean	GR sign	NW	775
15.033	90	11,9	Turn sharp right	Chemin des Prairies	N	783
15.034	800	12,7	Take the right fork down the hill on the gravel track	GR sign	NE	800
15.035	700	13,3	Bear left on the road through the housing development	GR sign	NE	792
15.036	900	14,2	After passing the hospital on the right, bear right on the road	Route de Chaudefeuille	E	782
15.037	280	14,5	At the T-junction, turn left on the pavement beside the road	D291	NE	788
15.038	150	14,6	Continue straight ahead on the road, D291	Rue des Lauries to the right	N	795

Tallard to Gap 17.9 km

Waypoint	Distance Between Waypoints (m)	Total (km)	Directions	Verification Point	Compass	Altitude (m)
15.039	1400	16,0	At the roundabout turn right on the D944, direction Gap	GR sign	E	830
15.040	400	16,4	Take the left fork, Ancienne route de Veynes	No entry sign	E	826
15.041	700	17,1	At the roundabout take the third exit, and then immediately bear right on the path leading under the railway bridge	GR sign	E	786
15.042	170	17,3	At the junction with the road, continue straight ahead downhill on the narrow road	Rue Ernest Cézanne, GR sign	E	771
15.043	280	17,6	At the T-junction, turn right	Keep hospital on your right, Cours Frédéric Mistral	SE	744
15.044	260	17,8	At the end of the road, beside the Office du Tourisme, turn sharp left	Towards the spire of the cathedral	NE	732
15.045	100	17,9	Arrive at Gap centre	Beside the cathedral		732

Tallard to Gap 17.9 km

B&B, Hotel, Gite d'Etapes	Price/ Opening
Hotel Carina Pavillon 2, Route de Veynes 05000 Gap, Hautes Alpes, France Tel:+33(0)4 92 51 02 52	B2
Hôtel le Pavillon, 27 Route de Chabanas 05000 Gap, Hautes Alpes, France Tel:+33(0)4 92 52 02 73 www.carina-hotel.com/ **Note:** Pilgrim price reduction	B2
Le Verdun, 20 Boulevard de la Libération 05000 Gap, Hautes Alpes, France Tel:+33(0)4 92 53 88 50	B2
Hôtel Bar Restaurant de la Cloche, 2 Place Alsace Lorraine 05000 Gap, Hautes Alpes, France Tel:+33(0)4 92 51 02 52	B2
Hôtel Napoléon, 19 Avenue Commdt Dumont 05000 Gap, Hautes Alpes, France Tel:+33(0)4 92 51 03 43	B2
Hôtel Restaurant Le Clos, 20 Ter Avenue du Commandant Dumont 05000 Gap, Hautes Alpes, France Tel:+33(0)4 92 51 37 04 www.hotel-restaurant-parc-golf.leclos.fr/	B2
PR La Canadienne Chez Mauzan (Marie Josée Bouliane-Poncet), Rue Mauzan,05000 Gap, Hautes Alpes, France Tel:+33(0)4 92 46 28 61 mjbp@club.fr **Note:** Pilgrim price reduction - also willing to collect pilgrims from station	B2
Hotel Formule 1 Gap, Espace Tokoro 05000 Gap, Hautes Alpes, France Tel:+33(0)8 91 70 52 53	B2
Hôtellerie Notre Dame du Laus, Notre Dame du Laus 05130 Saint Etienne le Laus, Hautes Alpes, France Tel:+33(0)4 92 50 95 51 www.notre-dame-du-laus.com/	B2
Le Moulin des Girons, Les Girons 05000 Rambaud, Hautes Alpes, France Tel:+33(0)4 92 52 71 24 orciere.lionel@wanadoo.fr	B2
Le Masdani, Terre Droite 05230 Avançon, Hautes Alpes, France Tel:+33(0)4 92 50 37 75 Mobile:+33(0)6 07 61 78 61 www.masdani.com	B3

Tallard to Gap 17.9 km

Religious Hostel	
PR Foyer Ste Anne La Providence, 20 Boulevard du Général Charles de Gaulle 05000 Gap, Hautes Alpes, France Tel:+33(0)4 92 46 12 57	Donation
Maison de Béthanie 05130 Saint Etienne le Laus, Hautes Alpes, France Tel:+33(0)4 92 50 30 73 accueil@notre-dame-du-laus.com	Donation

Camping	
Camping Le Napoleon, Sur RN 85,05000 Gap, Hautes Alpes, France Tel:+33(0)4 92 52 12 41	B1
Camping Alpes Dauphiné, Route Napoléon 05000 Gap, Hautes Alpes, France Tel:+33(0)4 92 51 29 95 www.alpesdauphine.com/	B1

Tourist Office

Office de Tourisme, 2 A Cours Frédéric Mistral 05000 Gap, Hautes Alpes, France   Tel:+33(0)4 92 52 56 56   www.gap-tourisme.fr/

Centrale d'info et de réservations sur les Gîtes du 05 Hautes Alpes,1 Place du Champsaur 05000 Gap, Hautes Alpes, France Tel:+33(0)4 92 52 52 92

Doctor

Grimmonprez Jean-Christian, 72 Avenue Jean Jaurès 05000 Gap, Hautes Alpes, France   Tel:+33(0)4 92 53 37 06

Tallard to Gap 17.9 km

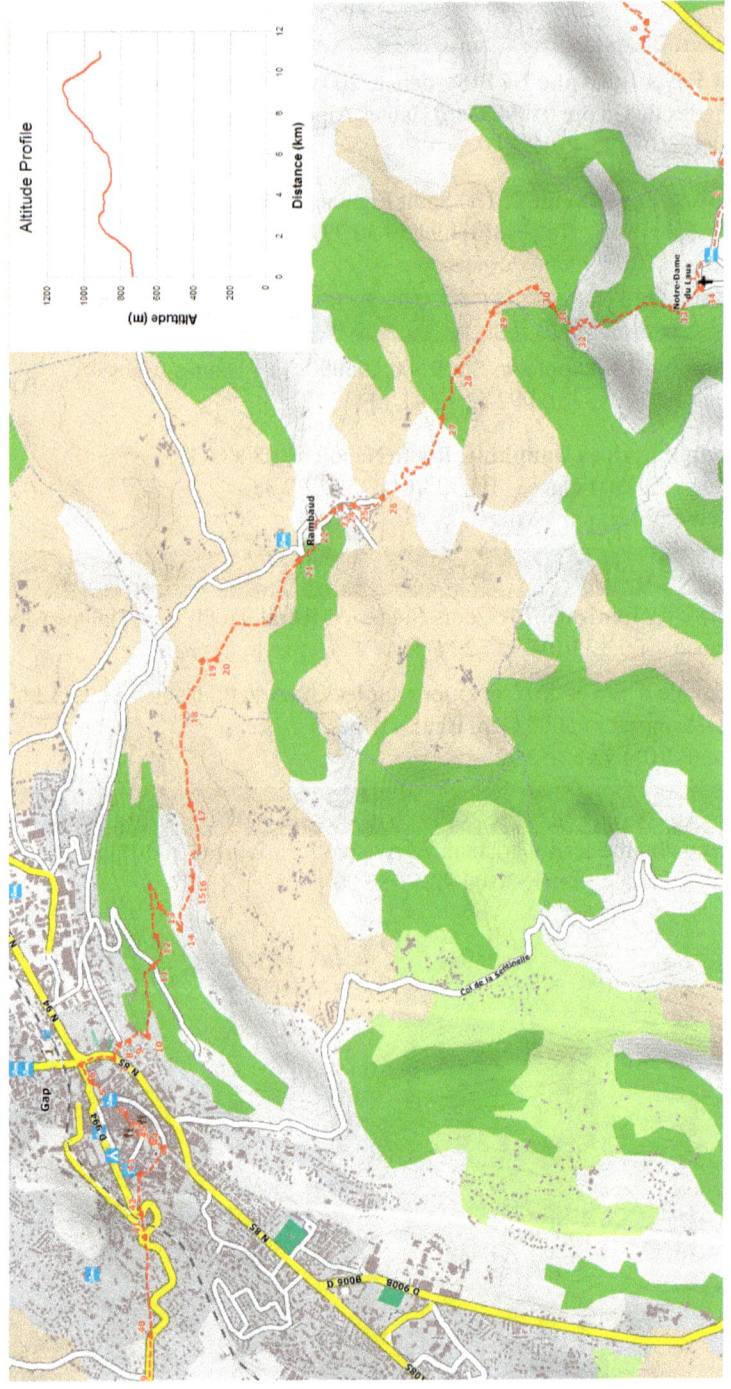

The route quickly leaves Gap on pleasant and broad forest tracks and then takes minor roads and farm tracks to Rambaud, before following increasingly narrow tracks to the the final steep descent to the sanctuary of Notre-Dame-de-Lurs

Distance from Arles: 279km **Distance to Vercelli: 343km**
Stage Ascent: 463m **Stage Descent: 283m**

Waypoint	Distance Between Waypoints (m)	Total (km)	Directions	Verification Point	Compass	Altitude (m)
16.001	0	0,0	Cross place Saint Arnoux and pass in front of the cathedral	Continue keeping the cathedral on your right side	NE	732
16.002	230	0,2	Cross place aux Herbes and bear left and then right	Rue de Mazel	NE	733
16.003	100	0,3	Cross place Jean Marcelin and bear left	Rue de France	NE	734
16.004	150	0,5	Cross the place de l'Alsace Lorraine and bear right on rue Carnot	Keep large car park on your left	NE	737
16.005	190	0,7	At the roundabout continue straight ahead	Rue Carnot	NE	739
16.006	140	0,8	At the next roundabout turn right on boulevard Pierre et Marie Curie	Pass park and concert halls on your left side	S	740
16.007	250	1,1	Turn left on rue de Saint-Mens	GR sign	E	739
16.008	100	1,2	Take the right fork	Keep the park to your left	S	742
16.009	80	1,2	On the apex of the bend to the right, bear left on the small road	GR sign	S	747
16.010	170	1,4	Turn sharp left onto a track, up hill	GR sign	E	766

Gap to Notre-Dame-de-Laus 11 km

Waypoint	Distance Between Waypoints (m)	Total (km)	Directions	Verification Point	Compass	Altitude (m)
16.011	600	1,9	Cross the minor road and continue straight ahead on the track	GR sign	E	843
16.012	240	2,2	Take the right fork and remain straight ahead at the next junction	GR sign	E	879
16.013	600	2,7	Continue straight ahead	Observation platform to your right	SW	916
16.014	240	2,0	At the junction with the minor road turn sharp left	Pass beside St Jacques Oratoire	E	915
16.015	300	3,3	On the apex of a bend, turn left onto the gravel track	GR sign	E	891
16.016	90	3,4	Take the left fork	GR sign	E	888
16.017	600	3,9	Join a minor road, chemin de Courbanion, and bear right down the hill	Equestrian centre to the left	E	891
16.018	700	4,6	Bear right on the road	GR sign	SE	854
16.019	400	4,0	Turn right onto a small road	GR sign	S	849
16.020	110	5,1	Take the left fork on the gravel track	GR sign, towards church spire	SE	849
16.021	1000	6,1	Just before the road junction, turn right on the path	GR sign	SE	880
16.022	300	6,4	At the road junction, cross over and bear right on the path	Church ahead at the junction, direction le Village	SE	914

Gap to Notre-Dame-de-Laus 11 km

Waypoint	Distance Between Waypoints (m)	Total (km)	Directions	Verification Point	Compass	Altitude (m)
16.023	200	6,6	At the road junction, bear left towards the centre of Rambaud	GR sign	SE	938
16.024	70	6,7	Bear right and then left, direction la Bàtie Vieille	Pass la Poste, GR sign	S	945
16.025	90	6,8	Continue straight ahead through the village	Football field to the right	S	949
16.026	240	6,0	Take the right fork, and bear right onto the track, direction le Sanctuaire de Notre Dame du Laus	Keep the cemetery on your left at the junction	SE	955
16.027	900	7,9	At the junction in the track, continue straight ahead	GR sign	E	1049
16.028	400	8,3	At the junction with the minor road turn left up the hill	GR sign, shrine ahead beside the road	SE	1083
16.029	500	8,8	Take the right fork onto the gravel track, then turn right	Chapel on left, chemin de Notre Dame du Laus	SE	1094
16.030	400	9,2	Take the left fork	GR sign	SW	1114
16.031	170	9,3	Take the left fork, down hill	Direction Notre Dame du Laus	SW	1113
16.032	250	9,6	At junction in tracks, after the Statue de l'Ange, turn left	GR sign	S	1092
16.033	1100	10,7	At the junction with the minor road, turn right across the bridge	Direction Notre Dame du Laus	SE	914
16.034	300	11,0	Arrive at Notre-Dame-de-Laus			911

Gap to Notre-Dame-de-Laus 11 km

B&B, Hotel, Gite d'Etapes	Price/ Opening
Hôtel de la Plaine, La Plaine 05230 Montgardin, Hautes Alpes, France Tel:+33(0)4 92 50 30 11	B3

Notre-Dame-de-Laus to Chorges 15.4 km

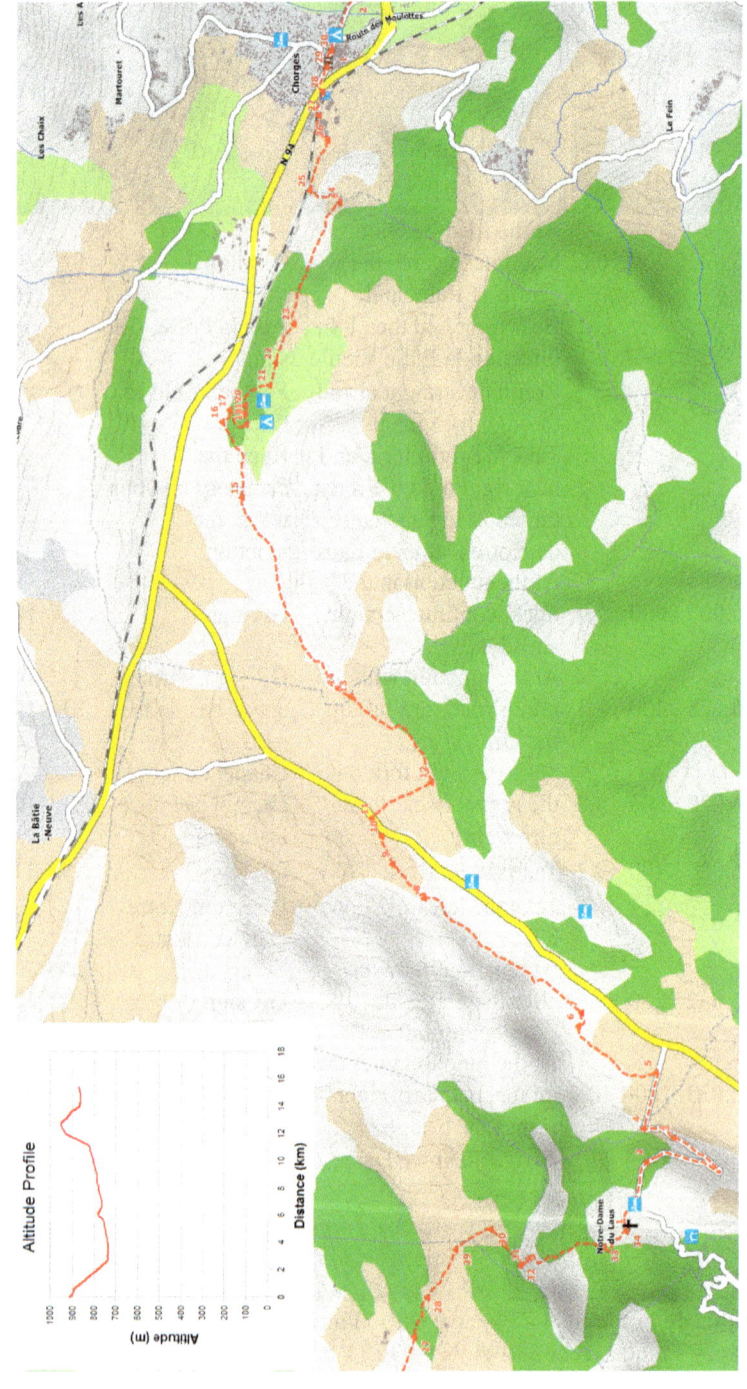

A short and generally easy section on small roads and farm tracks
Distance from Arles: 290km   **Distance to Vercelli: 332km**
Stage Ascent: 247m   **Stage Descent: 290m**

Waypoint	Distance Between Waypoints (m)	Total (km)	Directions	Verification Point	Compass	Altitude (m)
17.001	0	0,0	From the Sanctuary, pass the church, turn right, down the hill	Keep the sanctuary to the right, direction Saint Etienne	E	911
17.002	700	0,7	Take the left fork on the road. **Note:-** the GR descends steeply through the woods to the left rejoining the road below	Direction Montgardin	SE	887
17.003	1300	1,9	Continue straight ahead on the road. **Note:-** GR rejoins from the left	Direction Montgardin	N	790
17.004	300	2,2	Follow the road to the right	Directions les James	E	768
17.005	500	2,7	Turn left on the small road	Direction les James	NE	736
17.006	900	3,6	At the T-junction, turn right	GR sign	E	735
17.007	150	3,8	Turn left at the junction	GR sign, parallel to the main road	NE	736
17.008	1800	5,6	Turn sharp right across the stream and then shortly after turn left	GR sign	NE	757
17.009	500	6,0	At a crossroads in the track, continue straight ahead	Towards the main road	NE	783

Notre-Dame-de-Laus to Chorges 15.4 km

Waypoint	Distance Between Waypoints (m)	Total (km)	Directions	Verification Point	Compass	Altitude (m)
17.010	260	6,3	Shortly before reaching the main road, turn left up the steep narrow track	GR sign	NE	773
17.011	190	6,5	Bear right to cross the main road and take the track straight ahead	GR sign, direction Montgardin	SE	767
17.012	700	7,1	At the T-junction in the tracks, turn left	Direction Montgardin, GR sign	NE	766
17.013	1100	8,3	At the road junction, after crossing a stream, continue straight ahead on the road	GR sign, towards the mountains	NE	783
17.014	120	8,4	Take the right fork	Direction Montgardin	NE	784
17.015	1900	10,3	With a house to your right, turn left over a small bridge	GR sign	E	810
17.016	700	11,0	At the T-junction turn right	GR sign, house to the left "Auberge du Moulin"	SE	821
17.017	130	11,2	Just after passing "Auberge du Moulin", turn right and immediately left onto a small path through the trees	GR sign	SW	829
17.018	260	11,4	At the T-junction with a tarmac road, turn left and continue up the hill	GR sign	E	861

Notre-Dame-de-Laus to Chorges 15.4 km

Waypoint	Distance Between Waypoints (m)	Total (km)	Directions	Verification Point	Compass	Altitude (m)
17.019	120	11,5	Turn right onto the path	GR sign	E	875
17.020	70	11,6	At the junction with the road continue straight ahead on the path on the other side	GR sign	SE	884
17.021	300	11,9	At T-junction with road in Montgardin, turn left	Direction Chorges	E	926
17.022	210	12,1	At the fork in the road, keep left	Town below to your left	SE	936
17.023	400	12,5	On sharp bend right, turn left onto a road	Direction Chorges	E	948
17.024	1200	13,7	At the junction turn left	GR sign, direction Chorges	N	896
17.025	400	13,0	Before reaching the railway line, turn right	Direction Chorges	E	867
17.026	500	14,4	Bear left on the road	GR sign, industrial building on right	E	861
17.027	290	14,7	Turn left over the level-crossing and then bear right beside the supermarket car park	GR sign	E	862
17.028	230	14,0	In front of the railway station cross the main road and bear right	Direction Prunières, no GR sign	E	864
17.029	250	15,2	Continue ahead through centre of town	Grande Rue	E	868
17.030	170	15,4	Arrive at Chorges centre	Crossroads between Grande Rue and rue des Ecoles		869

Notre-Dame-de-Laus to Chorges 15.4 km

B&B, Hotel, Gite d'Etapes	Price/ Opening
Champ Peyron (Martine Bertrand) 05230 Montgardin, Hautes Alpes, France Tel:+33(0)4 92 50 33 04 Mobile:+33(0)6 11 95 15 45 les.aroncis.gite@wanadoo.fr	B3
La Chambre deVia Croze (Jacky Allègre), Route des Andrieux 05230 Chorges,Hautes Alpes, France Tel:+33(0)4 92 50 63 21 Mobile:+33(0)6 16 72 57 26 jacky.allegre@wanadoo.fr	B2
L'Air du Temps (Chantal Disdier),Vière 05230 Prunières, Hautes Alpes, France Tel:+33(0)4 92 50 29 28 Mobile:+33(0)6 71 45 84 34 chantal.disdier@tiscali.fr	B2
Roborg Gilles, L'Eglise 05160 Pontis, Hautes Alpes, France Tel:+33(0)4 92 44 34 57	B2
Chalets Les Vignes (Huguette Avignon) 05230 Prunières, Hautes Alpes, France Tel:+33(0)4 92 50 20 13 chaletstmichel@wizeo.fr	B1
Les Carlines (Louis Velay) 05230 Prunières, Hautes Alpes, France Tel:+33(0)4 92 50 63 27	B3
Camping	
Le Forest du Milieu (Maurice et Lucette Bertrand) 05230 Montgardin, Hautes Alpes, France Tel:+33(0)4 92 50 31 33	B1 Open 15/04 - 30/09
Camping La Clé des Champs, Aux portes du Parc des Ecrins 05230 Chorges, Hautes Alpes, France Tel:+33(0)4 92 50 69 62	B1
Camping Le Rio Claret, Les Chabès 05230 Chorges, Hautes Alpes, France Tel:+33(0)4 92 50 66 77 www.camping-lerioclaret.com/	B1
Les Blanchons (Yves Blanc), Les Gourres 05230 Prunières, Hautes Alpes, France Tel:+33(0)4 92 50 39 02 Mobile:+33(0)6 12 44 41 48 campinglesblanchons@yahoo.fr **Note:** Pilgrim price reduction	B1

Notre-Dame-de-Laus to Chorges 15.4 km

Tourist Office
Office du Tourisme, Grande Rue 05230 Chorges, Hautes Alpes, France
Tel:+33(0)4 92 50 64 25 www.otchorges.com/

Doctor
Arcangéli Richard, Chemin Moulin 05230 Chorges, Hautes Alpes, France
Tel:+33(0)4 92 50 66 66

Veterinary
Cabinet vétérinaire des Ecrins, RN 94 05230 Chorges, Hautes Alpes, France Tel:+33(0)4 92 20 26 40   www.cliniquevet-ecrins.com/

Notre-Dame-de-Laus to Chorges 15.4 km

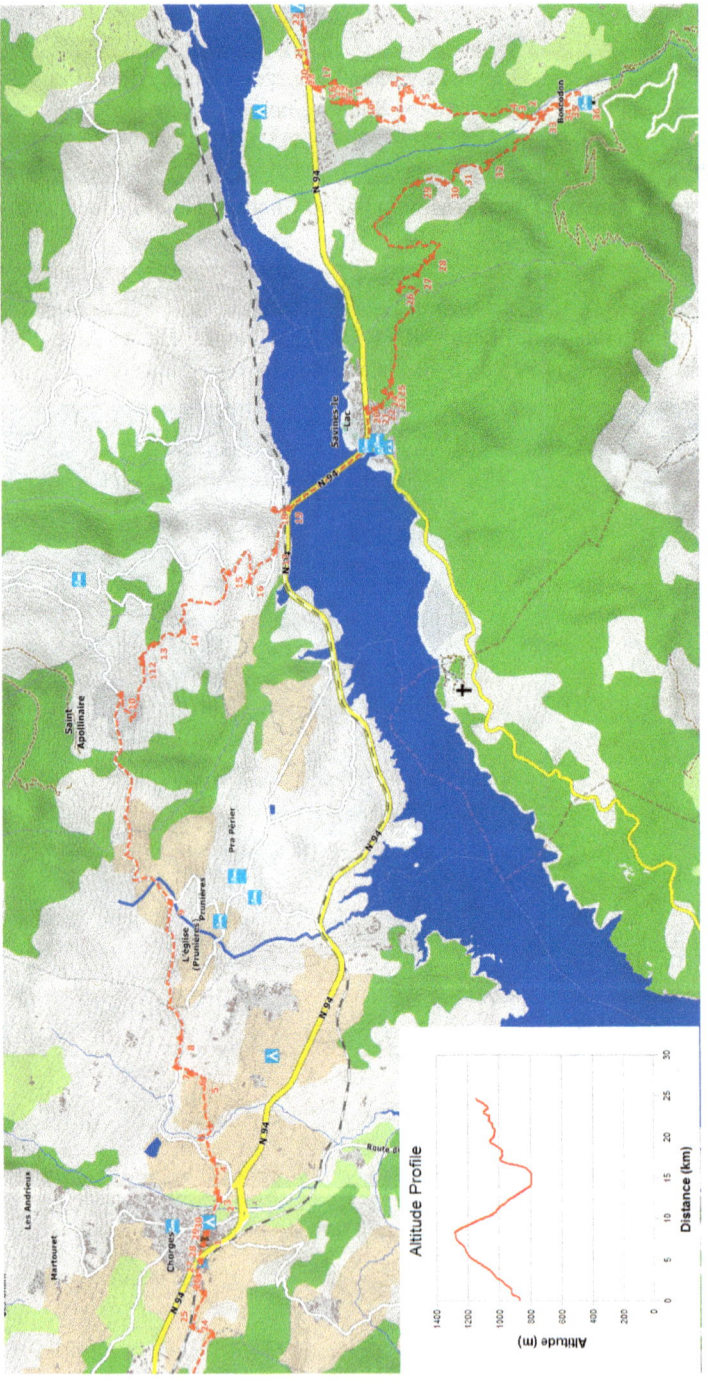

Chorges to Abbaye-de-Boscodon 24.6 km

After leaving Chorges the route generally follows very minor roads to the crossing of lac de Serre-Ponçon. The long road bridge can be very busy, but has a pavement for pedestrians. However this is too narrow to be used by riders who will need to carefully negotiate the main carriageway. The route from Savine-le-Lac returns to forest tracks for the approach to the Abbaye.

Distance from Arles: 305km **Distance to Vercelli:** 316km
Stage Ascent: 863m **Stage Descent:** 584m

Waypoint	Distance Between Waypoints (m)	Total (km)	Directions	Verification Point	Compass	Altitude (m)
18.001	0	0,0	Continue ahead on Grande Rue	Pass the Office du Tourisme on your left	SE	864
18.002	500	0,5	On the edge of the town turn left onto a grass track	GR sign	E	878
18.003	90	0,6	At the junction with the gravel track, turn left up the hill and continue on the grass track	Pass cemetery to your right	E	888
18.004	500	0,0	At the junction with the tarmac road, cross over and continue on the tarmac	Direction Camping, GR sign	E	910
18.005	1400	2,4	Turn left onto a gravel track	GR sign	NE	980
18.006	220	2,6	Beside the farm, turn right	Pass farmhouse, "Protonotaire", on your left, GR sign	N	1000
18.007	230	2,9	At the T-junction with the main road, turn right	Sign "Protonotaire"	E	1019
18.008	400	3,2	Take the left fork	Direction Saint Apollinaire	E	1033
18.009	1900	5,1	Take the left fork, remaining on the D9	GR sign	E	1171

Chorges to Abbaye-de-Boscodon 24.6 km

Waypoint	Distance Between Waypoints (m)	Total (km)	Directions	Verification Point	Compass	Altitude (m)
18.010	3400	8,5	In Saint-Apollinaire, turn right on the D541	Direction Savines le Lac, GR sign	SE	1279
18.011	1200	9,7	On the crown of a sharp bend to the right, turn left onto a gravel track	Chemin de la Côte de la Forêt, GR sign	E	1151
18.012	80	9,8	Take the left fork and then immediately turn right	Keep "Les Blaches" to your left, GR sign	SE	1142
18.013	280	10,0	Take the left fork	GR sign	S	1109
18.014	500	10,5	At the T-junction with the road turn left		SE	1041
18.015	1500	12,1	T-junction turn right	GR sign	S	951
18.016	800	12,9	Turn left on the road towards the lake shore. **Note:-** caution, you will travelling against the flow of traffic	Avoid the D41 towards Pont de Savines, GR sign	SE	891
18.017	600	13,5	Continue straight ahead on the road	Towards the lake bridge	E	842
18.018	600	14,1	At the roundabout turn take the first exit	Direction Savines le Lac, GR sign	S	797
18.019	260	14,4	At the junction with the major road continue straight ahead to cross the bridge	GR sign	SE	795
18.020	1800	16,2	Pass through the sentre of Savines-le-Lac and turn sharp right before reaching the "Super U"	Rue du Paradisier, GR sign	S	824
18.021	190	16,3	Turn sharp right onto a dirt track	GR sign	SE	838

Chorges to Abbaye-de-Boscodon 24.6 km

Waypoint	Distance Between Waypoints (m)	Total (km)	Directions	Verification Point	Compass	Altitude (m)
18.022	120	16,5	Turn sharp left and then immediately right keeping the house to your left	GR sign	SE	855
18.023	240	16,7	Turn sharp left	Direction "les Preis", GR sign	N	918
18.024	120	16,8	Turn right	GR sign	SE	945
18.025	170	16,0	At the T-junction with the broad gravel track, turn left	GR sign	E	975
18.026	1600	18,6	Turn sharp right	Direction Boscodon, GR sign	SE	995
18.027	400	18,0	Bear left to stay on the gravel track	No GR sign	SE	1022
18.028	500	19,4	At the fork in the tracks, take the left fork	Direction Boscodon, GR sign	E	1059
18.029	2100	21,5	Take the right fork	Direction Boscodon	S	1039
18.030	400	21,9	After passing through the hamlet of le Bois take the left fork and fork left again downhill	GR sign	SE	1064
18.031	290	22,2	Take the right fork towards the houses	GR sign	S	1061
18.032	600	22,8	Keep right	Parallel to the river below on the left	SE	1086
18.033	1000	23,8	With the farm buildings to your right, take the right fork onto a grassy track	GR sign	SE	1082

Chorges to Abbaye-de-Boscodon 24.6 km

Waypoint	Distance Between Waypoints (m)	Total (km)	Directions	Verification Point	Compass	Altitude (m)
18.034	270	24,0	At the junction with the tarmac road turn right and cross the bridge then turn right again on the track	Direction Abbaye, GR sign	S	1100
18.035	220	24,3	Turn sharp right	GR sign	S	1121
18.036	300	24,6	Arrive at Abbaye-de-Boscodon	Gîte d'Etape ahead		1147

B&B, Hotel, Gite d'Etapes	Price/
Hôtel Les Chaumettes, Rue du Bannafrat 05160 Savines le Lac, Hautes Alpes, France Tel:+33(0)4 92 44 29 00 www.hotel-leschaumettes.eu/	B2
Résidence Morgon (Alain Bellet), Rue du Morgon 05160 Savines le Lac, Hautes Alpes, France Tel:+33(0)4 92 44 33 22 Mobile:+33(0)6 87 87 44 15 info@hautes-alpes.org **Note:** Pilgrim price reduction	B2
Les Flots Bleus, Rue Sauze 05160 Savines le Lac, Hautes Alpes, France Tel:+33(0)4 92 44 20 89 www.les-flots-bleus.fr/	B3
Le Relais Fleuri, Rue Sauze 05160 Savines le Lac, Hautes Alpes, France Tel:+33(0)4 92 44 23 92 www.savinesrelaisfleuri.ifrance.com/	B2
L'Escharena (Jean-Pierre Guigue), Chérines 05160 Savines le Lac, Hautes Alpes, France Tel:+33(0)4 92 44 33 70 gite.escharena@wanadoo.fr	B1
PR Cellier des Moines (Pascal et Nicolas Albran), Boscodon 05200 Crots, Hautes Alpes, France Tel:+33(0)4 92 43 00 50 gite-boscodon@tiscali.frname	B2
Club Nautique Alpin, Chemin de Chadenas 05200 Embrun, Hautes Alpes, France Tel:+33(0)4 92 43 00 02 cnasp@wanadoo.fr	B1

Chorges to Abbaye-de-Boscodon 24.6 km

B&B, Hotel, Gite d'Etapes	Price/
Hotel les Peupliers, Chemin de Lesdier 05200 Baratier, Hautes Alpes, France Tel:+33(0)4 92 43 03 47 www.hotel-les-peupliers.com/	B2

Youth Hostel	
Auberge de Jeunesse, Rue du Bannafrat 05160 Savines le Lac, Hautes Alpes, France Tel:+33(0)4 92 44 20 16 oti.savineslelac@orange.fr www.hotel-leschaumettes.eu/	B1 Open 15/06 - 1/09

Camping	
Hotel et camping les Sources, Rue du Barnafret 05160 Savines le Lac, Hautes Alpes, France Tel:+33(0)4 92 44 20 52 www.hotel-les-sources.com/	B1
Camping Camp Municipal La Garenne 05200 Crots, Hautes Alpes, France Tel:+33(0)4 92 43 11 93 **Note:** on RN 94 between Savines and Embrun	B1
Camping La Pinede 05200 Crots, Hautes Alpes, France Tel:+33(0)4 92 43 13 55 **Note:** On the RN 94	B1
Monino Manu 05200 Crots, Hautes Alpes, France Tel:+33(0)4 92 43 13 14	B1
Camping Le Verger, Le Verger 05200 Baratier, Hautes Alpes, France Tel:+33(0)4 92 43 15 87 www.campingleverger.fr/	B1
Camping Les Airelles, Route Orres 05200 Baratier, Hautes Alpes, France Tel:+33(0)4 92 43 11 57 www.lesairelles.com/	B1
Camping Les Deux Bois 05200 Baratier, Hautes Alpes, France Tel:+33(0)4 92 43 54 14 www.camping-les2bois.com/	B1

Chorges to Abbaye-de-Boscodon 24.6 km

Tourist Office
Office Tourisme Serre Poncon, Avenue Combe D'Or 05160 Savines le Lac, Hautes Alpes, France   Tel:+33(0)4 92 44 31 00

Doctor
Sepulchre Philippe Jean-Marie, Rue Oratoire 05160 Savines le Lac, Hautes Alpes, France Tel:+33(0)4 92 44 20 55,

Veterinary

Clinique Vétérinaire,Avenue Acacias 05200 Embrun, Hautes Alpes, France Tel:+33(0)4 92 43 10 38

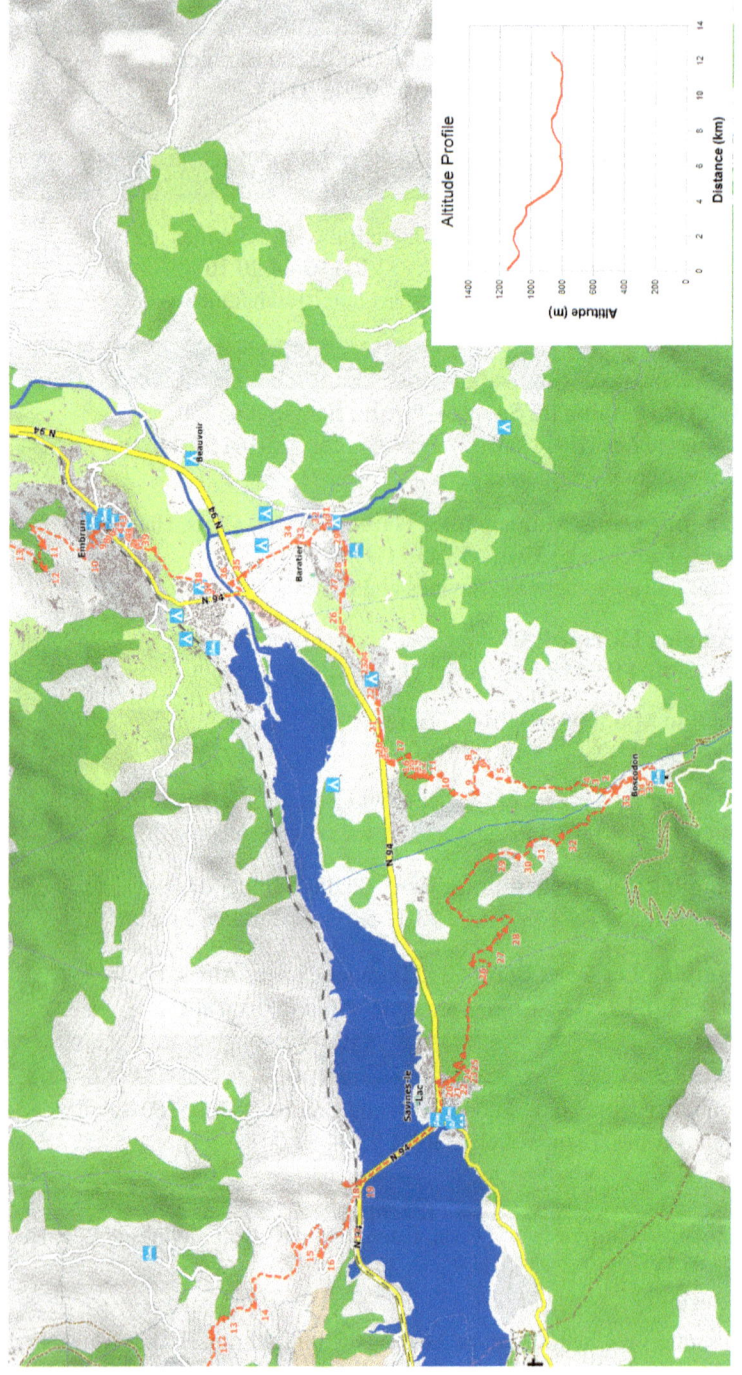

From the Abbaye to Crots the route again follows broad tracks and minor roads except for a very short section of the route nationale. The remainder of the section is undertaken on a flat canal-side path and minor roads before the entry to Embrun.

Distance from Arles: 330km   **Distance to Vercelli: 292km**
Stage Ascent: 188m   **Stage Descent: 468m**

Waypoint	Distance Between Waypoints (m)	Total (km)	Directions	Verification Point	Compass	Altitude (m)
19.001	0	0,0	Pass between the Abbaye and the Gîte d'Etape and follow the road	Keep the Abbaye to your left and the river to your right	N	1147
19.002	800	0,8	Continue straight ahead on the road	GR sign	N	1082
19.003	180	0,0	After crossing the bridge over the Torrent de Boscodon, turn right onto a path into the forest. **Note:-** riders and cyclists can take the broader track to the right to soften the climb	GR sign	N	1074
19.004	160	1,1	At the T-junction with the broad track, turn left	GR sign	N	1079
19.005	1300	2,4	At the junction with the tarmac road, cross straight over and take the lower of 2 dirt tracks	GR sign	N	1097
19.006	260	2,7	On rejoining the tarmac road turn right and then immediately left on the track	GR sign	NE	1070

Abbaye-de-Boscodon to Embrun 12.5 km

Waypoint	Distance Between Waypoints (m)	Total (km)	Directions	Verification Point	Compass	Altitude (m)
19.007	210	2,9	On entering the village of Beauvillard, go straight ahead on the road, then turn left	Direction la Cagnolle, GR sign	NW	1051
19.008	130	3,0	After passing through the village, bear left	GR sign	W	1044
19.009	300	3,3	In front of "Code Baille" turn right	GR sign	N	1027
19.010	300	3,7	Continue straight ahead onto a dirt track	Trees to your right, GR sign	NE	1029
19.011	400	4,0	At the intersection with a tarmac road, cross straight over and follow the track on the opposite side	GR sign	N	969
19.012	130	4,2	At the junction with the minor road, continue straight ahead on the track on the other side	GR sign	N	945
19.013	70	4,2	At the junction with the minor road, again continue straight ahead on the track on the other side	GR sign	N	933
19.014	60	4,3	Join a wider track, turn right and then left down the hill	GR sign	N	922
19.015	100	4,4	Take the right fork	Towards the town of Crots, no GR sign	N	905
19.016	110	4,5	Turn right down the hill	Do not cross the stream, GR sign	E	887

Abbaye-de-Boscodon to Embrun 12.5 km

Waypoint	Distance Between Waypoints (m)	Total (km)	Directions	Verification Point	Compass	Altitude (m)
19.017	400	4,0	At the T-junction in the tracks, turn left	GR sign	NW	841
19.018	210	5,2	At the T-junction with a gravel track, turn right	Direction Crots	N	826
19.019	50	5,2	At the crossroads, continue straight ahead on the grass track	Main road parallel on your left, GR sign	NE	823
19.020	70	5,3	Bear left on the track	Beside the main road on your left	E	819
19.021	300	5,6	Bear right onto the disused road	No GR sign	E	804
19.022	400	6,0	At the T-junction bear right	Towards town centre, GR sign	E	797
19.023	300	6,3	Turn right on chemin de Bellegrave	GR sign	E	804
19.024	160	6,5	Turn left onto a gravel track	Canal on your right, GR sign	NE	811
19.025	500	6,0	Take the right fork to remain close to the canal	GR sign	NE	807
19.026	210	7,2	Turn right over the bridge	Direction Baratier	E	808
19.027	400	7,6	At the junction with the minor road, continue straight ahead	Direction Baratier, GR sign	E	841
19.028	210	7,8	At the crossroads continue straight ahead	Chemin de Jouglare, GR sign	E	853

Abbaye-de-Boscodon to Embrun 12.5 km

Waypoint	Distance Between Waypoints (m)	Total (km)	Directions	Verification Point	Compass	Altitude (m)
19.029	400	8,2	At the crossroads, continue straight ahead	La Chènevière, GR sign	NE	864
19.030	250	8,4	At the junction continue straight ahead into the centre of Baratier	GR sign	E	865
19.031	130	8,6	At the crossroads, turn left	Rue Guillaume Apollinaire, GR sign	NW	865
19.032	190	8,8	After passing the church on your right, turn left and then immediately right on the gravel track	Le Pave	NW	860
19.033	300	9,1	At the junction with the road, turn right on the tarmac	Towards the main road, GR sign	N	836
19.034	180	9,2	At the roundabout, D40, continue straight ahead	Ancienne route de Baratier, GR sign	NW	831
19.035	800	10,0	At the T-junction continue straight ahead to take the underpass	Supermarket ahead, GR sign	NW	805
19.036	210	10,3	At the roundabout turn left and then turn right to cross over the river bridge	Keep the petrol station on your right	NW	802
19.037	500	10,8	Beside the restaurant "Le Truite qui Parle", turn right and immediately left	Direction "Camping la Vieille Ferme"	NE	805

Abbaye-de-Boscodon to Embrun 12.5 km

Waypoint	Distance Between Waypoints (m)	Total (km)	Directions	Verification Point	Compass	Altitude (m)
19.038	180	10,0	Take the left fork	Pass the camp site on your right	NE	802
19.039	900	11,9	At the junction turn left on the gravel track	Keep the rock outcrop to your right	N	811
19.040	300	12,2	At the top of the hill turn right and climb the flight of steps. **Note:-** riders can avoid the steps by crossing the car park and taking the first right towards the cathedral	GR sign	E	846
19.041	70	12,2	At the top of the steps, with the hospital on your right, turn left	GR sign	NE	854
19.042	120	12,4	At the T-junction turn right	Direction Hôtel de le Marie	E	863
19.043	100	12,5	Arrive at Embrun centre	Directly in front of the steps leading to the cathedral		868

Abbaye-de-Boscodon to Embrun 12.5 km

B&B, Hotel, Gite d'Etapes	Price/Opening
Les Echelettes (Fabrice Sergent), Rue Quatre Traverses 05200 Embrun, Hautes Alpes, France Tel:+33(0)4 92 43 41 84 Mobile:+33(0)6 23 76 16 09 lesechelettes.embrun@free.fr	B1
Hôtel du Commerce, Rue Saint-Pierre 05200 Embrun, Hautes Alpes, France Tel:+33(0)4 92 43 54 54 www.hotel-lecommerce-embrun.com/	B2
Le Rex,1 Rue Clovis Hugues 05200 Embrun, Hautes Alpes, France Tel:+33(0)4 92 43 00 06	B2
Hôtel Le Tourisme, Avenue Alexandre Didier 05200 Embrun, Hautes Alpes, France Tel:+33(0)4 92 43 20 17 www.hotel-le-tourisme.com/	B2
Hôtel Notre Dame, Avenue du Général Nicolas 05200 Embrun, Hautes Alpes, France Tel:+33(0)4 92 43 08 36 www.hotel-notredame-embrun.fr/	B2
Le Chalvet (Dominique et Michel Bonnafoux), Chalvet 05200 Embrun, Hautes Alpes, France Tel:+33(0)4 92 43 03 63 Mobile:+33(0)6 30 31 03 69 hotel_chalvet@orange.fr **Note:** Pilgrim price reduction	B2
Les Pinées (Domy et Philou Testou) 05380 Châteauroux les Alpes, Hautes Alpes, France Tel:+33(0)4 92 43 30 46 Mobile:+33(0)6 61 26 59 68 gite.lespinees@wanadoo.fr	B1
Le Relais des Ecrins, 11 Rue Des Aubergeries 05380 Châteauroux les Alpes, Hautes Alpes, France Tel:+33(0)4 92 43 27 93	B2

Camping	
Camping Les Tourelles,Sainte Marthe 05200 Embrun, Hautes Alpes, France Tel:+33(0)4 92 24 02 35 www.camping-alpes-les-tourelles.com/	B1
Camping La Vieille Ferme, La Clapiere 05200 Embrun, Hautes Alpes, France Tel:+33(0)4 92 43 04 08 www.campingembrun.com/	B1
Camping Le Petit Liou, Anciene route de Baratier 05200 Embrun, Hautes Alpes, France Tel:+33(0)4 92 43 19 10 www.camping-lepetitliou.com	B1

Abbaye-de-Boscodon to Embrun 12.5 km

Camping

Camping les Grillons, La Madeleine 05200 Embrun, Hautes Alpes France   Tel:+33(0)4 92 43 32 75   www.lesgrillons.com/ — B1

Camping La Madeleine, La Madeleine 05200 Embrun, Hautes Alpes, France   Tel:+33(0)4 92 43 01 16 — B1

Camping Les Esparons, La Madeleine 05200 Embrun, Hautes Alpes, France   Tel:+33(0)4 92 43 02 73 www.lesesparons.com/ — B1

Camping de la Tour, La Madeleine 05200 Embrun, Hautes Alpes, France   Tel:+33(0)4 92 43 17 66 — B1

Camping Les Pins 05380 Châteauroux les alpes, Hautes Alpes, France   Tel:+33(0)4 92 43 22 64 — B1

Camping Fontmolines 05380 Châteauroux les Alpes, Hautes Alpes, France Tel:+33(0)4 92 43 22 63
www.les.cariamas.free.fr/ — B1

Camping Les Eygas, Fontmolines 05380 Châteauroux les Alpes, Hautes Alpes, France   Tel:+33(0)4 92 43 63 80
www.alpescamping.fr/ — B1

Tourist Office

Office de Tourisme d'Embrun, Place Général Dosse 05200 Embrun, Hautes Alpes, France Tel:+33(0)4 92 43 72 72   www.tourisme-embrun.com/

Office de Tourisme, Les Aubergeries 05380 Châteauroux les Alpes, Hautes Alpes, France   Tel:+33(0)9 62 35 40 34

Doctor

Louchet Jean-Claude, Rue Capucines,05200 Embrun, Hautes Alpes, France   Tel:+33(0)9 79 54 58 17

Talweg, Les Aubergeries 05380 Châteauroux les Alpes, Hautes Alpes, France Tel:+33(0)6 87 12 36 00   www.talweg.net/

Farrier

Rochas Gilles, Jaumare 05200 Saint André d'Embrun, Hautes Alpes, France   Tel:+33(0)4 92 43 86 60

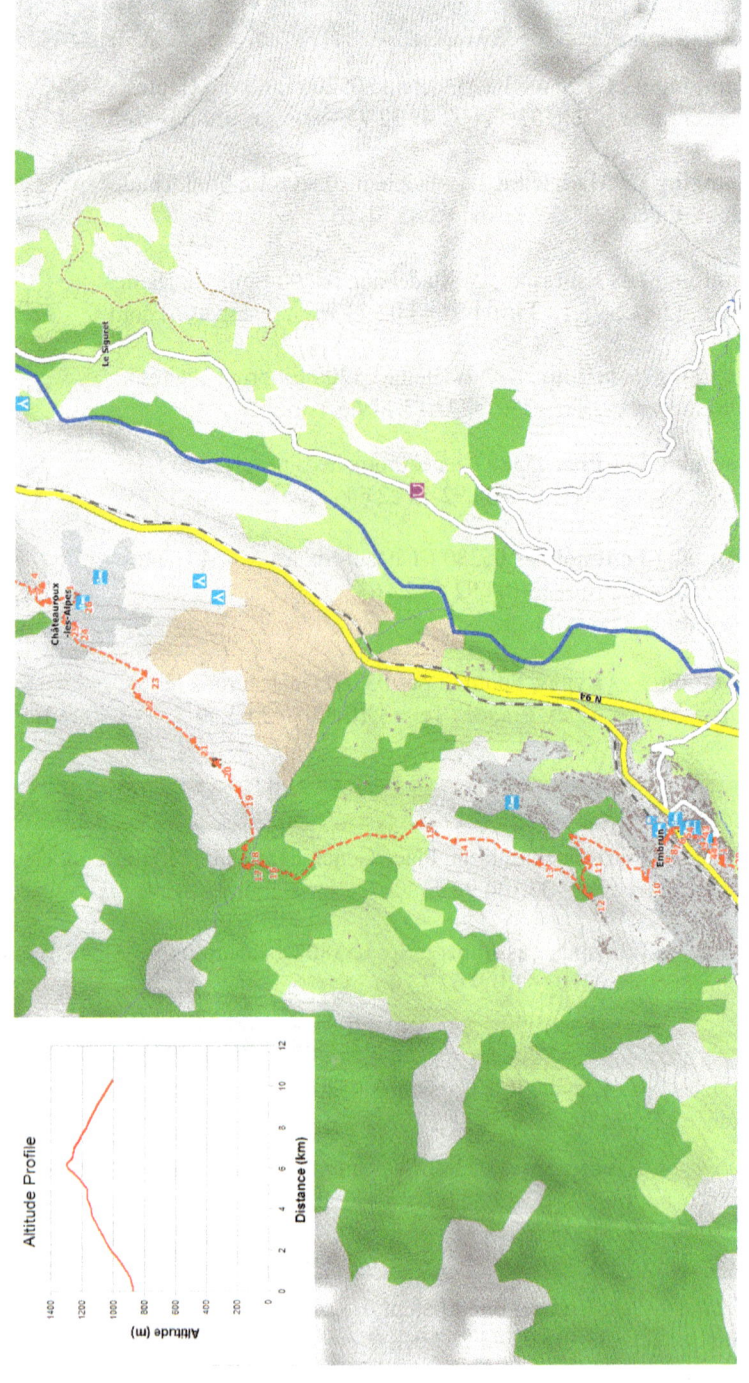

This very short section generally follows quiet tarmac roads.
Distance from Arles: 342km   **Distance to Vercelli: 279km**
Stage Ascent: 433m   **Stage Descent: 295m**

Waypoint	Distance Between Waypoints (m)	Total (km)	Directions	Verification Point	Compass	Altitude (m)
20.001	0	0,0	In front of the steps leading to the church, turn left on the narrow road	Rue Savine	NW	868
20.002	110	0,1	Turn right on the cobbled street on rue de la Liberté	Plaque to Jean-Antoine Savine	NE	870
20.003	160	0,3	After passing through Place Mazelière continue straight ahead	Rue Clovis Hughes	NE	873
20.004	200	0,5	At the broad intersection, turn left on rue Alexandre Didier	Keep Hotel Rex to your left	W	880
20.005	70	0,5	Turn right up the hill	Bibliothèque Municipale on the right	NW	882
20.006	70	0,6	At the junction continue straight ahead		NW	885
20.007	80	0,7	At the crossroads continue straight ahead and then bear left on Allée des Rosiers		NW	890

Embrun - Châteauroux to les-Alpes 10.3 km

Waypoint	Distance Between Waypoints (m)	Total (km)	Directions	Verification Point	Compass	Altitude (m)
20.008	50	0,7	Keep left on the small road. **Note:-** there is a flight of steps at the end of the road, riders should remain on Allée des Rosiers to the next waypoint	No through road sign	NW	893
20.009	90	0,8	At the top of the flight of steps turn left on route des Caleyères	GR sign	NW	890
20.010	500	1,3	Turn right onto the track	Ancienne chemin des Caleyères	N	940
20.011	1200	2,5	Take the right fork	GR sign	W	1052
20.012	600	3,1	At the T-junction with the road, turn right up the hill	GR sign	NE	1096
20.013	600	3,7	At the junction continue straight ahead	House to the right with distinctive arches	N	1135
20.014	800	4,5	Take the right fork and enter the commune of les Barthelons	GR sign	NE	1167
20.015	400	4,9	On the apex of a bend to the right and a house immediately on your right, turn left onto a dirt track	GR sign	N	1165

Embrun - Châteauroux to les-Alpes 10.3 km

Waypoint	Distance Between Waypoints (m)	Total (km)	Directions	Verification Point	Compass	Altitude (m)
20.016	1800	6,6	At T-junction in the tracks turn left	GR sign	N	1258
20.017	140	6,8	Bear right and cross the river		E	1256
20.018	210	6,0	Bear right down the hill	Direction Châteauroux	E	1252
20.019	600	7,6	Take the left fork	House just ahead	NE	1209
20.020	300	7,9	At the T-junction turn left	Direction Châteauroux, GR sign	NE	1183
20.021	300	8,2	Continue straight ahead on the road	GR sign points left to a track into woods	NE	1163
20.022	700	8,8	At the junction with the larger road, bear right		E	1122
20.023	270	9,1	After passing a restored chapel, turn left	Rue de Saint-Roch	NE	1103
20.024	900	9,0	Bear left on the road	Cemetery to the right	N	1035
20.025	90	10,0	Keep right on the road		SE	1028
20.026	280	10,3	Arrive at Châteauroux-les-Alpes	Crossroads, Marie 50m to the right		1006

Embrun - Châteauroux to les-Alpes 10.3 km

B&B, Hotel, Gite d'Etapes	Price/ Opening
Les Peschiers (Paul Piol), Avenue de la Gare 05380 Châteauroux les Alpes, Hautes Alpes, France Tel:+33(0)4 92 43 10 67 Mobile:+33(0)6 08 04 60 39 lespeschiers@free.fr	B2
L'Aster des Alpes (Véronique Durin), Serre Buzard 05380 Châteauroux les Alpes, Hautes Alpes, France Tel:+33(0)4 92 43 82 24 Mobile:+33(0)6 78 72 38 20 veronique.durin@orange.fr	B2
Le Gite de Saint-Alban, Saint-Alban 05380 Châteauroux les Alpes, Hautes Alpes, France Tel:+33(0)4 92 45 10 40 www.pagesperso-orange.fr/saint-alban/	B1
Camping	
Camping municipal St-James, Le Rabioux 05380 Châteauroux les Alpes, Hautes Alpes, France Tel:+33(0)4 92 43 43 78 www.sudrafting.fr/camping_rabioux.html	B1
Le Balcon de la Durance (Jean-Marie Barral), Les Chamousses 05380 Châteauroux les Alpes, Hautes Alpes, France Tel:+33(0)4 92 43 06 13	B1

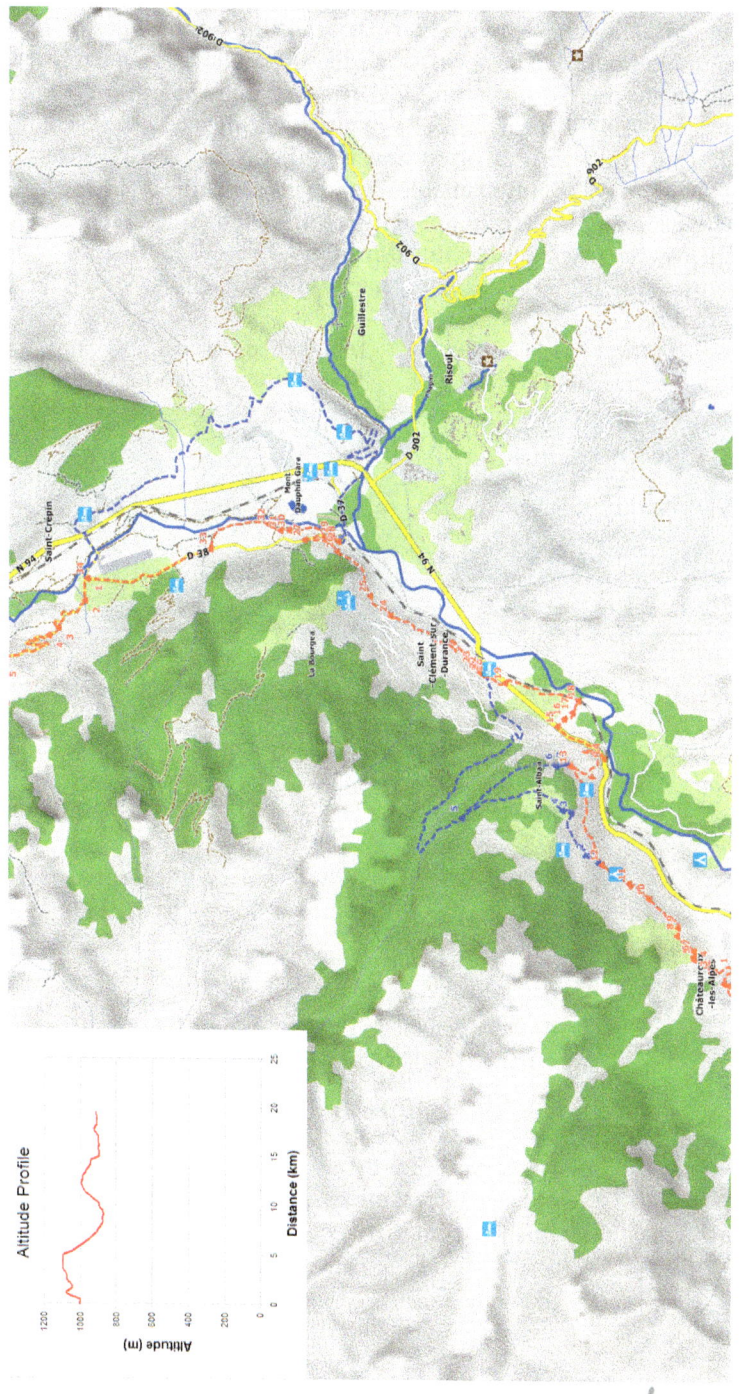

After initially following quiet tarmac roads the route climbs on broad mountain tracks. The approach to Saint-Alban follows a narrow track along a steep faced mountain-side – riders should consider the longer alternate route. At the time of writing the bridge over the torrent de Couleau had been destroyed and it was unsafe to cross the river. Unfortunately the only available diversion is along the main-road. The route from Saint-Clément to Saint-Crépin follows quiet tarmac roads and a cycle track beside the Durance. The GR653D crosses and recrosses the Durance passing through Mont-Dauphin. We prefer the more direct route.

Distance from Arles: 352km **Distance to Vercelli: 269km**
Stage Ascent: 304m **Stage Descent: 396m**

Waypoint	Distance Between Waypoints (m)	Total (km)	Directions	Verification Point	Compass	Altitude (m)
21.001	0	0,0	At the crossroads in Châteauroux-les-Alpes, turn left	Pass hotel on the right	N	1001
21.002	400	0,3	After crossing the bridge, turn left onto a gravel track		N	997
21.003	70	0,4	Pass through metal gates and then bear right	Behind the buildings on your right	E	998
21.004	200	0,6	At the junction with a minor road, turn left	GR sign	N	1010
21.005	400	1,0	At the top of the hill, continue straight ahead	Leaving, route de Viere, GR sign	E	1077
21.006	40	1,1	Take the right fork	Châteauroux below to the right	E	1078 7
21.007	80	1,1	At the end of rue Saint-Mercellin, continue straight ahead	Cemetery to your left	NE	1078
21.008	400	1,5	At the entry to the hamlet of Fontfourane continue straight ahead on the road	Ignore GR sign leading to a track on the left	E	1052

Châteauroux-les-Alpes to Saint-Crépin 19.4 km

Waypoint	Distance Between Waypoints (m)	Total (km)	Directions	Verification Point	Compass	Altitude (m)
21.009	130	1,6	At the T-junction turn left	Direction "Camping des Balcons de la Durance"	NE	1045
21.010	700	2,3	Take the right fork downhill	Wooden cross at the intersection	NE	1070
21.011	500	2,8	Continue straight ahead	Ignore the GR50 sign to the right	NE	1074
21.012	500	3,4	Turn right on the narrow track. **Note:-** riders can avoid the steep-sided and narrow track by continuing straight ahead on the Alternate route	Torrent de Couleau 4.7km	E	1091
21.013	1700	5,1	Turn sharp right and continue on the road down the hill. **Note:-** The GR653D leaves the road to the left on the apex of the bend. At the time of writing this route is impassable because of the washed-out bridge. In the event of the bridge being repaired the GR653D will rejoin our route in Saint Clément		S	1082
21.014	1600	6,7	At the T-junction with the major road, turn left		NE	943

Châteauroux-les-Alpes to Saint-Crépin 19,4 km

Waypoint	Distance Between Waypoints (m)	Total (km)	Directions	Verification Point	Compass	Altitude (m)
21.015	1000	7,6	Immediately after passing the parking area on your left, turn right on the stony track leading at right angles to the road	Remain parallel to the torrent	SE	899
21.016	170	7,8	Take the right fork remaining on the main track		SE	892
21.017	190	7,0	Take the left fork	Towards the railway line	SE	884
21.018	220	8,2	At the T-junction, turn left	Keep railway track to your right	N	876
21.019	1300	9,5	At the intersection with the main road, turn right and then left to take the minor road on the other side	Towards the church in Saint Clément	N	873
21.020	400	9,9	Bear left	Uphill towards the village centre	N	895
21.021	70	9,9	With a fountain to your right, turn right. **Note:-** the GR653D rejoins from the left	Towards the church	NE	896
21.022	60	9,0	After passing the church, continue straight ahead on the road along the hill-side	Lavoir on the left	NE	895
21.023	120	10,1	At the T-junction, turn left	Direction Reotier	NE	893

Châteauroux-les-Alpes to Saint-Crépin 19,4 km

Stage Ascent: 171m   Stage Descent: 218m

Waypoint	Distance Between Waypoints (m)	Total (km)	Directions	Verification Point	Compass	Altitude (m)
21A1.001	0	0,0	Continue straight ahead on the broader track	Torrent de Couleau par La Béguë	NE	1112
21A1.002	220	0,2	At the T-junction with the minor road, turn right	River to your right	E	1131
21A1.003	900	1,2	Take the left fork	Uphill	N	1263
21A1.004	180	1,3	At the T-junction in the track, turn right	Direction Torrent de Couleau	N	1277
21A1.005	1900	3,2	Turn sharp right. **Note:-** continuing straight ahead to Torrent de Couleau on the GR653D leads to the washed-out bridge	Direction Les Blaches, Cockleshell sign	SE	1249
21A1.006	2000	5,2	Take the left fork to continue down the hill		S	1111
21A1.007	180	5,4	Rejoin the main route at the junction with a minor road and continue straight ahead down the hill	Saint Aubin to the right at the junction		1070

Alternative Route 5.4 km

Châteauroux-les-Alpes to Saint-Crépin 19,4 km

Waypoint	Distance Between Waypoints (m)	Total (km)	Directions	Verification Point	Compass	Altitude (m)
21.023	120	10,1	At T-junction, turn left	Direction Reotier	NE	893
21.024	2100	12,2	Take the right fork downhill	Direction Saint Crépin	NE	994
21.025	500	12,7	Take the left fork	Water trough on the left	NE	987
21.026	1000	13,7	Take the right fork, downhill	Direction le Cros	N	963
21.027	600	14,2	Turn sharp right on the road	D37, towards the railway bridge	S	942
21.028	600	14,8	Turn left off the road and follow VTT route N° 3. **Note:-** the GR653D continues ahead into Mont Dauphin, Eygliers and St Crépin and rejoins our shorter, less strenuous route via the airfield in Saint Crépin	Turn beside the restaurant "Peche a la Truite"	NE	919
21.029	190	15,0	Bear left	VTT route N° 3	N	898
21.030	700	15,7	Take the right fork	Between the camp site and the river	N	898
21.031	150	15,9	Bear right	Parallel to river	NE	898
21.032	240	16,1	Bear right and then left, remaining on the broad track	Pass Camp site toilet block on the right	N	896
21.033	1200	17,3	At the T-junction with the D38, turn right	Towards the town of Saint Crépin	N	911
21.034	2200	19,4	Arrive at Saint-Crépin, village centre to right	T-junction beside the airfield		914

B&B, Hotel, Gite d'Etapes	Price/ Opening
Chambres et table d'hôtes Maison Estienne, 5 route des Ecrins 05120 Les Vigneaux, Hautes Alpes, France Tel:+33(0)4 92 20 26 71 www.maisonestienne.com/	B2
Gîte d'Etape Le Montbrison, Le Village 05120 LesVigneaux ,Hautes Alpes, France Tel:+33(0)4 92 23 10 99	B1
Gîte les Carlines, Le village 05120 Les Vigneaux, Hautes Alpes, France Tel:+33(0)4 92 23 02 74 www.gitelescarlines.com/	B1
Le Moulin Papillon (Bénédicte Voruz), Rue du Fournel 05120 L'Argentière la Bessée, Hautes Alpes, France Tel:+33(0)4 92 21 85 14 Mobile:+33(0)6 83 25 27 95 moulin-papillon@orange.fr	B1
Hotel de la Mairie, 32 Avenue Charles de Gaulle 05120 L'Argentière la Bessée, Hautes Alpes, France Tel:+33(0)4 92 23 12 70 www.hotel-argentiere.fr/	B1
Apoutiak (Madame Astier), Rue du Lys des Alpes 05120 L'Argentière la Bessée, Hautes Alpes, France Tel:+33(0)4 92 23 16 93 Mobile:+33(0)6 13 29 36 62 romainepautier@hotmail.fr	B3
La Gare, Avenue la Gare 05120 L'Argentière la Bessée, Hautes Alpes, France Tel:+33(0)4 92 23 10 02	B2
Glaizette, 32 Rue de la République 05120 L'Argentière la Bessée, Hautes Alpes, France Tel:+33(0)4 92 23 10 05	B2
Hôtel de la Gyronde, 18 Avenue Vallouise 05120 L'Argentière la Bessée, Hautes Alpes, France Tel:+33(0)4 92 23 11 31	B2
Lucas Sébastien, Seyes 05310 Champcella, Hautes Alpes, France Tel:+33(0)4 92 20 97 56	B2
Le Relais des Vaudois, Les Ribes 05310 Freissinières, Hautes Alpes, France Tel:+33(0)4 92 20 93 01 www.relais-vaudois.com/	B2
Les 5 Saisons (Julie et Laurent), Les Meyries 05310 Freissinières, Hautes Alpes, France Tel:+33(0)4 92 20 94 40	B2
Au Cœur d'Ici, Maison Neuve 05310 Freissinières, Hautes Alpes, France Tel:+33(0)4 92 20 94 50 info@aucoeurdici.fr	B1

Châteauroux-les-Alpes to Saint-Crépin 19.4 km

B&B, Hotel, Gite d'Etapes	Price/Opening
Le Relais des Vaudois, Les Ribes 05310 Freissinières, Hautes Alpes, France Tel:+33(0)4 92 20 93 01 www.relais-vaudois.com/	B2
Gîte de la Cure 05310 Freissinières, Hautes Alpes, France Tel:+33(0)4 92 20 94 40 saisons5@clubinternet.fr	B1
Le Rucher du Martagon, Les Faures 05310 Champcella, Hautes Alpes, France Tel:+33(0)4 92 20 97 56 le.rucher.martagon@free.fr	B2
Le Chalet des les Faures (Christine & Jean-Pierre Zoellin), Les Faures 05310 Champcella, Hautes Alpes, France Tel:+33(0)4 92 20 92 74 Mobile:+33(0)6 64 91 31 76 zoellinjeanpierre@wanadoo.fr	B2
La Bergerie (Karin Kloosterman Jos Kleverwal) 05310 Champcella, Hautes Alpes, France Tel:+33(0)4 92 20 96 69 info@gite-labergerie.com	B1
Les Tables de Gaspard (Virginie et Sébastien) 05600 Saint Crépin, Hautes Alpes, France Tel:+33(0)4 92 24 85 28 lestablesdegaspard@gmail.com	B2
Le Balcon (Michèle & Francis Breuza), Les Eymards 05600 Saint Crépin, Hautes Alpes, France Tel:+33(0)4 92 45 01 36 Mobile:+33(0)6 25 33 71 52	B2
Le Pigeonnier 05600 Eygliers, Hautes Alpes, France Tel:+33(0)4 92 45 33 64 funkytoupi@yahoo.fr	B2
Auberge de l'Echauguette,Catinat 05600 Mont Dauphin, Hautes Alpes, France Tel:+33(0)4 92 45 07 13 www.echauguette.com/	B2
Gîte Auberge Glacier Bleu, Rue Catinat 05600 Mont Dauphin, Hautes Alpes, France Tel:+33(0)4 92 45 18 47 www.leglacierbleu.fr/	B1
La Taverne Du Roy, Route De Reotier 05600 Eygliers, Hautes Alpes, France Tel:+33(0)4 92 45 03 15	B2
Hotel Restaurant Lacour, Mont-dauphin gare RN 94 05600 Eygliers, Hautes Alpes, France Tel:+33(0)4 92 45 03 08 www.hotel-lacour.com/	B2
Gîte Auberge de Pinfol (Mireille et Christophe) 05600 Réotier, Hautes Alpes, France Tel:+33(0)4 92 45 01 58	B1

Châteauroux-les-Alpes to Saint-Crépin 19.4 km

B&B, Hotel, Gite d'Etapes	Price/ Opening
J.P.Certain Hôtel, 32 Avenue Charles de Gaulle 05120 L'Argentière la Bessée, Hautes Alpes, France Tel:+33(0)4 92 23 12 58	B2
La Grange de mon Père (Janine & Alain Gérard), Les Traverses 05600 Saint Clément sur Durance, Hautes Alpes, France Tel:+33(0)4 92 45 37 80 Mobile:+33(0)6 27 89 26 46 lagrangedemonpere@free.fr	B2
Religious Hostel	
Maison Paroissiale, Les Ribes 05310 Freissinières, Hautes Alpes, France Tel:+33(0)4 92 20 93 74 maisons-paroissiales@wanadou.fr	Donation
Maison Paroissiale, Pallon 05310 Champcella, Hautes Alpes, France Tel:+33(0)4 92 20 93 74 maisons-paroissiales@wanadoo.fr	Donation
Camping	
La Pierre d'Oran, Plan Léothaud 05120 L'Argentière la Bessée, Hautes Alpes, France Tel:+33(0)9 64 01 67 64	B1
Camping des Ecrins, Avenue de la Pierre Sainte 05120 L'Argentière la Bessée, Hautes Alpes, France Tel:+33(0)4 92 23 03 38 Mobile:+33(0)6 20 97 09 73 contact@camping-les-ecrins.com	B1
Camping des Allouviers, Les Allouviers 05310 Freissinières, Hautes Alpes, France Tel:+33(0)4 92 20 93 24 www.camping-freissinieres.fr/	B1
Camping la Cabane, La Cabane 05600 Saint Crépin, Hautes Alpes, France Tel:+33(0)4 92 45 07 33 www.campinglacabane.com/	B1
Camping Municipal Les Iscles, Les Iscles 05600 Eygliers, Hautes Alpes, France Tel:+33(0)4 92 45 14 18 www.iscles.com/	B1
Camping la Fontaine 05600 Réotier, Hautes Alpes, France Tel:+33(0)4 92 45 16 84 www.camping-reotier.com/	B1
Camping Les Mille Vents, Route de St André 05600 Saint Clément sur Durance, Hautes Alpes, France Tel:+33(0)4 92 45 10 90 www.camping-les-mille-vents.com	B1

Châteauroux-les-Alpes to Saint-Crépin 19.4 km

Tourist Office

Office de Tourisme du Pays des Ecrins, 23 Avenue de la République 05120 L'Argentière la Bessée, Hautes Alpes, France
Tel:+33(0)8 10 00 11 12   www.paysdesecrins.com/

Office de tourisme du Pays des Ecrins 05120 L'Argentière la Bessée, Hautes Alpes, France   Tel:+33(0)8 10 00 11 12
www.paysdesecrins.com/

Doctor

Lecerf Thierry, 8 Rue Plan d'ergue 05120 L'Argentière la Bessée, Hautes Alpes, France   Tel:+33(0)4 92 23 13 53

Châteauroux-les-Alpes to Saint-Crépin 19.4 km

The section begins on quiet tarmac roads, but proceeds on stony mountain tracks overlooking the Durance and returning to the road to take the river bridge in Pallon and for the approach to l'Argentière-la-Bess

Distance from Arles: 372km   Distance to Vercelli: 249km
Stage Ascent: 496m   Stage Descent: 438m

Waypoint	Distance Between Waypoints (m)	Total (km)	Directions	Verification Point	Compass	Altitude (m)
22.001	0	0,0	At the T-junction beside the airfield, take the road towards Champcella. **Note:-** GR635D rejoins from the right	D38, GR sign	W	914
22.002	400	0,4	Turn right and cross the bridge	Direction Champcella	NW	932
22.003	900	1,3	Bear right remaining on the road	Ignore GR sign	NW	998
22.004	210	1,5	Continue straight ahead on the road. **Note:-** the GR will cut the corner on a number of hairpins ahead, but we suggest remaining on the quiet road	Ignore GR sign	NW	1013
22.005	1900	3,4	Turn left on the path	GR sign	W	1160
22.006	500	3,9	At the T-junction turn right	Towards the centre of Champcella	N	1179
22.007	400	4,4	At the junction in Champcella, continue straight ahead	Towards church	N	1181
22.008	600	4,9	At the junction, continue straight ahead	Direction Fressinières, GR sign	N	1175

Saint-Crépin to l'Argentière-la-Bessée 13.1 km

Waypoint	Distance Between Waypoints (m)	Total (km)	Directions	Verification Point	Compass	Altitude (m)
22.009	280	5,2	Bear right onto a dirt track, direction Pallon	Wooden crucifix at the junction	NE	1158
22.010	240	5,4	At the junction in the tracks, continue straight ahead	Water treatment plant on the right	NW	1138
22.011	500	5,0	At the T-junction with the road, turn right	GR sign	N	1144
22.012	600	6,6	In Pallon, turn right and cross over the bridge	La Biaysse	E	1135
22.013	400	6,9	Continue straight ahead on the road	Direction Col d'Aiguille	N	1136
22.014	190	7,1	Turn left onto the track. **Note:**- the track ahead is very demanding and unsuitable for horse and bike riders who should remain on the road until l'Argentière-la-Bessée	Direction l'Argentière-la-Bessée, GR sign	NW	1143
22.015	60	7,2	With a house on your right, bear right onto the gravel track	GR sign	N	1147
22.016	500	7,7	Turn sharp right onto a narrow track	Direction col de l'Aiguille	N	1191
22.017	900	8,5	Bear right	Direction la Bessée, GR sign	N	1319
22.018	3100	11,6	At the T-junction with the road, turn left	GR sign	N	968

Saint-Crépin to l'Argentière-la-Bessée 13.1 km

Waypoint	Distance Between Waypoints (m)	Total (km)	Directions	Verification Point	Compass	Altitude (m)
22.019	400	12,0	Immediately after passing the entry sign for l'Argentière-lal-Bessée, turn left onto the small road	GR sign	N	964
22.020	130	12,2	Take the left fork and then go straight ahead between the houses		N	969
22.021	1000	13,1	Arrive at l'Argentière-la-Bessée	River Bridge		973

Saint-Crépin to l'Argentière-la-Bessée 13.1 km

B&B, Hotel, Gite d'Etapes	Price/ Opening
Les Carlines (Sandrine et Gary), Bouchier 05120 Saint Martin de Queyrières, Hautes Alpes, France Tel:+33(0)4 92 23 02 74 gite.lescarlines@wanadoo.fr	B1
Gite Refuge Le Pas du Loup Observatoire Astronomie, Serre Crozet – Bouchier 05120 Saint Martin de Queyrières, Hautes Alpes, France Tel:+33(0)4 92 23 09 25 www.lepasduloup.com/	B2

Camping	
Camping Campéole Le Courounba, Le Village 05120 Les Vigneaux, Hautes Alpes, France Tel:+33(0)4 92 23 02 29 www.camping-courounba.com/	B1

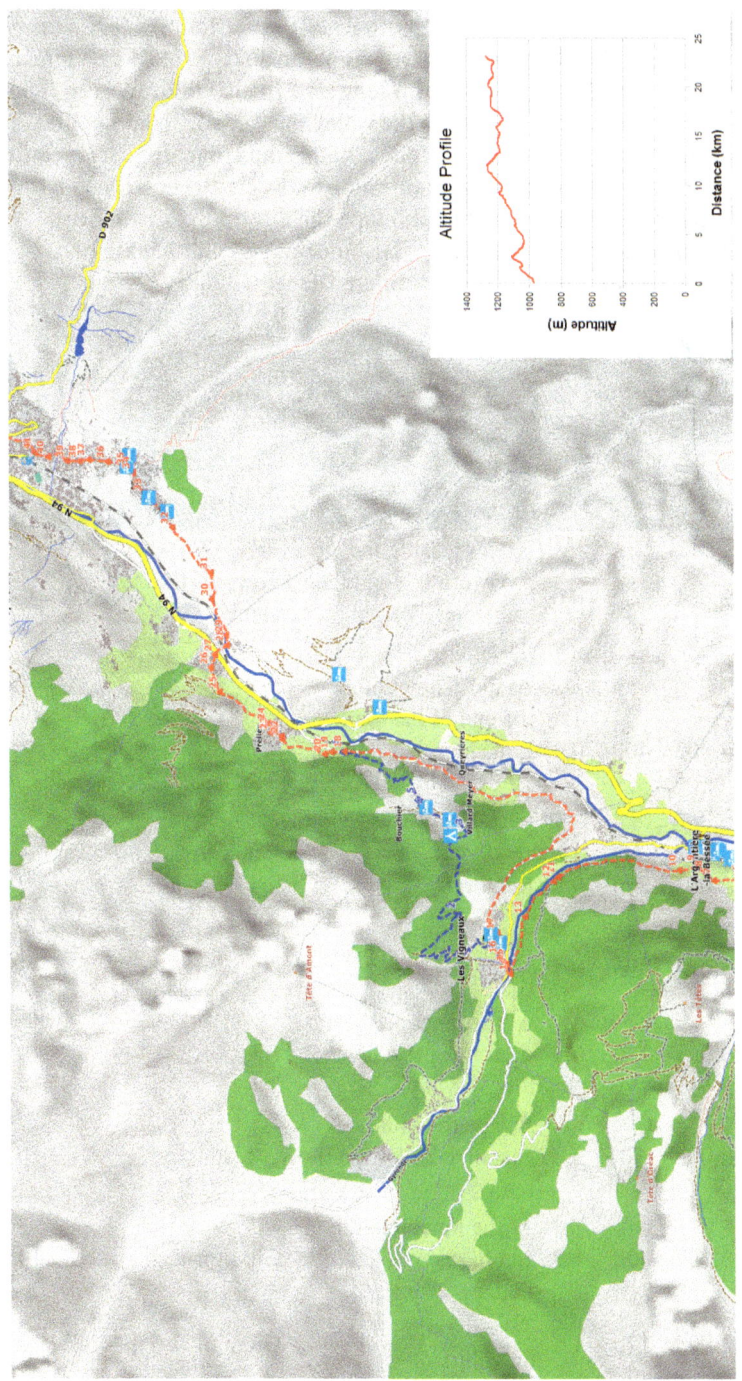

The route climbs from l'Argentière-la-Bessée joining forest tracks leading to the river crossing at Les Vigneaux. From Les Vigneaux there is the difficult choice of a long and tiring climb to over 1600m and the subsequent descent to the valley floor or a long and unpleasant stretch of tarmac road to Prelles, before approaching Briançon on quieter tarmac roads. The main route to the citadel in Briançon is not suitable for riders who should follow the alternatives with care.

Distance from Arles: 385km   Distance to Vercelli: 236km
Stage Ascent: 630m   Stage Descent: 330m

	Waypoint	Distance Between Waypoints (m)	Total (km)	Directions	Verification Point	Compass	Altitude (m)
l'Argentière-la-Bessée to Briançon 23.1 km	23.001	0	0,0	After crossing the river turn left and then immediately right on the small road	Towards the church	NW	973
	23.002	400	0,4	At the T-junction at the end of the road, turn sharp left on rue du Château and then turn right on the path	Uphill with a wall and exposed rock on the left	NW	979
	23.003	260	0,7	Bear left	Water trough on the right, GR sign	W	997
	23.004	70	0,7	At the junction bear right	GR sign	N	1006
	23.005	180	0,9	At the junction, bear right towards the clock tower	GR sign	NE	1020
	23.006	70	0,0	Beside the round chapel, bear left on the road	GR sign	N	1023
	23.007	500	1,5	At the junction at the end of chemin des Fonzes, bear right	GR sign	NE	1058
	23.008	170	1,6	Take the right fork downhill	GR sign	NE	1059

Waypoint	Distance Between Waypoints (m)	Total (km)	Directions	Verification Point	Compass	Altitude (m)
23.009	160	1,8	Take the left fork uphill	Stone wall on your left	N	1046
23.010	300	2,1	Fork left onto a narrow track	Direction Les Vigneaux	N	1056
23.011	2000	4,1	At the T-junction with a minor road turn left	GR sign	NW	1036
23.012	90	4,2	Take the right fork	GR sign	NW	1034
23.013	700	4,0	After crossing the camp site, continue straight ahead on the road	"Camping Les Vaudois"	W	1049
23.014	1000	5,9	Turn right to take the bridge over the river, then turn right again on the road	Direction Briançon, D994e	E	1092
23.015	200	6,1	Turn left on the road	Direction Briançon, D4	NE	1085
23.016	170	6,3	Continue straight ahead on the road. **Note:-** the GR turns left at this point and involves a steep climb to over 1600m before descending to rejoin the road		E	1090
23.017	400	6,7	At the junction continue straight ahead on the road		NE	1103
23.018	6700	13,4	Continue straight ahead on the road. **Note:-** GR653D rejoins from the left	GR sign	N	1189

l'Argentière-la-Bessée to Briançon 23.1 km

Waypoint	Distance Between Waypoints (m)	Total (km)	Directions	Verification Point	Compass	Altitude (m)
23.019	200	13,6	On the crown of the bend to the right, fork left onto a gravel track	GR sign	N	1185
23.020	140	13,7	Take the right fork	GR sign	N	1189
23.021	800	14,5	At the junction, continue straight ahead towards the church in Prelles	Water trough to your right, GR sign	E	1196
23.022	60	14,5	Bear left	Keep the church to your right	N	1195
23.023	190	14,7	Bear right on chemin des Noyers	GR sign	E	1199
23.024	150	14,9	At the crossroads, continue straight ahead	Cemetery on your left	NE	1195
23.025	900	15,8	At the T-junction with a minor road, turn right downhill	Ignore the red and white "X" on the tree.	E	1208
23.026	400	16,2	At the crossroads, continue straight ahead	Pass supermarket on your left, GR sign	E	1187
23.027	210	16,4	At the junction with the main road continue straight ahead	Towards river bridge	SE	1179
23.028	240	16,7	Bear left and continue on the road	GR sign	E	1166
23.029	160	16,8	On the crown of the bend to the right, turn left onto the grass track	GR sign	NE	1171
23.030	600	17,5	Bear right, uphill	GR sign	E	1200
23.031	400	17,9	At the T-junction with a minor road, turn left	GR sign	NE	1241

l'Argentière-la-Bessée to Briançon 23.1 km

Waypoint	Distance Between Waypoints (m)	Total (km)	Directions	Verification Point	Compass	Altitude (m)
23.032	1000	18,8	Just after entering the village of Villar-Saint-Pancrace turn left	Rue Principal du Bourg, GR sign	NE	1244
23.033	700	19,5	At the crossroads, continue straight ahead on rue de l'Ecole	Church on your right	NE	1238
23.034	400	19,9	At the T-junction turn left	Pass information point on your left	NE	1248
23.035	120	20,0	At the junction after passing the bar on your right, keep left on the road	GR sign	N	1257
23.036	400	20,4	At the roundabout, continue straight ahead	Direction Z.A. de la Tour	N	1255
23.037	300	20,7	At the junction, keep left on rue du Rencurel	GR sign	N	1250
23.038	150	20,8	At the junction with the main road, bear left, towards Briançon	GR sign	N	1239
23.039	200	21,0	At the roundabout take the first exit. **Note:-** a number of GR routes pass through Briançon and as a result the GR signing can be misleading in the town. Please follow the written instructions with care	"Toutes Directions", GR sign	N	1229

l'Argentière-la-Bessée to Briançon 23.1 km

Waypoint	Distance Between Waypoints (m)	Total (km)	Directions	Verification Point	Compass	Altitude (m)
23.040	400	21,4	At the roundabout, take the second exit, rue Jouseph Silvestre	"Toutes Directions"	N	1229
23.041	220	21,6	At the roundabout take the first exit on rue des Toulousannes	Apartment building to the right	NE	1235
23.042	700	22,2	At the T-junction with the main road, turn left	Downhill	NW	1234
23.043	140	22,4	Turn right into the park. **Note:-** the route ahead includes flights of steps and is not suitable for riders who should continue straight ahead and follow then turn right on chemin Vieux to rejoin the main route as it leaves the park	Direction Parc de la Schappe, keep the river to your left in the park	NE	1226
23.044	100	22,5	Turn left to cross the bridge and then turn right on the path	GR sign	NE	1221
23.045	200	22,7	Take the left fork, up the hill		NE	1231
23.046	80	22,8	Continue straight ahead on the path		NE	1242
23.047	200	22,0	At the junction with the road turn right	Towards the citadel	N	1269
23.048	140	23,1	Arrive at Briançon	Entrance to the citadel		1273

l'Argentière-la-Bessée to Briançon 23.1 km

Stage Ascent: 738m   Stage Descent: 646m

Waypoint	Distance Between Waypoints (m)	Total (km)	Directions	Verification Point	Compass	Altitude (m)
23A1.001	0	0,0	Turn left on the road	GR sign	NE	1093
23A1.002	3800	3,8	Take the left fork and continue to climb the hill	GR sign	E	1482
23A1.003	2300	6,1	At the junction bear left		NE	1562
23A1.004	700	6,8	After passing through the village of Bouchier take the right fork		NE	1515
23A1.005	290	7,1	Take the left fork		NE	1478
23A1.006	2100	9,2	At the T-junction with the main road, turn left. **Note:**- Main Route approaches from the left	GR sign		1192

Alternate Route 9.2 km

B&B, Hotel, Gite d'Etapes	Price/ Opening
Le Duranccau (Marc et Karine), La Vachette 05100 Val des Prés, Hautes Alpes, France Tel:+33(0)4 92 21 19 57 contact@leduranceau.com	B1
Le Petit Phoque (Walter), Hameau Le Fontenil 05100 Briançon, Hautes Alpes, France Tel:+33(0)4 92 20 07 27 Mobile:+33(0)6 63 18 03 57 corinne.palomero@wanadoo.fr	B1
Inter Hôtel, 8 Avenue Galibier 05100 Briançon, Hautes Alpes, France Tel:+33(0)4 92 21 12 55 www.inter-hotel.fr/	B1
Hôtel Des Remparts, 14 Avenue Vauban 05100 Briançon, Hautes Alpes, France Tel:+33(0)4 92 21 08 73 www.hotel-des-remparts.com/	B2
Hotel Edelweiss à Briançon, 32 Avenue de la République 05100 Briançon, Hautes Alpes, France Tel:+33(0)4 92 21 02 94 www.hotel-edelweiss-briancon.fr/ **Note:**Pilgrim price reduction	B3

l'Argentière-la-Bessée to Briançon 23.1 km

B&B, Hotel, Gite d'Etapes	Price/
Hotel Mont-Brison, 3 Avenue général de Gaulle 3 05100 Briançon, Hautes Alpes, France Tel:+33(0)4 92 21 14 55 www.hotelmontbrison.com/	B2
La Ferme de la Tour (Thierry & Nadine Moya), 38 Rue du Mélézin 05100 Villar Saint Pancrace, Hautes Alpes, France Tel:+33(0)4 92 20 58 68 fermedelatour@free.fr	B1
Le Bois de Barracan (Danièle et Mathieu), 3 Allée Sainte-Barbe 05100 Villar Saint Pancrace, Hautes Alpes, France Tel:+33(0)4 92 21 27 79 barracan@free.fr	B1
Les Tanneries (Pascale Martin), 10 Chemin de la Croix de Bretagne 05100 Villar Saint Pancrace, Hautes Alpes, France Tel:+33(0)4 92 43 88 19 Mobile:+33(0)4 92 43 88 19	B3
Le Bacha (Monique et Philippe Long), Impasse de la Fontaine 05100 Villar Saint Pancrace, Hautes Alpes, France Tel:+33(0)4 92 20 18 46 Mobile:+33(0)6 17 35 53 84 contact@lebacha.com	B3
Le Brin de Paille (David et Lydie) 05120 Saint Martin de Queyrières, Hautes Alpes, France Tel:+33(0)4 92 24 77 83 d.monnet1@libertysurf.fr	B2
Le Rocher Baron, Rocher Baron 05120 Saint Martin de Queyrières, Hautes Alpes, France Tel:+33(0)4 92 21 06 02	B1
Religious Hostel	
Paroisse Ste Catherine, 17 Rue Alphand 05100 Briançon, Hautes Alpes, France Tel:+33(0)4 92 20 04 10	B1
Presbytère de la Collégiale St Nicolas (Père Guy Corpataux), Place de l'Europe,05100 Briançon, Hautes Alpes, France Tel:+33(0)4 92 21 05 15 Mobile:+33(0)6 25 68 56 17 guy-corpataux@wanadoo.fr	B1
Camping	
Camping Caravaning de l'Iscle de Prelles, L'iscle 05120 Saint Martin de Queyrières, Hautes Alpes, France Tel:+33(0)4 92 20 28 66	B1
Tourist Office	
Office de Tourisme, Route d'Italie 05100 Briançon, Hautes Alpes, France Tel:+33(0)4 92 21 52 52 info@montgenevre.com	
Office de Tourisme, 1 Place Temple 05100 Briançon, Hautes Alpes, France Tel:+33(0)4 92 21 08 50 www.ot-briancon.fr/	

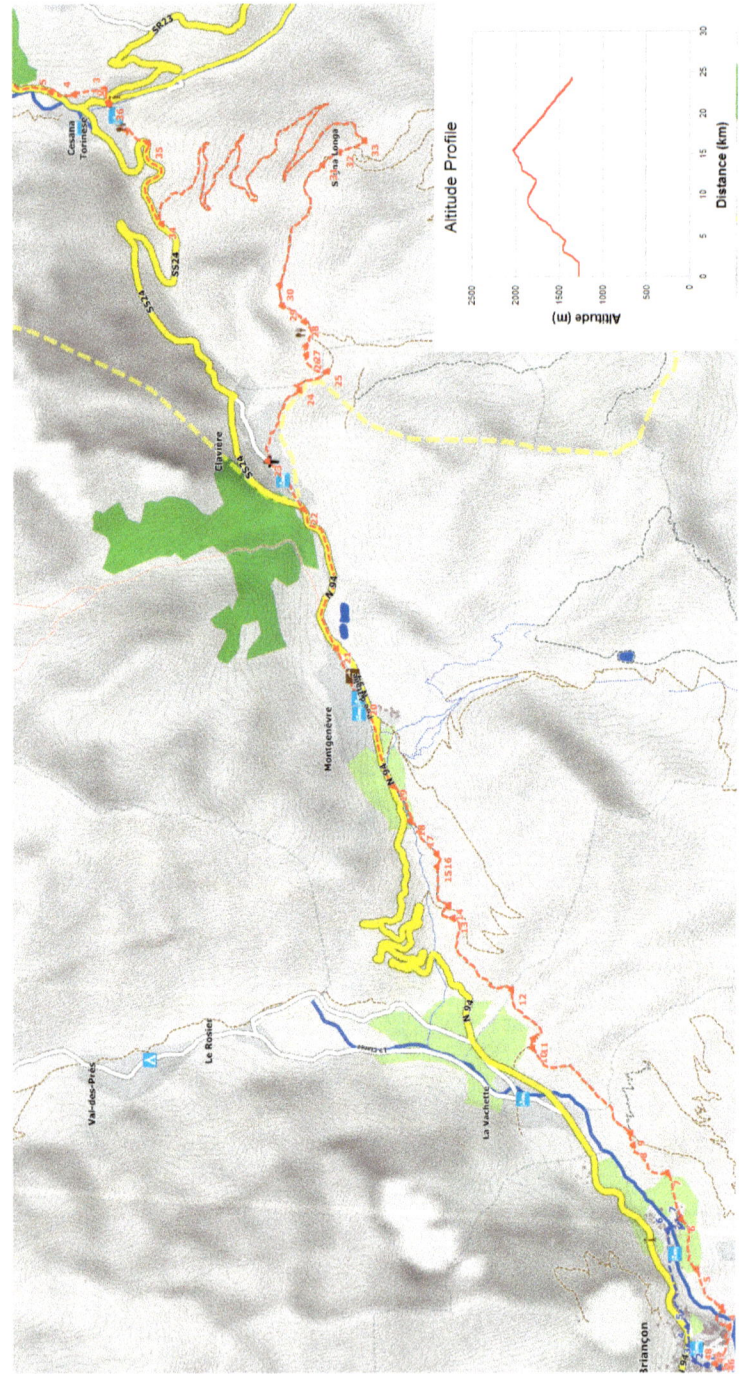

After passing through the citadel the route takes to generally broad and well signed forest tracks to Montgenevre. In the event of snow then the main road should be considered. From Montgenevre to Cesana the route climbs to over 2200m on broad tracks. Unfortunately the route is pisted for skiing in the winter and early spring making progress difficult and potentially dangerous.

Distance from Arles: 408km **Distance to Vercelli: 213km**
Stage Ascent: 883m **Stage Descent: 803m**

Waypoint	Distance Between Waypoints (m)	Total (km)	Directions	Verification Point	Compass	Altitude (m)
24.001	0	0,0	Turn right and enter the citadel	Porte d'Embrun	E	1273
24.002	80	0,1	At the T-junction turn right and follow the ramparts		SE	1273
24.003	400	0,5	Leave the ramparts, cross the bridge and continue straight ahead	Pont d'Asfeld	NE	1272
24.004	400	0,9	At the apex of a bend to the right, turn left on the track	Parallel to the river	NE	1272
24.005	500	1,4	At the T-junction, bear left	Towards the village	E	1272
24.006	600	1,9	At the junction in the village, turn right. **Note:-** alternate route rejoins from the left	Direction l'Envers du Fontenil, GR sign	E	1286
24.007	500	2,4	Take the left fork	GR sign	NE	1343
24.008	500	2,9	Bear right on the track, uphill	GR sign	E	1428
24.009	130	3,0	At a T-junction in tracks, turn left on the wider track	GR sign	NE	1447

Briançon to Cesana-Torinese 24.3 km

Waypoint	Distance Between Waypoints (m)	Total (km)	Directions	Verification Point	Compass	Altitude (m)
24.010	1400	4,4	Cross over the wooden bridge and then immediately turn right. **Note:-** in event of bad weather, it is possible to rejoin the main road by avoiding the right turn and continuing on the track for 400m. At the time of writing a further bridge ahead has been destroyed ahead and we suggest that riders also take to the road at this point	GR sign	E	1429
24.011	120	4,5	At the T-junction, turn right and then immediately bear left	GR sign	NE	1436
24.012	700	5,2	Bear left and cross over a small stream	GR sign	NE	1507
24.013	1100	6,3	Take the right fork, uphill	GR sign	E	1601
24.014	220	6,5	At the junction, bear right continuing uphill	Direction Montgenèvre, GR sign	E	1627
24.015	500	6,9	Take the right fork, uphill	GR sign	E	1686
24.016	130	7,1	Continue straight ahead on the track	GR sign	NE	1701
24.017	270	7,3	Continue straight ahead at the junction	GR signs	NE	1735
24.018	180	7,5	Bear right away from the river	Derelict bridge	NE	1748
24.019	400	7,9	At the junction with the road, turn right	Entry to Montgenèvre	E	1786

Briançon to Cesana-Torinese 24.3 km

Waypoint	Distance Between Waypoints (m)	Total (km)	Directions	Verification Point	Compass	Altitude (m)
24.020	900	8,8	Turn left and then right into the centre of Montgenèvre, rue de l'Eglise	Towards the church	NE	1847
24.021	600	9,4	At the roundabout, continue straight ahead on the N94	Direction Turin	E	1857
24.022	1500	10,9	At the frontier continue straight ahead on the road	Towards the centre of Claviere	NE	1799
24.023	600	11,5	Immediately after passing the church, turn right and follow the road over the river bridge and up the hill	Towards ski slope on Strada Communale Valle Gimont	SE	1771
24.024	800	12,3	Bear left and then right, continuing uphill	Towards the Gimont refuge	SE	1818
24.025	400	12,7	Approaching the top of the rise, turn left	Direction "La Coche"	NE	1879
24.026	290	13,0	Bear right between the pond and the buildings		E	1928
24.027	70	13,1	Continue straight ahead between the 2 bar/restaurants and then bear left		E	1931
24.028	300	13,4	Take the right fork, on the higher track	Signpost "Restaurant" on your left	NE	1930
24.029	250	13,7	Continue straight ahead	Avoid left turn to Rocca Clari	E	1935
24.030	240	13,9	Continue straight ahead	Signpost Sagna Longa	E	1948
24.031	1400	15,3	Take the right fork	Pass radio mast on the left	SE	2015

Briançon to Cesana-Torinese 24.3 km

Briançon to Cesana-Torinese 24.3 km

Waypoint	Distance Between Waypoints (m)	Total (km)	Directions	Verification Point	Compass	Altitude (m)
24.032	200	15,5	Continue straight ahead	Pass sign for Sagna Longa on your right	SE	2023
24.033	270	15,7	Turn left and proceed down the hill towards Cesana	Pass Sport Hotel on your right	N	2004
24.034	6900	22,6	At the T-junction with the main road, turn right	SS24, towards the town	E	1475
24.035	1000	23,6	Take the right fork on the road	Follow via Roma into the centre of Cesana Torinese	NE	1395
24.036	700	24,3	Arrive at Cesana-Torinese	Beside river bridge		1354

Stage Ascent: 80m   Stage Descent: 65m

Waypoint	Distance Between Waypoints (m)	Total (km)	Directions	Verification Point	Compass	Altitude (m)
24A1.001	0	0,6	Just in front of the entrance to the citadel, porte d'Embrun, turn left and then immediately right keeping the walls to your right	GR sign on the tree	N	1278
24A1.002	140	0,8	Cross the road and take the gravel path into the car park	Keep the walls of the citadel close on your right, GR sign	N	1289
24A1.003	150	0,9	Bear right and follow the flight of steps	GR sign	E	1307
24A1.004	170	1,1	At the junction with the main road turn right	Pass porte de Pignerol and the car park on your right	E	1327
24A1.005	190	1,3	Bear right to take the small road	Direction Fontenil	E	1332
24A1.006	1000	2,3	In Fontenil, turn right to cross the river bridge and continue straight ahead on the other side		SE	1267
24A1.007	400	2,7	At the top of the hill turn left and rejoin the main track	Direction l'Envers du Fontenil, GR sign		1293

Alternate Route 2.7 km

B&B, Hotel, Gite d'Etapes	Price/ Opening
Hôtel Valérie, Rue Eglise 05100 Montgenèvre, Hautes Alpes, France Tel:+33(0)4 92 21 90 02	B2
Gîte La Maita, Les Alberts 05100 Montgenèvre, Hautes Alpes, France Tel:+33(0)4 92 20 29 72	B1
Albergo Miramonti Di Franco, Strada Rio Secco, 1,10050 Claviere (TO), Italy Tel:+39 0122878804	B2
Opera Diocesana Pier Giorgio Frassati, Via Carlo Ferragut 10054 Cesana Torinese (TO), Italy Tel:+39 012289460	B1
B&B La Tana degli Orsi,Frazione Rhuilles, 96,10054 Cesana Torinese (TO), Italy Tel:+39 0122845149	B3
L'ibarus, Piazza Europa, 2,10054 Cesana Torinese (TO), Italy Tel:+39 0122856004 www.ibarus.com/	B3
Croce Bianca, Via Roma, 33,10054 Cesana Torinese (TO), Italy Tel:+39 012289192	B3
Camping	
L'Iscle du Rosier 05100 Val des Prés, Hautes Alpes, France Tel:+33(0)4 92 21 06 01	B1
Tourist Office	

Briançon to Cesana-Torinese 24.3 km

Comune Di Cesana Torinese, Ufficio Tributi, Piazza Vittorio Amedeo, 5,10054 Cesana Torinese (TO), Italy   Tel:+39 012289333
www.comune.cesana.to.it/

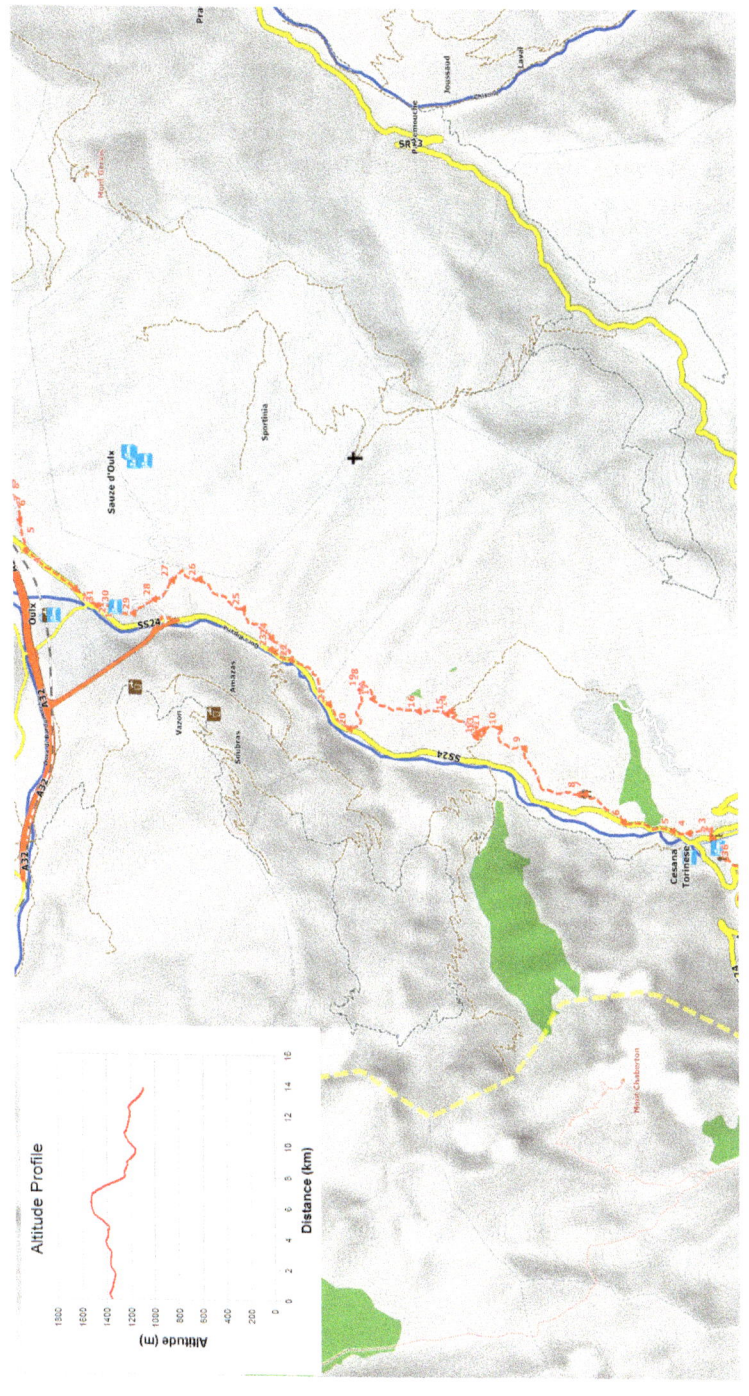

The route initially follows the main SS24, but quickly takes to woodland pathways and tracks through tiny and sometimes derelict mountain villages.

Distance from Arles: 432km   **Distance to Vercelli: 189km**
Stage Ascent: 370m   **Stage Descent: 635m**

Cesana-Torinese to Oulx 13.8 km

Waypoint	Distance Between Waypoints (m)	Total (km)	Directions	Verification Point	Compass	Altitude (m)
25.001	0	0,0	Continue straight ahead	Cross the river bridge	NE	1353
25.002	30	0,0	Continue straight ahead at the roundabout and then bear left uphill onto via Alessandro Voyron	Tourist office on your right at roundabout	E	1355
25.003	140	0,2	Turn sharp left and then bear right	Towards the church	N	1365
25.004	400	0,5	Continue straight ahead on via Augusto Plancia	Yellow pilgrim sign on telegraph pole	N	1365
25.005	250	0,8	At the T-junction, turn right beside the main road	Direction Torino, yellow pilgrim sign on the wall	N	1353
25.006	800	1,5	Turn right onto the small road, Frazione Mollieres	Direction "la Selvaggia"	NE	1332
25.007	700	2,2	In the village of Mollières, take the left fork	Follow white arrows	N	1367
25.008	100	2,3	Join a dirt track and bear right	Following white arrows	NE	1369
25.009	1200	3,6	Continue straight ahead avoiding the fork up the hill	Cross the stream	NE	1401

Waypoint	Distance Between Waypoints (m)	Total (km)	Directions	Verification Point	Compass	Altitude (m)
25.010	600	4,2	Bear left and cross the bridge before continuing straight ahead on the track		N	1385
25.011	270	4,4	Turn left on the road	Entering the small village of Solomiac	NW	1391
25.012	200	4,6	At the T-junction after passing through the village, turn right. **Note:-** the signed route turns left at this point to join the main road. We will continue on the wooded hillside		SE	1380
25.013	190	4,8	Take the left fork up the hill	Wooden sign for "Loc. Solomiac" and direction Colombière	NE	1395
25.014	800	5,6	Turn sharp left, between the houses	Derelict hamlet of Colombières	NW	1505
25.015	70	5,7	Continue straight ahead, grass track between the wall and the derelict house	Beside water trough	N	1509
25.016	500	6,1	Take the left fork	Downhill	N	1526
25.017	700	6,8	Take the left fork	Track to the right signed "GS"	NE	1518
25.018	280	7,1	Bear left down the hill	Pass derelict building on your right	W	1546

Cesana-Torinese to Oulx 13.8 km

Waypoint	Distance Between Waypoints (m)	Total (km)	Directions	Verification Point	Compass	Altitude (m)
25.019	100	7,2	Continue straight ahead	Between broken walls	W	1454
25.020	800	7,0	Shortly before reaching the main road, turn right on a grass track	Track proceeds parallel to the main road	NE	1250
25.021	500	8,5	Take the left lower fork	Blue painted pathway signs	NE	1242
25.022	1000	9,4	T-junction with the main road, turn right	Opposite the village of Amazas	NE	1174
25.023	400	9,7	After the bend to the right, turn right onto the partly made road	Warning sign for car drivers	E	1155
25.024	700	10,4	Take the left fork and continue parallel to the main road	Electricity pylons ahead	NE	1227
25.025	700	11,1	Cross the bridge over the stream and bear left		NE	1231
25.026	900	11,9	Continue straight ahead	Wooden crucifix to your right	N	1208
25.027	600	12,4	In front of the church in San Marco turn left onto the broad tarmac road	Beside water trough	NW	1214
25.028	400	12,8	Turn left onto a gravel track	Towards the church with the "onion" spire	NW	1186
25.029	400	13,2	At the bottom of the hill turn right and continue on via des Ambrois	Church on your left	N	1131
25.030	400	13,6	At the junction, continue straight ahead	Via Vittoria Emanuele	N	1101
25.031	230	13,8	Arrive at Oulx centre	Junction with via Roma		1088

Cesana-Torinese to Oulx 13.8 km

B&B, Hotel, Gite d'Etapes	Price/ Opening
Edil Gio.Roc. Srl, Casa Vacanza, Corso Montenero, 63,10056 Oulx (TO), Italy Tel:+39 0122830898	B3
Hotel Chez Toi Di Buono Francesca, Via des Ambrois, 28,10056 Oulx (TO), Italy Tel:+39 0122830883	B3
Albergo Ristorante Sayonara, Via Monfol, 21,10050 Sauze d'Oulx (TO), Italy Tel:+39 0122850269	B1
Villa Cary, Via Monfol, 13,10050 Sauze d'Oulx (TO), Italy Tel:+39 0122850191 www.villacary.com/	B2
Ristorante Albergo Villa Daniela, Via Monfol, 3,10050 Sauze d'Oulx (TO), Italy Tel:+390122850196	B1
Albergo Stella Alpina, Via Miramonti, 22,10050 Sauze d'Oulx (TO), Italy Tel:+39 0122858731 www.stellalpinahotel.it/	B2
Derby, Via Monfol, 8,10050 Sauze d'Oulx (TO), Italy Tel:+39 0122850176	B2
Camping	
Campeggi Ostelli Villaggi, Corso Torino, 141,10056 Oulx (TO), Italy Tel:+39 0122833005	B1

Cesana-Torinese to Oulx 13.8 km

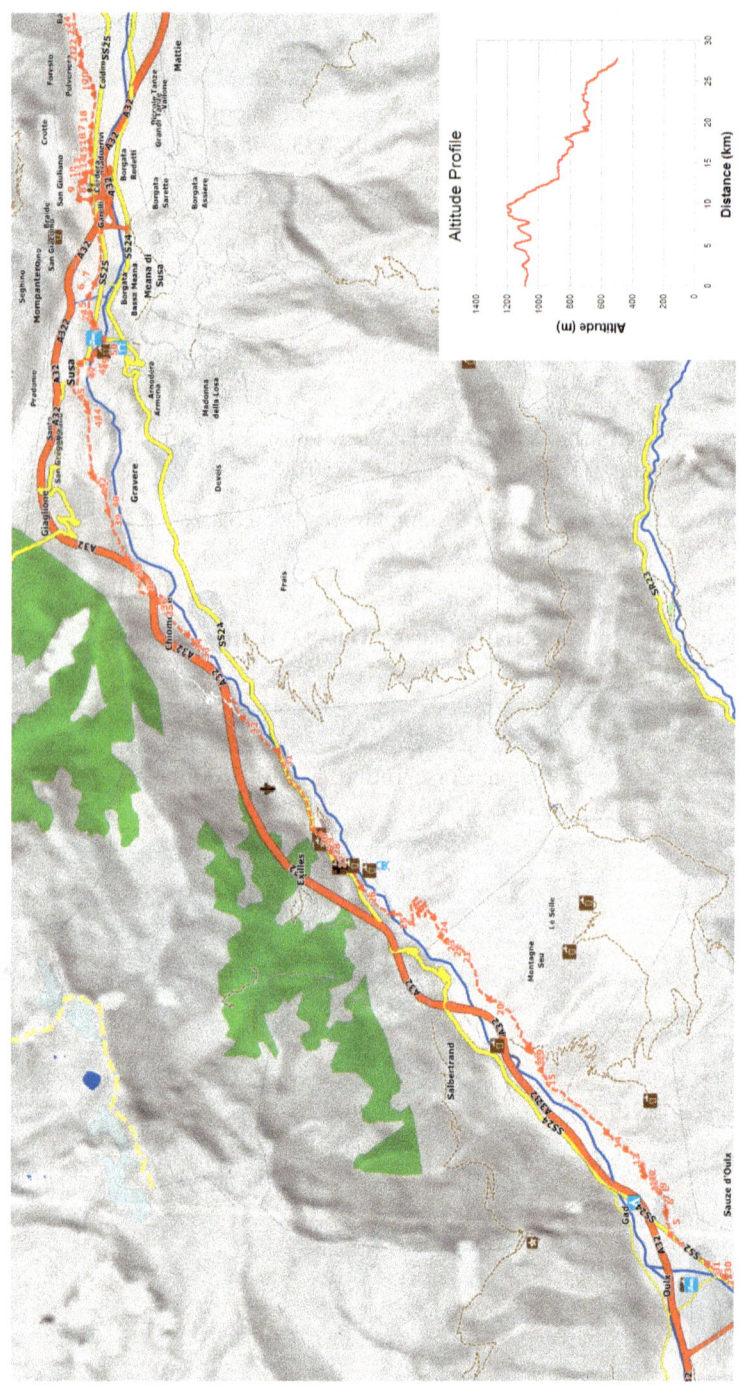

Oulx to Susa 27.7 km

The route returns to the SS24 for the exit from Oulx, before returning to wooded hillsides. The yellow pilgrim signs of the via Francigena are generally well placed from this point. Following the village of Exilles, the signed route leads to a destroyed bridge – the route maybe passable in the summer with care. However, we were forced to return to the main road for 1.7km, before taking the quiet roads and tracks on the north-side of the valley for the remainder of the route to Susa. There are few opportunities for eating and accommodation.

Distance from Arles: 446km   **Distance to Vercelli: 175km**
Stage Ascent: 621m   **Stage Descent: 1211m**

Waypoint	Distance Between Waypoints (m)	Total (km)	Directions	Verification Point	Compass	Altitude (m)
26.001	0	0,0	At the T-junction, turn right	Via Roma	NE	1088
26.002	120	0,1	At the junction, continue straight ahead	Via Roma, parallel to the main road	NE	1086
26.003	290	0,4	At the junction with the main road continue straight beside the SS24	Yellow pilgrim signs on the roadside	NE	1084
26.004	900	1,3	At the roundabout, turn right	Direction Gad, yellow pilgrim sign	E	1071
26.005	500	1,7	At the junction, continue straight ahead	Via Ricardo Ghiotti	E	1072
26.006	500	2,2	Continue onto a gravel track and bear left	Follow yellow pilgrim sign	NE	1086
26.007	120	2,3	Turn right and immediately left	Yellow pilgrim sign, "Sentiero dei Franchi"	E	1096

Oulx to Susa 27.7 km

Waypoint	Distance Between Waypoints (m)	Total (km)	Directions	Verification Point	Compass	Altitude (m)
26.008	170	2,5	At the junction in the track, continue straight ahead	Red and white footpath sign on your right	NE	1104
26.009	80	2,5	Bear left	White arrow	N	1103
26.010	190	2,7	At the junction, bear right	Wooden "Sentiero dei Franchi" sign	E	1093
26.011	100	2,8	Continue straight ahead	White arrow	E	1086
26.012	100	2,9	Bear right and cross wooden bridge	SF sign	NE	1080
26.013	500	3,4	Continue over the wooden bridge	Yellow pilgrim sign	NE	1058
26.014	500	3,9	Continue straight ahead on the narrow track	Follow SF signs	NE	1079
26.015	1900	5,8	At the T-junction, turn right along the "Percorso Atletico"	"Sentiero dei Franchi" sign	NE	1053
26.016	500	6,2	Turn left then left again onto the broad track	Follow the white arrows	N	1060
26.017	30	6,3	Bear right over the wooden bridge	"Sentiero dei Franchi"	NE	1063
26.018	60	6,3	After crossing the bridge, quickly turn right	SF and yellow pilgrim signs	SE	1069
26.019	80	6,4	Take the left fork	White arrow	NE	1076
26.020	1300	7,7	After crossing a small footbridge fork right	SF sign	NE	1065
26.021	1300	8,0	At the fork in the track, continue straight ahead on the main track		NE	1192

Oulx to Susa 27.7 km

Waypoint	Distance Between Waypoints (m)	Total (km)	Directions	Verification Point	Compass	Altitude (m)
26.022	220	9,2	Bear right, around the gorge		NE	1177
26.023	190	9,4	Bear right	"Sentiero dei Franchi"	E	1178
26.024	500	9,8	Continue straight ahead on the broad track	The "Sentiero dei Franchi" leaves to the right	N	1203
26.025	3200	13,0	Bear left on the road over the bridge and pass through the hamlet of Chambons Inferiore	White arrow	NE	885
26.026	800	13,8	At the T-junction turn right towards Exilles	Large stone wall ahead at the junction	NE	876
26.027	1000	14,8	After passing through Exilles, take the right fork	Towards the fortress	NE	875
26.028	300	15,1	At the T-junction turn left	Keep fortress to your right	NE	873
26.029	160	15,2	At the junction continue straight ahead towards the main road. **Note:-** at the time of writing the marked route turns right at this point. However, a river bridge has been destroyed leaving a potentially dangerous crossing		NE	869
26.030	150	15,4	At the T-junction with the main road, turn right and proceed with great care	SS24	NE	860

Oulx to Susa 27.7 km

Waypoint	Distance Between Waypoints (m)	Total (km)	Directions	Verification Point	Compass	Altitude (m)
26.031	1700	17,1	Turn left on the minor road, direction Ramats. **Note:-** the signed route rejoins at this point	Main road crosses the river after junction	NE	779
26.032	900	17,0	Take the right fork, downhill	Yellow pilgrim sign	NE	827
26.033	2000	19,9	Beside the bridge over the river leading to Chiomonte, continue straight ahead	Yellow pilgrim, direction Giaglione	NE	673
26.034	210	20,1	After passing the electricity plant, continue straight ahead on the road	White arrow	NE	679
26.035	1100	21,2	Take the right fork down hill	Small road under the motorway	NE	707
26.036	500	21,6	Bear left under the motorway	White arrow	NE	691
26.037	600	22,2	Pass again under the motorway	Beside tunnel entrance	NE	687
26.038	400	22,7	Continue straight ahead	White arrow	NE	717
26.039	1100	23,8	In Gaglione, continue straight ahead on the road		E	703
26.040	400	24,1	Continue straight ahead through the village		NE	699
26.041	400	24,5	Continue straight ahead, direction Susa	White arrow	NE	693
26.042	90	24,6	Continue straight ahead, avoid the left turn to Susa	White arrow	E	693

Oulx to Susa 27.7 km

Waypoint	Distance Between Waypoints (m)	Total (km)	Directions	Verification Point	Compass	Altitude (m)
26.043	1100	25,8	At the junction, continue straight ahead	White arrow	E	623
26.044	130	25,9	Keep right at the junction		NE	618
26.045	600	26,5	Shortly before reaching the main road, turn sharp right		SE	562
26.046	600	27,0	At the T-junction with the main road turn right	White arrow, SS25	SE	524
26.047	40	27,1	Bear left on the smaller road	Via Montenero	S	521
26.048	240	27,3	After crossing the river bridge, bear left	Towards archway, white arrow	SE	511
26.049	130	27,4	At the entrance to the piazza Savoia, continue straight ahead and parallel to the river	Corso Trieste	SE	504
26.050	290	27,7	Arrive at Susa centre	Beside museum		499

Oulx to Susa 27.7 km

B&B, Hotel, Gite d'Etapes	Price/ Opening
Hotel Napoleon Susa, Via Mazzini, 44,10059 Susa (TO), Italy Tel:+39 0122622855 www.hotelnapoleon.it/	B3
Albergo Du Parc, Via Rocchetta, 15,10059 Susa (TO), Italy Tel:+39 0122622273	B2

Religious Hostel	
Convento S. Francesco Frati Minori Conventuali, Via San Francesco, 3,10059 Susa (TO), Italy Tel:+39 0122622548 www.sanfrancescosusa.com/	B2

Doctor

Bianco Dolino - Studio Medico, Via Fratelli Vallero, 48,10059 Susa (TO), Italy   Tel:+39 0122623078

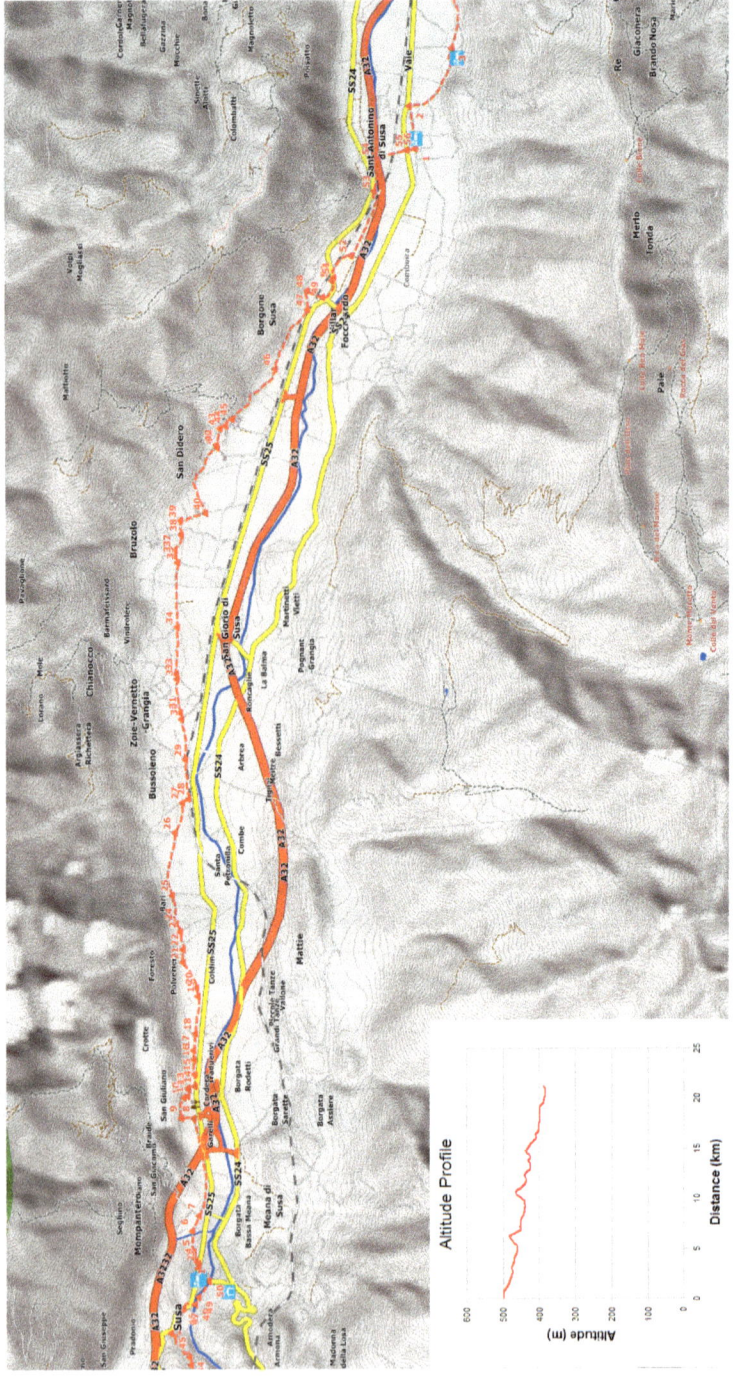

Susa to Sant'Antonio-di-Susa 21.2 km

The route follows quiet tarmac roads and farm tracks parallel to motorway and railway tracks on the valley floor.
Distance from Arles: 474km   **Distance to Vercelli: 147km**
Stage Ascent: 88m   **Stage Descent: 199m**

Waypoint	Distance Between Waypoints (m)	Total (km)	Directions	Verification Point	Compass	Altitude (m)
27.001	0	0,0	Turn left over the river bridge and then immediately bear right into via Roma	Pass Museum on your left	NE	498
27.002	270	0,3	At the crossroads turn right on the main road	Pass tourist office on your left	E	497
27.003	90	0,4	Take the first turning on the left	Immediately after passing the park	NE	497
27.004	70	0,4	At the crossroads, turn right	Corso Luciano Couvert	E	498
27.005	130	0,6	Continue straight ahead on the road	Corso Luciano Couvert	E	498
27.006	300	0,9	At the crossroads after crossing the watercourse, continue straight ahead	Via Montello	SE	496
27.007	260	1,2	At the junction, continue straight ahead direction San Giacomo	Yellow pilgrim	E	490
27.008	1600	2,7	Just before passing under the railway, turn left onto a gravel track	White arrow	N	474
27.009	210	2,9	At the T-junction, turn right		E	475

Susa to Sant'Antonio-di-Susa 21.2 km

Waypoint	Distance Between Waypoints (m)	Total (km)	Directions	Verification Point	Compass	Altitude (m)
27.010	300	3,3	At the T-junction with the road turn right	Towards the railway	S	475
27.011	80	3,3	Before reaching the railway, turn left on the track		E	474
27.012	120	3,5	Turn left and then right to pass through the houses		E	473
27.013	30	3,5	Turn right and proceed across the railway		S	473
27.014	110	3,6	Before reaching the main road, turn left on the track		E	471
27.015	180	3,8	At the road junction, continue straight ahead	Beside modern houses	E	469
27.016	230	4,0	Bear left and then right	Recross the railway	E	468
27.017	150	4,2	Continue straight ahead	Parallel and close to the railway	E	468
27.018	260	4,4	At the crossroads, continue straight ahead	Remain beside the railway	E	464
27.019	600	5,0	At the road junction bear left	Industrial building on the left	E	460
27.020	130	5,2	Take the left fork		NE	460
27.021	500	5,6	Bear right on the road	Towards Foresto	E	470

Susa to Sant'Antonio-di-Susa 21.2 km

Waypoint	Distance Between Waypoints (m)	Total (km)	Directions	Verification Point	Compass	Altitude (m)
27.022	200	5,8	At the junction, continue straight ahead on the road		E	475
27.023	290	6,1	At the road junction, continue straight ahead	Pass church on your left	NE	482
27.024	150	6,3	Take the right fork	Via San Rocco	E	482
27.025	500	6,7	At the crossroads, continue straight ahead		E	461
27.026	1000	7,7	At the crossroads, continue straight ahead	Via Guido Olmo	E	452
27.027	500	8,2	At the T-junction turn right	Via Massimo d'Azeglio	SE	447
27.028	140	8,3	At the T-junction, turn left	Railway directly ahead at the junction	E	444
27.029	600	8,0	Take the right fork	Initially remaining close to the railway	E	441
27.030	600	9,6	Take the left fork	Strada Chianoco	E	439
27.031	110	9,7	Continue straight ahead	Remain on Strada Chianocco	E	440
27.032	500	10,2	At the T-junction, bear left		E	454
27.033	110	10,3	Turn right	Cross over the waterway	E	459
27.034	800	11,1	At the junction continue straight ahead	Frazione Crotte	E	452
27.035	1000	12,1	At the road junction, turn left		NE	438

Susa to Sant'Antonio-di-Susa 21.2 km

Waypoint	Distance Between Waypoints (m)	Total (km)	Directions	Verification Point	Compass	Altitude (m)
27.036	120	12,2	Take the right fork	Via Cavour	E	440
27.037	100	12,3	Take the right fork	Via dei Mille	SE	441
27.038	270	12,6	At the junction in Bruzolo, continue straight ahead	Via dei mille	E	438
27.039	220	12,8	At the T-junction, turn right on via Carlo Emanuele 1	Pass beside il Castello	S	433
27.040	400	13,2	Turn left	Via San Didero	E	424
27.041	1200	14,4	Take the left fork	Towards the centre of San Didero	E	429
27.042	30	14,4	Bear right	Via Roma	E	429
27.043	260	14,7	At the T-junction in the centre of San Didero, turn right	Beside the tower - la Casaforte	SE	438
27.044	120	14,8	Take the left fork	Via Maometto	SE	436
27.045	170	14,0	At the junction, continue straight ahead	At the foot of the hills	SE	432
27.046	1200	16,1	At the junction continue straight ahead	Parallel to the railway on your right	SE	409
27.047	1100	17,2	Bear left	Via 4 Novembre	E	400
27.048	300	17,5	At the crossroads in Bargone, turn right	Via Guido Bobba	SW	400
27.049	280	17,8	After crossing the railway, bear left	Via Moncenisio	SE	400

Susa to Sant'Antonio-di-Susa 21.2 km

Waypoint	Distance Between Waypoints (m)	Total (km)	Directions	Verification Point	Compass	Altitude (m)
27.050	400	18,2	Before recrossing the railway, turn right		SE	400
27.051	70	18,3	Turn left	Railway close on your left	SE	400
27.052	600	18,8	Turn left on Strada Garitta Terza	Between the motorway and the railway	E	400
27.053	1200	19,9	Continue ahead beside the river		E	387
27.054	500	20,5	At the T-junction with road turn right	Pass over Dora Riparia and under the motorway	S	383
27.055	600	21,0	At the crossroads with the SS25, continue straight ahead		S	385
27.056	140	21,2	Arrive at Sant'Antonio-di-Susa	Via Torino		388

Susa to Sant'Antonio-di-Susa 21.2 km

B&B, Hotel, Gite d'Etapes	Price/Opening
PR Bed & Breakfast Sanpancrazio, Via San Pancrazio, 24,10050 Vaie (TO), Italy Tel:+39 0119634028 Mobile:+39 3387580678 estella@sanpancrazio.net www.sanpancrazio.it	B2
Dell'Angelo, Via Torino, 130,10050 Sant'Antonino di Susa (TO), Italy Tel:+39 0119640493 **Note:** 5km from the main route	B2

Religious Hostel	
Sacra Di San Michele - Santuario Padri Rosminiani Via alla Sacra San Michele, 10050 Chiusa di San Michele (TO), Italy Tel:+39 011939706 www.sacradisanmichele.com/	Donation
Parrocchia di S. Giovanni Vincenzo,10057 Sant'Ambrogio di Torino (TO), Italy Tel:+39 011939132 canto-s.ambrogio1802@libero.it	Donation

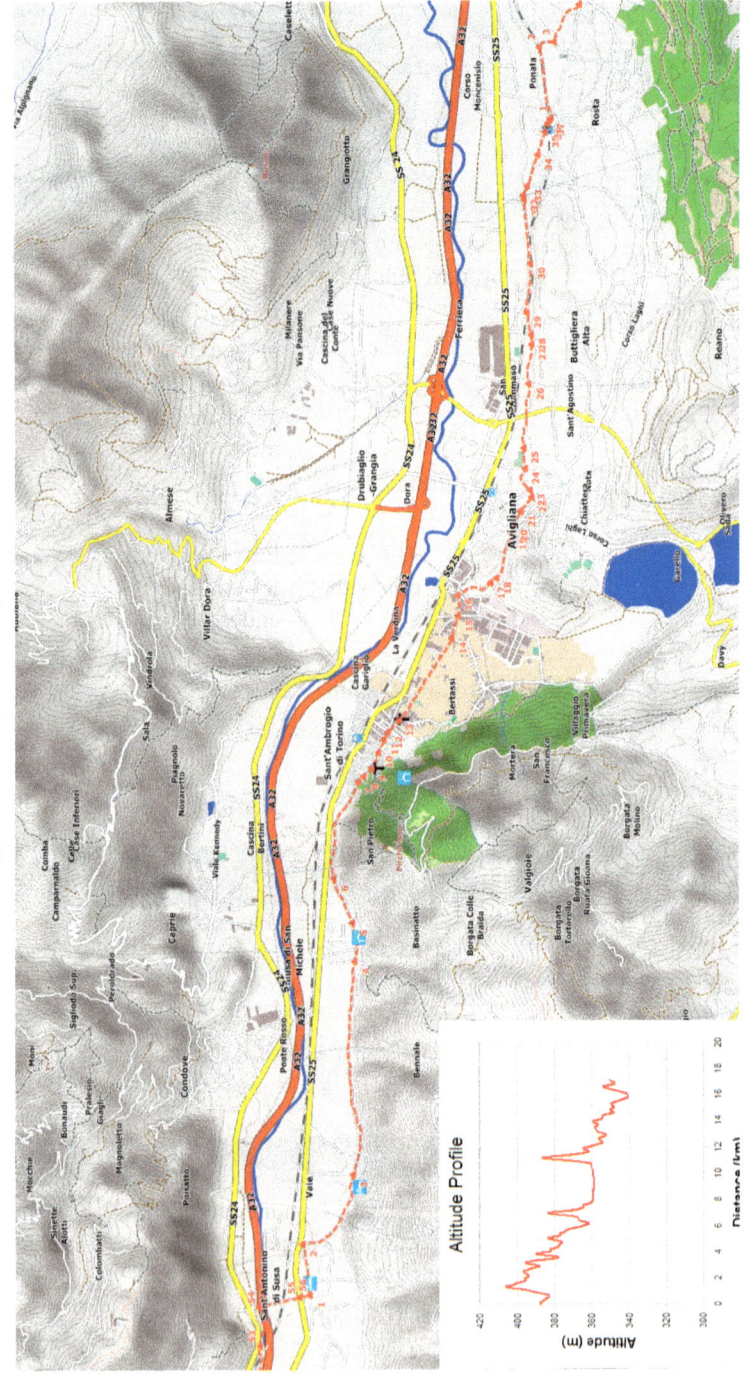

The route follows quiet tarmac roads and cycle tracks of the via Antica di Francia on the south side of the valley floor and passing beside the promontory surmounted by Sacra di San Michele.
Distance from Arles: 495km   Distance to Vercelli: 126km
Stage Ascent: 142m   Stage Descent: 179m

Waypoint	Distance Between Waypoints (m)	Total (km)	Directions	Verification Point	Compass	Altitude (m)
28.001	0	0,0	From the crossroads turn left and take via Torino	Towards the centre of Sant'Antonio di Susa	E	387
28.002	700	0,7	After passing through Sant'Antonio and shortly before the intersection with the SS25, turn right	Via Vaie	SE	383
28.003	1300	1,0	In centre of Vaie, continue straight ahead	Via Roma, via Antica di Francia	E	396
28.004	2900	4,8	At the junction at the entrance to Chiusa di San Michele, continue straight ahead	Via Roma	E	377
28.005	500	5,3	Continue straight ahead	Via Antica di Francia	NE	377
28.006	700	5,0	Continue straight ahead	Sacra di San Michele high on the right	E	365
28.007	1400	7,3	At the end of the cycle track, turn right on the road - towards the centre of Sant'Ambrogio di Torino	White arrow	SE	366
28.008	90	7,4	At the junction continue straight ahead on the narrow street	No Entry sign, via Umberto 1	SE	365

Sant'Antonio-di-Susa to Rosta 17.2 km

Waypoint	Distance Between Waypoints (m)	Total (km)	Directions	Verification Point	Compass	Altitude (m)
28.009	160	7,6	Continue straight ahead through the town	Road to Sacra di San Michele to the right	SE	364
28.010	240	7,8	At the crossroads, continue straight ahead	Pass Tabacchi on the left	SE	360
28.011	180	8,0	Continue straight ahead on the broad road	Parking area on the left	SE	360
28.012	110	8,1	At the roundabout beside the memorial, bear right	Yellow pilgrim sign	SE	360
28.013	210	8,3	At the junction beside the chapel, continue straight ahead	Cycle route to Avigliana, yellow pilgrim	SE	359
28.014	1300	9,6	At the junction, bear slightly left	White arrow	E	359
28.015	300	9,9	At the roundabout, continue straight ahead	Pass industrial buildings on the right	E	359
28.016	270	10,2	At the next roundabout turn right and then immediately bear left on the small road	Dynamite factory museum on your left	S	359
28.017	500	10,7	At the junction continue straight ahead with the wire fence on your left	White arrow	SE	360
28.018	100	10,8	At the T-junction with the tarmac road, turn left	Yellow pilgrim sign	E	363
28.019	600	11,4	Take the left fork	Under the archway	E	370
28.020	100	11,5	At the end of the cobbled road, continue straight ahead	Via Alliaud	SE	365

Sant'Antonio-di-Susa to Rosta 17.2 km

Waypoint	Distance Between Waypoints (m)	Total (km)	Directions	Verification Point	Compass	Altitude (m)
28.021	230	11,8	At the crossroads with via San Giuseppe, continue straight ahead	Yellow pilgrim	SE	363
28.022	230	12,0	At the roundabout, take the second exit	Pass shopping centre on the left	E	363
28.023	90	12,1	At the traffic lights, cross the main road continue straight ahead with great care beside the road	Via Don Luigi Balbiano	E	360
28.024	400	12,5	At the next crossroads, again continue straight ahead, on the small road	Cemetery to the left	E	355
28.025	260	12,7	Continue straight ahead on the small road	Mobile phone masts on the left	E	355
28.026	900	13,6	At the crossroads with a stop sign, continue straight ahead	Yellow pilgrim	E	358
28.027	500	14,1	Take the left fork, following the cycle route signs	Yellow pilgrim	E	356
28.028	120	14,2	At the T-junction with the main road, turn left	Yellow pilgrim	E	354
28.029	300	14,5	Pass under the railway bridge and then immediately turn right	Cycle route and yellow pilgrim signs	E	351
28.030	700	15,2	Continue straight ahead	Railway track on the embankment to the right	E	350
28.031	900	16,0	Bear right on the gravel track	Sant'Antonio di Ranverso on the right	E	341

Sant'Antonio-di-Susa to Rosta 17.2 km

Waypoint	Distance Between Waypoints (m)	Total (km)	Directions	Verification Point	Compass	Altitude (m)
28.032	70	16,1	At the T-junction with the tarmac road, turn right and follow the road		SE	342
28.033	130	16,2	At the junction, continue straight ahead on the road	Following cycle route signs, yellow pilgrim	E	345
28.034	400	16,7	At the road junction, continue straight ahead. **Note:-** the route immediately ahead follows a subway under the railway line. To avoid this riders should turn right at this point and then turn left after crossing the railway bridge to rejoin the main route beside the railway station	Yellow pilgrim	E	353
28.035	300	16,0	Bear right between the car park and the Trattoria	Towards the Rosta railway station	E	348
28.036	120	17,1	Turn right and take the pedestrian subway under the railway. Then turn left on the road		SE	350
28.037	90	17,2	Arrive at Rosta	In front of the railway station		350

Sant'Antonio-di-Susa to Rosta 17.2 km

B&B, Hotel, Gite d'Etapes	Price

Hotel des Alpes, Corso Moncenisio, 25 10090 Rosta - Rivoli (TO), Italy Tel: +39 011 956 7777 www.hoteldesalpes.com

The route leaves Rosta on stony tracks through woodland before joining a busy and potentially dangerous minor road, via Rosta. The centre of Rivoli is partially pedestrianized but the signed route from Rivoli to the centre of Turin follows an exceptionally busy dual carriageway. There are pavements for much of its length, but also a long bridge crossing where walkers and riders would need to take the main carriageway. We have chosen to leave the signed route and divert to the south of Corso Francia. Pedestrians have the option to take the bus from Rivoli to the centre of Turin. Bus 36 will take you to Paradiso, where the metro line will then take you to XVIII Decembre, just a short walk from piazza Castello.

Distance from Arles: 512km   Distance to Vercelli: 109km
Stage Ascent: 72m   Stage Descent: 188m

	Waypoint	Distance Between Waypoints (m)	Total (km)	Directions	Verification Point	Compass	Altitude (m)
Rosta to Turin 20.4 km	29.001	0	0,0	At the roundabout take the last exit	Parallel to the railway track, via 20 Settembre	E	350
	29.002	1000	0,0	Bear right away from the railway		S	348
	29.003	230	1,2	At the junction, turn left	Pass metal gates on your right	SE	355
	29.004	700	1,8	At the T-junction, bear left	Yellow pilgrim	E	394
	29.005	170	2,0	At the subsequent T-junction, again bear left with great care on the busy road	Towards Rivoli	E	401
	29.006	1600	3,6	At the roundabout, bear right	Via Rosta	E	391
	29.007	170	3,8	In the piazza, bear left on the narrow street	Via Roma	E	394

Waypoint	Distance Between Waypoints (m)	Total (km)	Directions	Verification Point	Compass	Altitude (m)
29.008	800	4,6	After passing through the archway, Porto Giacomo Matteotti, bear left across the piazza and take the narrow street downhill	Via Fratelli Piol	E	368
29.009	500	5,1	At the large roundabout go straight ahead on the long straight road.	Corso Francia	E	358
29.010	4900	9,0	There is no pavement on the railway bridge ahead forcing pedestrians and riders into the traffic. Turn right on the tree lined viale Antonio Gramsci	Shortly after passing bus stop 969 on Corso Francia	S	295
29.011	800	10,7	At the roundabout, turn left on the cycle-track beside the divided highway	Corso Torino	E	294
29.012	2500	13,2	At the roundabout after crossing the railway, continue straight ahead	After passing sports ground on the left	NE	278
29.013	90	13,3	Shortly before the road bends to the left, turn right on short road	Beside apartment buildings	E	278

Rosta to Turin 20.4 km

Waypoint	Distance Between Waypoints (m)	Total (km)	Directions	Verification Point	Compass	Altitude (m)
29.014	60	13,3	At the T-junction turn left on via Asiago	Torino sign to the left	N	278
29.015	700	14,0	At the T-junction with Corso Francia turn right	Traffic lights	E	278
29.016	2900	16,9	At the roundabout continue straight ahead	Piazza Rivoli	E	255
29.017	1100	17,9	At the next roundabout again continue straight ahead	Piazza Lorenzo Bernini	E	252
29.018	1200	19,1	In Piazza Statuto, bear right beside the portico and take via Garibaldi	Enter pedestrian zone	SE	245
29.019	1400	20,4	Arrive at Turin centre	Piazza Castello		235

Rosta to Turin 20.4 km

B&B, Hotel, Gite d'Etapes	Price/ Opening
Albergo Antico Distretto, Corso Valdocco, 10,10122 Torino (TO), Italy Tel:+39 0115213713	B2
Pensione Kitty, Piazza Statuto, 9,10122 Torino (TO), Italy Tel:+39 0115627383	B2
Hotel Frejus,Via Castagnevizza, 27,10093 Collegno (TO), Italy Tel:+39 0114112907	B3

Camping	
Camping Sofia Sas, Strada Provinciale di Cuorgnè, 50,10156 Torino (TO), Italy Tel:+39 0112623695 www.campingsofia.com/	B1
Ostello Torino, Via Alby, 1,10131 Torino (TO), Italy Tel:+39 0116602939 www.ostellotorino.it/	B1
Camping Villa Rey, Strada Val San Martino Superiore, 27, 10131 Torino (TO), Italy Tel:+39 0118190117 www.campingvillarey.it/	B1

Diocesan House	
Parrocchia San Giuseppe Cafasso, Via Giovanni Battista Gandino, 1,10148 Torino (TO), Italy Tel:+39 0112201022	Donation
Duomo (San Giovanni Battista), Piazza San Giovanni, 10121 Torino (TO), Italy Tel:+39 0114361540	Donation
Parrocchia San Giovanni Battista, 87,Via 20 Settembre, 10122 Torino (TO), Italy Tel:+39 0114361540 www.provincia.torino.it/	Donation
Parrocchia Gesu' Redentore, Piazza Giovanni XXIII, 26, 10137 Torino (TO), Italy Tel:+39 0113095026	Donation

Tourist Office
Torino Porta Nuova S.C.A.R.L., Via Paolo Sacchi, 5,10125 Torino (TO), Italy   Tel:+39 011535181   info.torino@turismotorino.org
Piazza Castello, 10122 Torino (TO), Italy Tel:+39 011535181   info.torino@turismotorino.org

Doctor
Berta - Studio Medico, Via San Paolo, 1,10138 Torino (TO), Italy Tel:+39 0113833765

Veterinary
Clinica Veterinaria Europa, Corso Guglielmo Marconi, 17,10125 Torino (TO), Italy   Tel:+39 0116690207   www.clinicaveterinariaeuropa.eu/

Rosta to Turin 20.4 km

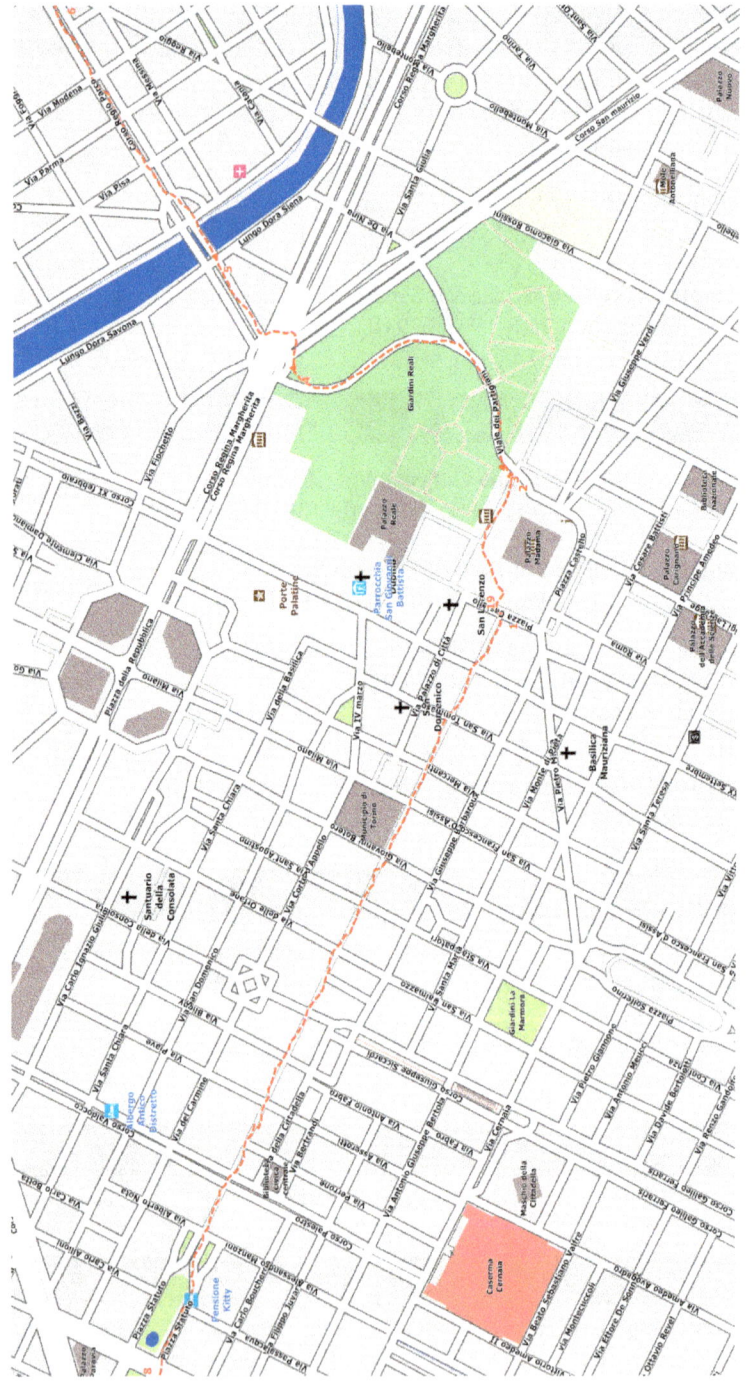

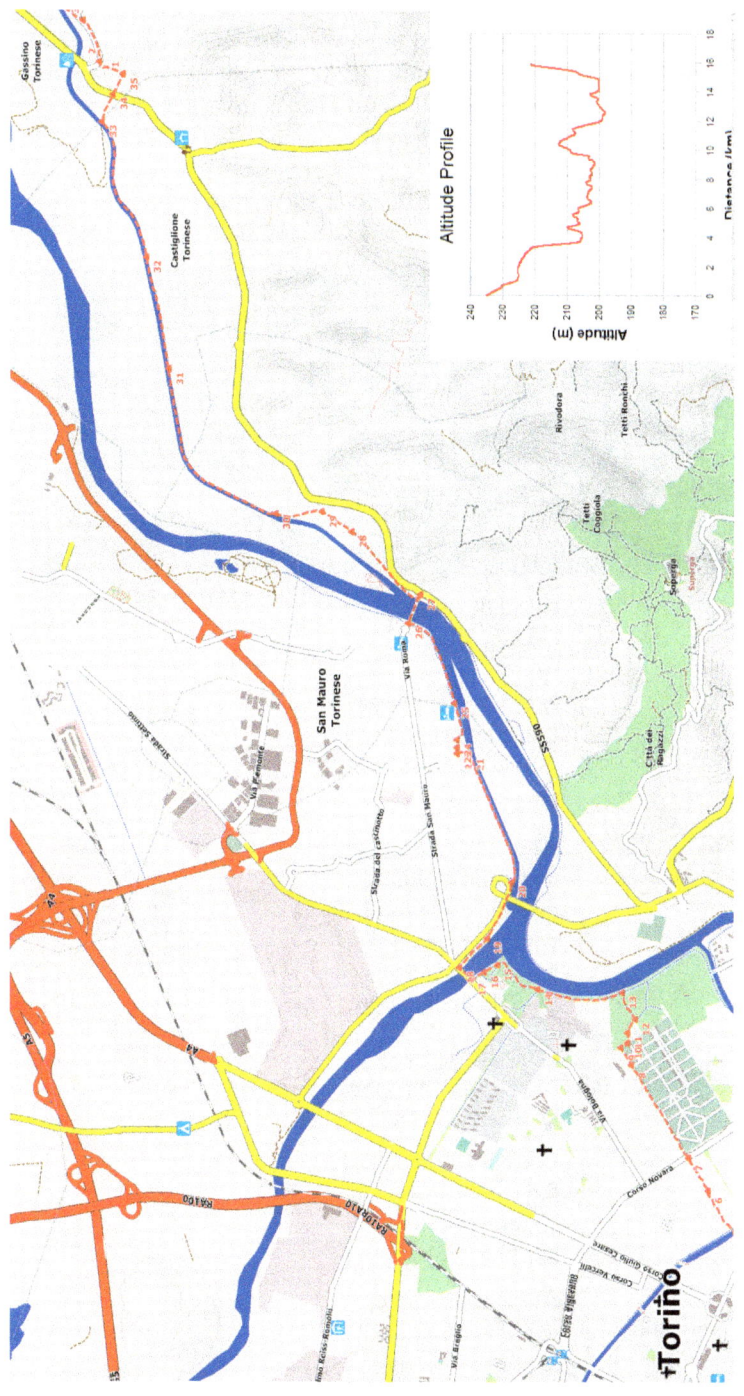

After 2kms following the broad boulevards or Turin, the signed route joins the pathways along the banks of the Po, occasionally returning to the tarmac roads to negotiate river and canal crossings. The approach to Gassino-Torinese is along a broad canal path before finally entering the old town centre.

Distance from Arles: 533km Distance to Vercelli: 89km
Stage Ascent: 51m Stage Descent: 64m

Waypoint	Distance Between Waypoints (m)	Total (km)	Directions	Verification Point	Compass	Altitude (m)
30.001	0	0,0	Bear left across piazza Castello	Between palazzo Reale and palazzo Madama	E	235
30.002	240	0,2	In the corner piazza of Castello turn left and follow the road under the portico	Traffic lights as you pass under the building	NE	233
30.003	30	0,3	After emerging from under the building, take the cycle track with the park on the left and viale Primo Maggio on the right	Pass under the archway and bear left through the park	NE	233
30.004	500	0,8	Cross the large roundabout and take broad road opposite	Corso Regio Parco, between towered buildings	NE	229
30.005	260	1,0	Cross the bridge over the Dora Riparia and continue straight ahead	Tree lined road	NE	225
30.006	500	1,5	At the roundabout, continue straight ahead	Remain on Corso Regio Parco	NE	225

Turin to Gassino-Torinese 15.9 km

Waypoint	Distance Between Waypoints (m)	Total (km)	Directions	Verification Point	Compass	Altitude (m)
30.007	400	1,9	At the crossroads, continue straight ahead	Cemetery on the right	NE	225
30.008	1000	2,9	Take the right fork	Remain beside the cemetery	NE	223
30.009	180	3,1	At the end of the cemetery wall turn right	Via Giacomo Zanella	SE	222
30.010	80	3,2	Turn left into the car park	Parco della Colletta	E	222
30.011	90	3,3	Continue straight ahead on the broad track	Beside poplar trees	SE	221
30.012	150	3,4	Turn left	At the end of the line of trees	NE	219
30.013	280	3,7	At the T-junction beside the river turn left	Sign "Confluenza fiume Po - fiume Stura"	N	207
30.014	800	4,5	Take the right fork	Closer to the river	NE	207
30.015	500	5,0	Take the right fork beside the river	Sports area on the left	NW	206
30.016	140	5,1	Again take the right fork and remain beside the river	Towards the bridge	NW	207
30.017	140	5,3	At the T-junction with the road, turn right and cross the bridge	Petrol station on the left at the junction	NE	206
30.018	150	5,4	After crossing the bridge, immediately turn right onto the track	River close on the right	SE	207

Turin to Gassino-Torinese 15.9 km

Waypoint	Distance Between Waypoints (m)	Total (km)	Directions	Verification Point	Compass	Altitude (m)
30.019	400	5,8	Take the left fork	Towards the road	SE	206
30.020	600	6,4	After passing under the road bridge, turn right on the tarmac path, beside the canal	Yellow pilgrim	E	203
30.021	1300	7,6	Bear left on the path into the village of Bertolla	Sluice gates ahead	N	203
30.022	140	7,8	On reaching the parking area, turn sharp right	Yellow pilgrim painted on the ground	E	204
30.023	60	7,8	Cross the piazza and bear right	Piazza Monte Tabor	E	204
30.024	90	7,9	Bear right onto the cycle track and return to the canal-side	Yellow pilgrim	E	203
30.025	400	8,3	Take the right fork and remain close to the wooden fence beside the water	Yellow pilgrim	NE	203
30.026	900	9,2	At the junction with the brick pedestrian bridge turn right and cross the bridge, Ponte Vittorio Emanuele II	Via Francigena Map beside the path	SE	201
30.027	290	9,4	At the road junction at the end of the bridge, turn right and right again to pass under the bridge with the river now on your left	Yellow pilgrim signs	NE	203

Turin to Gassino-Torinese 15,9 km

Waypoint	Distance Between Waypoints (m)	Total (km)	Directions	Verification Point	Compass	Altitude (m)
30.028	1000	10,4	At the roundabout, continue straight ahead on the road	Via 25 Aprile	NE	213
30.029	400	10,7	Take the left fork	Yellow pilgrim	N	210
30.030	500	11,2	As the road bends to the right, turn left towards the bridge and then immediately turn right on the track with the canal on your left	Yellow pilgrim sign	NE	207
30.031	1900	13,1	Continue straight ahead on the track beside the canal	Pass under road bridge	E	200
30.032	1000	14,1	Continue straight ahead on the track. **Note:-** to visit Castiglione Torinese, turn right and then left on the farm road that runs obliquely away from the canal	Bridge to the left and barrier across the track	E	200
30.033	1300	15,4	Beside the bridge run right on via Armondo Diaz - towards the centre of Gassino Torinese	Tarmac road on the immediate right before the junction	E	207
30.034	270	15,7	At the crossroads, continue straight ahead		SE	216
30.035	210	15,9	Arrive at Gassino-Torinese centre	Beside the domed Chiesa della Confraternita		221

Turin to Gassino-Torinese 15.9 km

211

B&B, Hotel, Gite d'Etapes	Price/ Opening
La Corte Agriturismo, Strada Sant'Antonio, 54,10090 Gassino Torinese (TO), Italy Tel:+39 0119607773	B3
Girarrosto, Via Torino, 6,10090 San Raffaele Cimena (TO), Italy Tel:+39 0119602060	B2
Hotel La Pace, Via Roma, 36,10099 San Mauro Torinese (TO), Italy Tel:+39 0118221945 www.hotelapace.it/	B2
Hotel Elite, Via Trento, 35,10099 San Mauro Torinese (TO), Italy Tel:+39 0118221888 www.hotelelitetorino.it/	B2

Religious Hostel	
Parrocchia di Castiglione Torinese, Piazza Beata Vergine Assunta, 10090 Castiglione Torinese (TO), Italy Tel:+39 0119607178	Donation

Turin to Gassino-Torinese 15.9 km

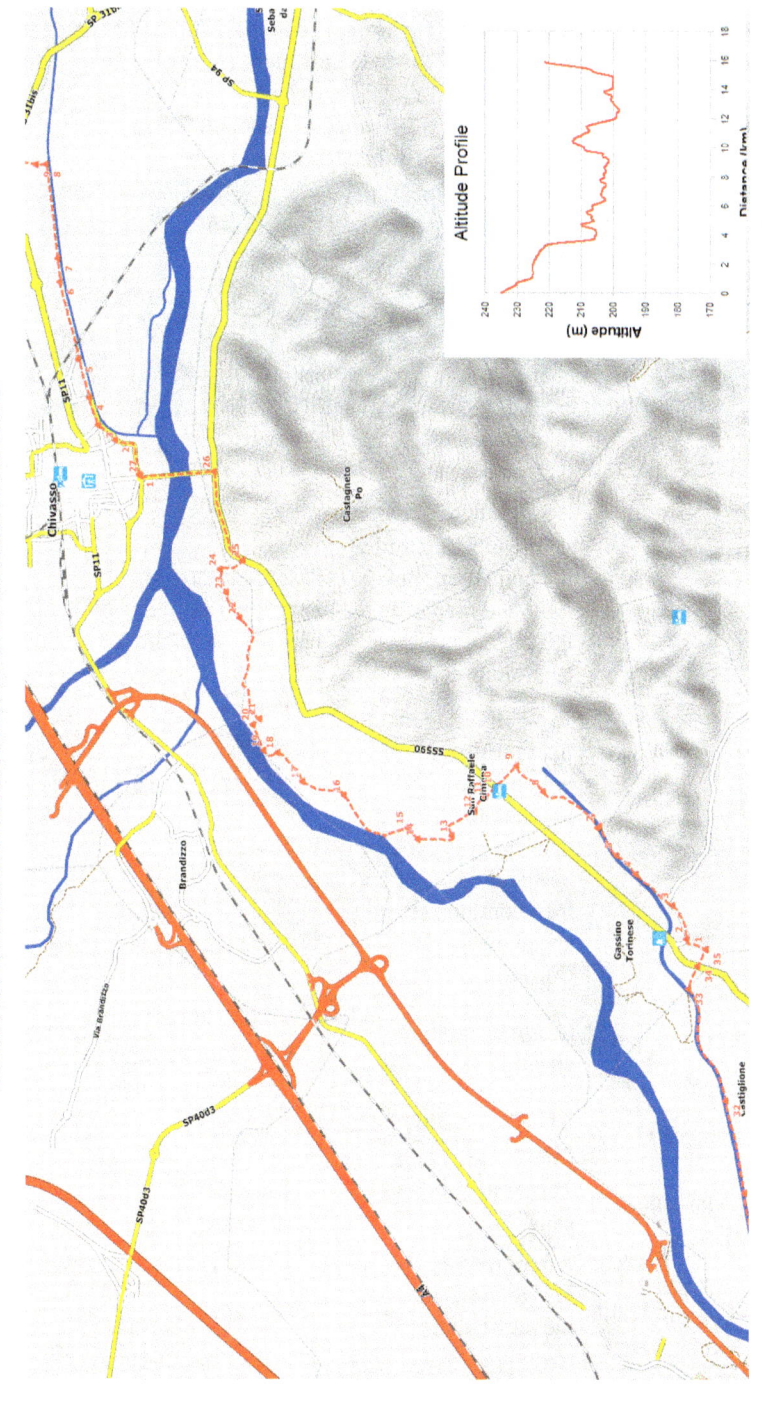

Shortly after leaving Gassino-Torinese, the route returns to the canal-side path before crossing San Raffaele and then following farm tracks to the outskirts of Chivasso.
Distance from Arles: 549km   Distance to Vercelli: 73km
Stage Ascent: 30m   Stage Descent: 71m

Waypoint	Distance Between Waypoints (m)	Total (km)	Directions	Verification Point	Compass	Altitude (m)
31.001	0	0,0	At the crossroads in the centre of the old town turn left	Away from la Chiesa della Confraternita	NE	221
31.002	270	0,3	At the junction with the main road, turn right and then keep left on strada Bussolino	Pass the church of Santi Pietro e Paolo on the right	NE	218
31.003	500	0,7	Just before the main road turns right, turn left and then immediately right onto the small road beside the houses and then continue straight ahead on strada Cerreto	Yellow pilgrim	NE	204
31.004	600	1,3	Continue straight ahead	Canal on your left, house N° 48 on the right	NE	215
31.005	300	1,6	Keep to the left on the road	Close to the canal	NE	214
31.006	400	1,0	Turn left and cross the canal bridge	Yellow pilgrim on crash barrier	NW	208
31.007	20	1,0	After crossing the bridge, turn right on the narrow tarmac road	Via Rivalta	NE	207

Gassino-Torinese to Chivasso 11.6 km

Waypoint	Distance Between Waypoints (m)	Total (km)	Directions	Verification Point	Compass	Altitude (m)
31.008	800	2,8	Continue straight ahead into the village of San Raffaele Cimena	Pass via Don Lupo Domenico on the right	NE	199
31.009	400	3,2	At the crossroads in piazzetta San Bernado, turn left	Church on your left	NW	199
31.010	400	3,5	At the traffic lights continue straight ahead	Yellow pilgrim	NW	197
31.011	160	3,7	At the mini-roundabout, go straight ahead then take the left fork	Via Moie	NW	196
31.012	220	3,9	Take the right fork remaining on via Moie	Yellow pilgrim	NW	195
31.013	500	4,4	At the crossroads in the tracks go straight ahead and then quickly bear right	Pilgrim painted on posts of sign board	N	194
31.014	500	4,8	Bear right and pass the metal barrier	Yellow pilgrim	NE	193
31.015	170	4,0	Turn left onto the gravel path	Sluice gate ahead at the junction	NE	193
31.016	1000	5,0	Bear left to remain on the main track	Proceed parallel to the river	N	193
31.017	500	6,5	Bear right, remaining on the main track	White arrow	NE	190
31.018	400	6,9	At the T-junction, turn left	Equestrian centre to the right	N	190

Gassino-Torinese to Chivasso 11.6 km

Gassino-Torinese to Chivasso 11.6 km

Waypoint	Distance Between Waypoints (m)	Total (km)	Directions	Verification Point	Compass	Altitude (m)
31.019	180	7,1	Take the right fork, away from the river	White arrow	NE	190
31.020	300	7,4	At the T-junction, turn right	Towards metal gate	SE	189
31.021	100	7,5	At the T-junction after the metal gates, turn left	Yellow pilgrim	E	189
31.022	1300	8,8	Pass around a clump of trees and follow the narrow path	White arrow on pylon on the right	NE	185
31.023	300	9,1	Turn left and bear right	Line of trees to your right	E	184
31.024	280	9,4	At the T-junction, turn right	Pass pylon on your right as you continue	S	181
31.025	300	9,7	At the T-junction with the main road turn left over the bridge and then keep right on the main road using the parallel track to avoid the traffic	Pass electricity plant on your right	E	179
31.026	1100	10,8	At the roundabout, turn left onto the river bridge	Towards Chivasso	N	188
31.027	900	11,6	Arrive at Chivasso, town centre directly ahead	Beside large roundabout		180

B&B, Hotel, Gite d'Etapes	Price

Albergo D'Italia, Piazza Giuseppe Garibaldi, 7,10034 Chivasso (TO), Italy   Tel:+39 0119103679

Diocesan House	

Santa Maria Assunta, Piazza della Repubblica, 4,10034 Chivasso (TO), Italy   Tel:+39 0119101282

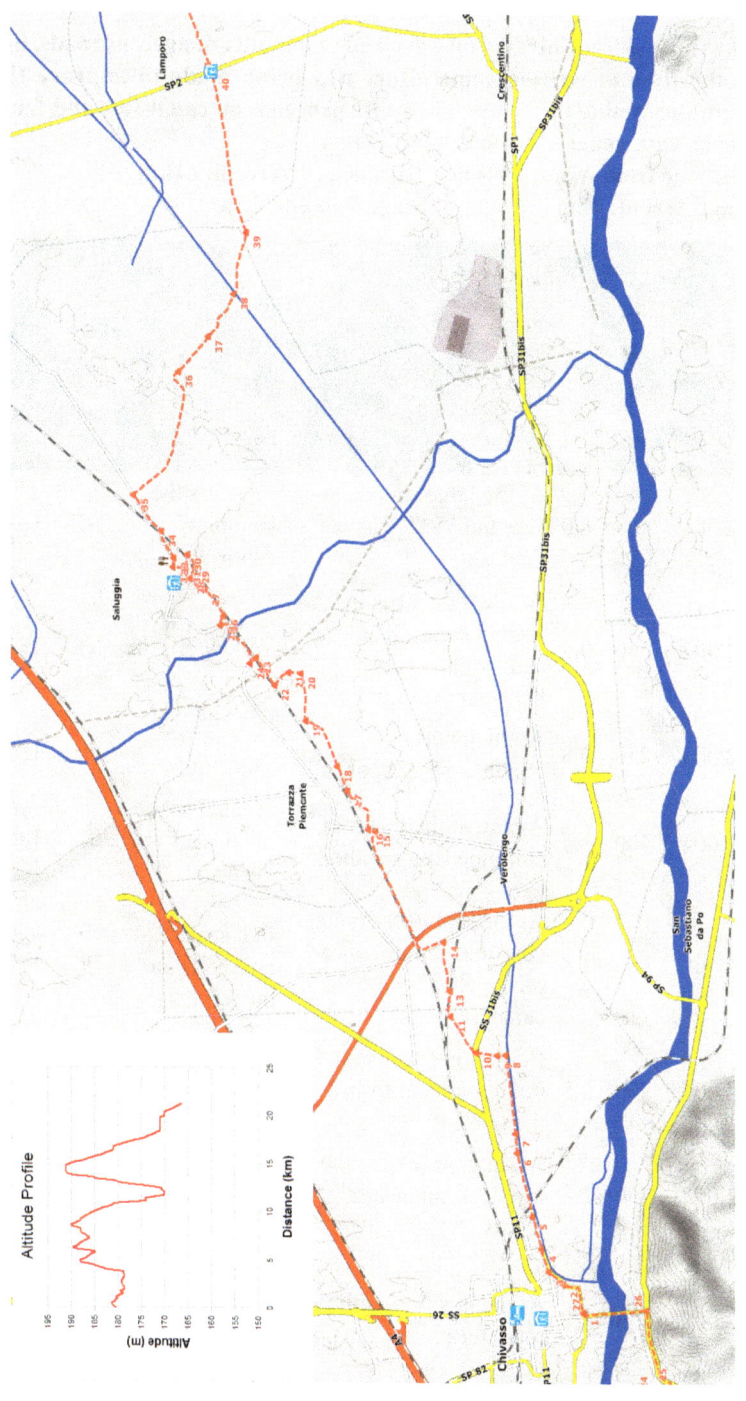

The route skirts Chivasso on busy and potentially dangerous roads, but at the time of writing some effort was being made to improve the footpaths beside the roads. The route proceeds on canal-side and farm tracks with generally good sign-posting.

Distance from Arles: 560km   **Distance to Vercelli: 61km**
Stage Ascent: 42m   **Stage Descent: 56m**

Chivasso to Lamporo 21.2 km

Waypoint	Distance Between Waypoints (m)	Total (km)	Directions	Verification Point	Compass	Altitude (m)
32.001	0	0,0	At the large roundabout take the SS11, via Gerbido	Towards the shopping centre	NE	180
32.002	600	0,6	At the roundabout, continue parallel to the canal on the path between the trees	Yellow pilgrim	NE	181
32.003	250	0,8	At the junction, continue straight ahead		E	180
32.004	400	1,2	Again, at the junction, continue straight ahead	Parallel to the main road and the canal	E	180
32.005	500	1,6	At the roundabout, continue straight ahead on the road beside the canal	Industrial buildings on the left	E	179
32.006	900	2,5	Bear right to leave the main road and follow the track	Canal close on your right	E	179
32.007	250	2,8	At the bridge over the canal, continue straight ahead	Keep canal on your right	E	179
32.008	1100	3,8	At the junction with the road, turn left	Brick built road bridge to the right at the junction	N	180

Waypoint	Distance Between Waypoints (m)	Total (km)	Directions	Verification Point	Compass	Altitude (m)
32.009	120	3,9	At the crossroads, continue straight ahead on via Cimitero	Towards the church in Castelrosso	N	182
32.010	290	4,2	At the T-junction with via Casale, bear left towards the church and then turn right	Via Santa Maria	NE	184
32.011	600	4,8	Shortly before the level-crossing turn right on the track. **Note:-** the track ahead involves a subway under the railway. Riders should remain on the road and then take the first turning to the right and rejoin the track at the exit from the subway	Yellow pilgrim and Rolandini signs	E	188
32.012	400	5,2	Turn left and pass under the railway		N	187
32.013	10	5,2	After emerging from the subway, bear right on the track		E	187
32.014	700	5,9	At the T-junction with the road, cross the road, turn left and then bear right on the small road below the bridge ramp	Towards the railway track	NE	185
32.015	2100	7,9	At the T-junction with the main road, turn left	Towards Torrazza Piemonte	N	188
32.016	110	8,0	Shortly before the level crossing, turn right	Over a bridge onto a track	NE	188

Chivasso to Lamporo 21.2 km

Waypoint	Distance Between Waypoints (m)	Total (km)	Directions	Verification Point	Compass	Altitude (m)
32.017	700	8,7	At the crossroads, continue straight ahead	Canal bridge to the left, yellow pilgrim	NE	190
32.018	400	9,0	Continue straight ahead	Avoid the bridge	NE	188
32.019	800	9,8	At the T-junction with a minor road turn right	Farmhouse immediately to right, yellow pilgrim	E	184
32.020	600	10,4	At a T-junction turn left	Wire fence on the left	N	183
32.021	180	10,6	At the crossroads continue straight ahead	Pass metal barrier	NW	181
32.022	270	10,9	Turn right	Railway on the left	NE	181
32.023	500	11,3	At the T-junction, turn left	Pass under the railway	NW	174
32.024	120	11,4	At the T-junction with the road, turn sharp right on the road	Approach railway on the right	NE	174
32.025	700	12,2	After crossing the bridge over the Dora Baltea, turn right on the track	Yellow pilgrim	E	170
32.026	140	12,3	Cross a small bridge over an irrigation channel and then turn left	Railway immediately to the right	NE	171
32.027	500	12,7	Bear left over the bridge and then bear right	Water treatment plant close on your right	NE	175

Chivasso to Lamporo 21.2 km

Waypoint	Distance Between Waypoints (m)	Total (km)	Directions	Verification Point	Compass	Altitude (m)
32.028	280	13,0	Turn right just before crossing the canal	Shrine on the right, yellow pilgrim	SE	180
32.029	160	13,2	Pass under the railway and then turn left	Over the canal bridge	NE	181
32.030	210	13,4	At the T-junction at the end of via Canal Farini, turn left	Pass church on the right	W	184
32.031	190	13,6	Turn right onto via Roma	Direction Livorno Ferraris	N	186
32.032	180	13,8	At the crossroads in the centre of Saluggia, turn right	Direction Vercelli	E	189
32.033	120	13,9	Bear left on the main road	Pass the railway station on the right	NE	190
32.034	400	14,3	After crossing the railway bridge, keep left on the main road		NE	191
32.035	600	14,9	Immediately after passing the farmhouse "Cascina Primavera", turn right on a gravel track	Hand-painted sign to Lamporo and Roma	E	190
32.036	2000	16,9	At a crossroads in the track, continue straight ahead	Lamporo, Vercelli, Roma sign	SE	180
32.037	600	17,5	Continue straight ahead over the bridge	Lamporo, Roma sign	SE	176

Chivasso to Lamporo 21.2 km

Waypoint	Distance Between Waypoints (m)	Total (km)	Directions	Verification Point	Compass	Altitude (m)
32.037	600	17,5	Continue straight ahead over the bridge	Lamporo, Roma sign	SE	176
32.038	700	18,2	At the crossroads, continue straight ahead and cross the bridge over canal Cavour	Lamporo, Roma sign	E	172
32.039	900	19,0	At the junction bear left towards the village	Lamporo Roma sign on a sluice gate	E	171
32.040	2200	21,2	Arrive at Lamporo	Crossroads beside the church		166

Chivasso to Lamporo 21.2 km

Diocesan House	Price

Parrochia Lamporo, 13046 Lamporo (VC), Italy
Tel:+39 0161848125

Parrocchia S. Grato,Vicolo Parrocchia, 13040 Saluggia (VC), Italy   Tel:+39 0161480113

Entry to Lamporo

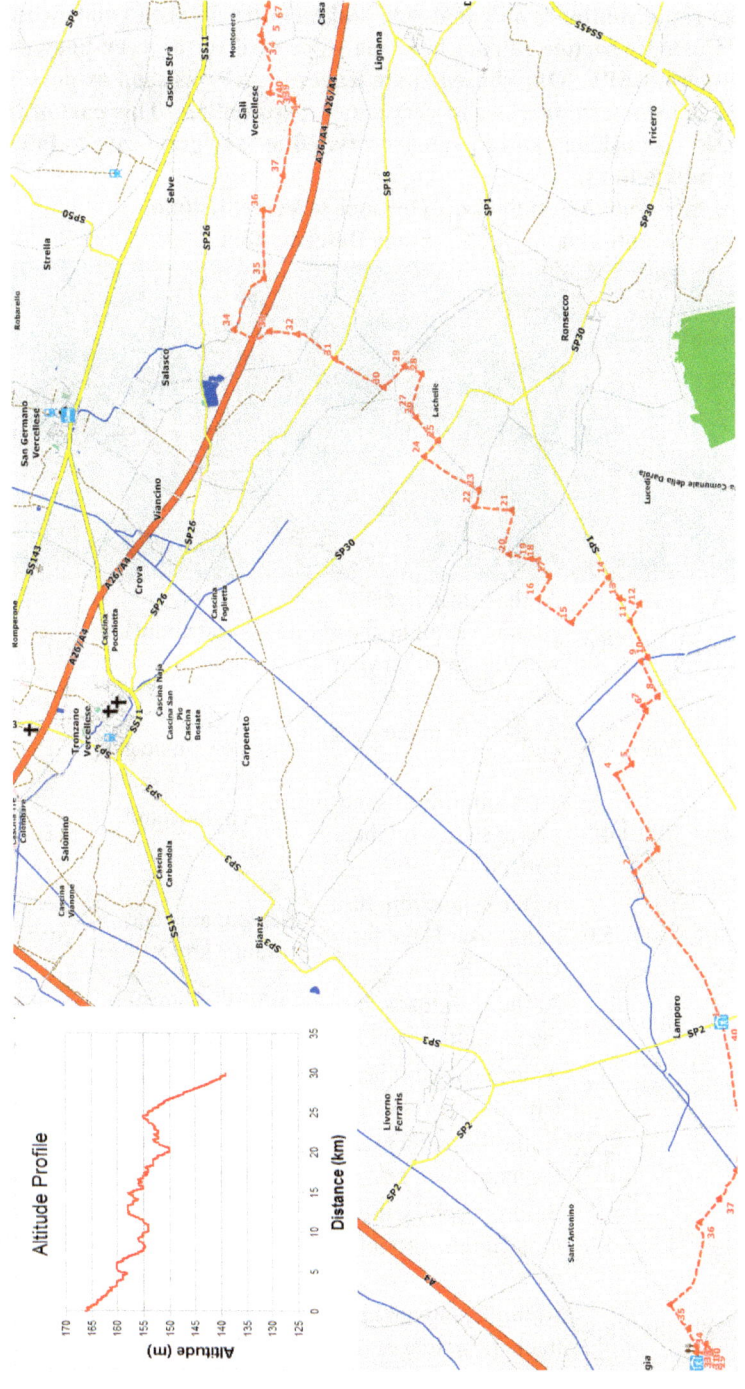

The route continues on canal-side and farm tracks with good signing to Castell'Apertole. From here the signs lead to the very busy and dangerous SP1. Our chosen route leaves the SP1 as soon as possible and follows farm tracks and very small roads to Sali. This part of the section is unsigned and so you are advised to take great care to follow the instructions.

Distance from Arles: 581km **Distance to Vercelli: 40km**
Stage Ascent: 21m **Stage Descent: 48m**

Waypoint	Distance Between Way-points (m)	Total (km)	Directions	Verification Point	Compass	Altitude (m)
33.001	0	0,0	At the traffic lights continue straight ahead with the canal on your left	Pass restaurants on the right	NE	166
33.002	3600	3,6	At the fork in the track, bear right	Sign on sluice gate	SE	60
33.003	700	4,3	Turn left, towards the power station on the horizon	Green, blue and orange sign	NE	159
33.004	1700	5,0	At the T-junction, turn right towards the farm, Cascina Mandria	Green, blue and orange arrow	SE	160
33.005	400	6,4	At the crossroads, beside the farm, turn left	White arrow on the sluice-gate	E	159
33.006	1200	7,5	At the next farm bear left	Towards the Give-Way sign	NE	155
33.007	110	7,7	At the T-junction with the main road, turn right	Pass Pony Club on your left	SE	155
33.008	400	8,0	Before reaching the roundabout, turn left on the track	Green, blue and orange sign	NE	155
33.009	800	8,8	At the T-junction in the track, turn right	Towards the main road	SE	156

Lamporo to Sali-Vercellese 29.9 km

Waypoint	Distance Between Waypoints (m)	Total (km)	Directions	Verification Point	Compass	Altitude (m)	
33.010	170	8,0	At the junction, turn left with great care on the busy main road, SP1	Towards fly-over	NE	156	
33.011	800	9,8	Shortly after passing under the road bridge, bear right onto the track and then turn right between the fields		SE	155	Lamporo to Sali:Vercellese 29.9 km
33.012	400	10,1	At the T-junction turn left	Towards the power lines and main road	N	154	
33.013	400	10,6	On returning to the main road, turn right	Cross the bridge over the waterway	NE	154	
33.014	500	11,1	Turn left onto a small road	Towards the church tower	NW	155	
33.015	1200	12,3	After passing through the hamlet of Leri Cavour, turn right	Between the derelict farm buildings	NE	158	
33.016	900	13,1	After passing through the next farm complex, Castelmerlino, turn right at the junction	Towards the main road	SE	158	
33.017	500	13,6	Turn left over the water way	Towards the line of trees	NE	157	
33.018	500	14,1	After crossing the bridge, bear left on the same track	Towards the farm buildings	N	156	
33.019	140	14,2	At the next junction continue straight ahead		N	156	

Waypoint	Distance Between Waypoints (m)	Total (km)	Directions	Verification Point	Compass	Altitude (m)
33.020	500	14,7	At the junction in the tracks, track joins from the left, continue straight ahead towards the houses	After 150 metres the track ahead turns right	E	157
33.021	1000	15,7	After passing the farm, Cascina Fantino, turn left on the gravelled road	Pass through metal gates	N	155
33.022	800	16,5	At the T-junction with the tarmac road, turn right		E	156
33.023	400	16,8	Turn left off the road onto a gravelled track	Towards buildings on the sky-line	NE	155
33.024	1300	18,1	At the T-junction with the tarmac road, turn right	Large farm ahead, Casina Corte	SE	154
33.025	500	18,6	Immediately after a crossing a small bridge, turn left onto a dirt track towards a line of trees	Near the sign for Ronsecco	NE	153
33.026	700	19,2	At a fork in the track, continue straight ahead on the grass track	Keep irrigation channel on the left	NE	153
33.027	190	19,4	Shortly before the track bears left, turn right	Clump of trees ahead at the turning	E	152
33.028	800	20,2	Turn left on the stony track		NE	150
33.029	400	20,6	At the T-junction, turn left	Towards the large sluice gate	NW	150

Lamporo to Sali:Vercellese 29.9 km

Waypoint	Distance Between Waypoints (m)	Total (km)	Directions	Verification Point	Compass	Altitude (m)
33.030	600	21,2	After passing the large sluice, turn right	Cross the concrete canal bridge	NE	152
33.031	1200	22,3	At the intersection with the tarmac road, continue straight ahead	Direction Salasco	NE	152
33.032	1000	23,2	Take the right fork	Towards the motorway bridge	N	153
33.033	600	23,8	Bear left onto the tarmac road	Cross the motorway bridge	N	154
33.034	800	24,6	Turn right on the part made road	Strada Provinciale Salasco - Sali Vercellese	SE	154
33.035	1300	25,9	Bear left on the road	Roughly parallel to the motorway	E	152
33.036	1400	27,2	Turn sharp right to remain on the road	Towards the motorway	SE	147
33.037	1000	28,2	At the junction, continue straight ahead parallel to the motorway	Towards the village	E	144
33.038	1400	29,6	At the junction, continue straight ahead	Enter the village of Sali Vercellese	E	140
33.039	180	29,7	Continue straight ahead	Over the bridge	NE	139
33.040	150	29,9	Arrive at Sali-Vercellese centre	Via Roma to the left		139

Lamporo to Sali-Vercellese 29.9 km

B&B, Hotel, Gite d'Etapes	Price/ Opening
Delle Miniere, Corso Giacomo Matteotti, 91, 13047 San Germano Vercellese (VC), Italy Tel:+39 0161933111	B2

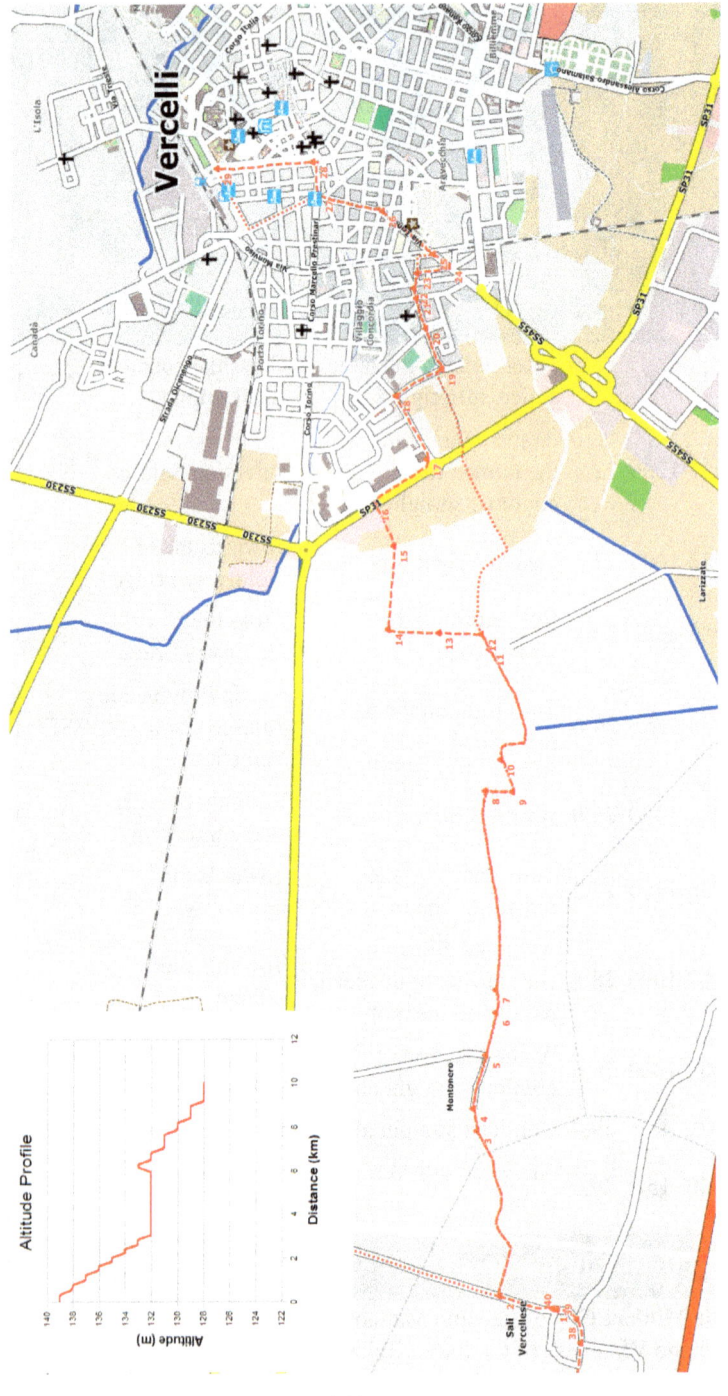

Stage Summary: the route quickly joins the principal route of the via Francigena from Canterbury with the larger but less frequent signs and follows farm tracks separating the rice fields to the edge of Vercelli.

Distance from Arles: 611km **Distance to Vercelli: 10km**
Stage Ascent: 1m **Stage Descent: 12m**

Waypoint	Distance Between Waypoints (m)	Total (km)	Directions	Verification Point	Compass	Altitude (m)
34.001	0	0,0	From the centre of Sali Vercellese continue straight ahead	Towards the cemetry	N	139
4.002	400	0,4	Shortly after leaving Sali Vercellese turn right	Cemetery on the left at the junction	E	139
34.003	1100	1,5	Continue straight ahead towards Montonero. Note:- the via Francigena from Canterbury joins from the left at this point and the official government signs begin		E	136
34.004	120	1,6	Continue straight ahead on the tarmac road	Pass beside the church and sign for Area di Sosta	E	136
34.005	300	1,9	Pass through the village and continue straight ahead on the unmade road		E	135
34.006	270		At the fork in the track continue straight ahead	Ignore the turning to the right	E	134

Sali-Vercellese to Vercelli 10 km

229

Waypoint	Distance Between Waypoints (m)	Total (km)	Directions	Verification Point	Compass	Altitude (m)
34.007	130	2,3	Take the right fork	Broken VF sign	E	134
34.008	1200	3,5	Turn right. Note:- riders should cross the broad water course and turn right to the next waypoint	Cross over the bridge	S	132
34.009	160	3,7	Continue straight ahead	Pass a farm on the right	NE	132
34.010	210	3,9	Cross a sluice-gate and continue straight ahead		E	132
34.011	800	4,7	Continue straight ahead	Pass a farm on the right	NE	132
34.012	120	4,8	Turn left on the broad track. Note:- at the time of writing the "official route", straight ahead at the junction was overground and impassable	Line of wooden telegraph poles on the left side of the track	N	132
34.013	260	5,1	At the end of the broad track, continue straight ahead	Cross narrow concrete bridge	N	132

Sali-Vercellese to Vercelli 10 km

Waypoint	Distance Between Waypoints (m)	Total (km)	Directions	Verification Point	Compass	Altitude (m)	
34.014	300	5,4	With the farm buildings on your left, turn right onto the grass track. Note:- at the time of writing the track ahead was poorly maintained, in the event that it is impassable, continue straight ahead here to join the SS11, then turn right on the ring road to join this track beside the hypermarket	Towards the hypermarket	E	132	
34.015	500	5,9	Continue straight ahead	Across the bridge, pass houses on your left	NE	132	Sali-Vercellese to Vercelli 10 km
34.016	290	6,2	At the junction with the ring road, cross over the road and turn right in the hypermarket car park	Pass commercial centre on the left	SE	133	
34.017	500	6,7	At the road junction, turn left	Via Giulio Sambonet	SE	132	
34.018	500	7,1	At the crossroads, turn right	Via Giovanni Baratto	SE	131	
34.019	300	7,4	At the junction, turn left	Sports ground to the left, via Francigena sign	NE	131	

Waypoint	Distance Between Waypoints (m)	Total (km)	Directions	Verification Point	Compass	Altitude (m)
34.020	280	7,7	At the roundabout continue straight ahead	Via Francigena sign ahead	E	131
34.021	190	7,9	At the next roundabout again continue straight ahead	No sign	E	130
34.022	40	7,9	Bear right, cross the road and continue on via Puccini	VF sign	E	130
34.023	90	8,0	Turn right	Via Einaurdi, VF sign	S	130
34.024	220	8,2	At the T-junction, turn left	Via Trino	NE	130
34.025	110	8,3	Via Trino	Across the railway tracks	NE	129
34.026	400	8,8	At the roundabout bear left	Direction Il Centro	N	129
34.027	400	9,2	At the roundabout, turn right on Largo Brigata Cagliari	Petrol station ahead at the roundabout	E	128
34.028	190	9,4	Turn left on the broad tree lined boulevard	Shortly after passing the tall military monument	N	128
34.029	700	10,0	Arrive at Vercelli centre	Piazza Roma		128

Sali-Vercellese to Vercelli 10 km

B&B, Hotel, Gite d'Etapes	Price/ Opening
Alexi's Hotel,Via Cairoli,12-14,27027 Gropello Cairoli(PV),Italy Tel:+39(0)382815391	B2
Albergo Italia Ristorante,Via Libertà,144,27027 Gropello Cairoli(PV),Italy Tel:+39(0)382815082	B2
Religious Hostel	
Parrochia S Martino,27020 Tromello(PV), Italy Tel:+39(0)38286020	Donation
Convento di Billimemme,Corso Alessandro Salamano, 13100 Vercelli (VC), Italy Tel:+39 0161250167	Donation
Diocesan House	
Parrocchia Di S. Bernardo, Via Lavini Fratelli, 40,13100 Vercelli (VC), Italy Tel:+39 0161254567	

Sali-Vercellese to Vercelli 10 km

"One's destination is never a place, but a new way of seeing things."

Henry Miller

www.ingramcontent.com/pod-product-compliance
Lightning Source LLC
Chambersburg PA
CBHW071949160426
43198CB00011B/1607